INTENSIVE READING INTERVENTIONS
FOR THE ELEMENTARY GRADES

The Guilford Series on Intensive Instruction
Sharon Vaughn, *Editor*

This series presents innovative ways to improve learning outcomes for K–12 students with challenging academic and behavioral needs. Books in the series explain the principles of intensive intervention and provide evidence-based teaching practices for learners who require differentiated instruction. Grounded in current research, volumes include user-friendly features such as sample lessons, examples of daily schedules, case studies, classroom vignettes, and reproducible tools.

Essentials of Intensive Intervention
*Rebecca Zumeta Edmonds, Allison Gruner Gandhi,
and Louis Danielson*

Intensive Reading Interventions
for the Elementary Grades
*Jeanne Wanzek, Stephanie Al Otaiba,
and Kristen L. McMaster*

Intensive
Reading Interventions
for the Elementary
Grades

Jeanne Wanzek
Stephanie Al Otaiba
Kristen L. McMaster

Series Editor's Note by Sharon Vaughn

THE GUILFORD PRESS
New York   London

Copyright © 2020 The Guilford Press
A Division of Guilford Publications, Inc.
370 Seventh Avenue, Suite 1200, New York, NY 10001
www.guilford.com

Printed in the United States of America

This book is printed on acid-free paper.

Last digit is print number: 9 8 7 6 5 4 3

Library of Congress Cataloging-in-Publication Data is available from the the publisher.

ISBN 978-1-4625-4111-9 (paperback)
ISBN 978-1-4625-4112-6 (hardcover)

About the Authors

Jeanne Wanzek, PhD, is Professor in the Department of Special Education and the Currey-Ingram Endowed Chair at Peabody College of Vanderbilt University. Dr. Wanzek conducts research examining effective reading instruction and intervention for students with reading difficulties and disabilities. Prior to receiving her doctorate, she worked as a special educator and as an elementary teacher. In addition to several federally funded research projects, she has over 100 publications in the areas of early reading, learning disability, and adolescent reading intervention. She has worked with several elementary and secondary schools conducting research to improve core classroom instruction and reading intervention implementation. In addition, Dr. Wanzek has consulted with several schools and districts across the country on the implementation of effective reading instruction.

Stephanie Al Otaiba, PhD, is Professor of Teaching and Learning at Southern Methodist University in Dallas, Texas. She received her doctorate in special education from Vanderbilt University. A former special education teacher, her research focuses on early literacy interventions for students with, or at risk for, disabilities, response to intervention, and teacher training. Her research has been supported by the Institute of Education Sciences (IES), the Office of Special Education Programs, and the National Institute of Health (NIH). She is the author or coauthor of over 150 articles and chapters. Dr. Al Otaiba serves as the editor of the *Journal of Learning Disabilities.*

Kristen L. McMaster, PhD, is Professor of Special Education in the Department of Educational Psychology at the University of Minnesota in Minneapolis. Dr. McMaster's research interests include creating conditions for successful RTI for students at risk and students with disabilities. Specific research focuses on promoting teachers' use of data-based decision making and evidence-based instruction, and developing intensive, individualized interventions for students for whom generally effective instruction is not sufficient.

Series Editor's Note

What is intensive instruction and how can we (teachers, paraprofessionals, and educational leaders) effectively implement intensive instruction? This book, *Intensive Reading Interventions for the Elementary Grades*, provides the thorough background knowledge and—even more valuable to educators—sets of instructional lessons to address intensive instruction in reading. These lessons are much more than examples, ideas, practices, and suggestions—they provide specific scripts for teachers about what to do, materials needed, and how to effectively implement multiple practices related to foundation reading skills, such as phonemic awareness and phonics, as well as fluency, comprehension, and writing.

Are you wondering what you might do as a school leader to ensure that all of your students are making adequate gains in reading? This book defines the plan to address that question. As a teacher, are you perplexed as to what else you could do to enhance your instruction in the foundation skills, such as phonological awareness, phonics, and fluency? This book not only enhances your background knowledge, but it also provides you with highly specific lessons that you can implement immediately in your classroom. What about writing and comprehension—for which it is always a challenge to develop appropriately intensive instruction? The methods, activities, and guidelines included here will increase your confidence and skills across all of the essential areas related to literacy development.

As Series Editor for The Guilford Series on Intensive Instruction, I am particularly excited about *Intensive Reading Interventions for the Elementary Grades*, written by the team of outstanding research-to-practice authors Jeanne Wanzek, Stephanie Al Otaiba, and Kristen McMaster. This book reflects the extraordinary evidence-based knowledge of the author team as well as their classroom expertise. In addition to the instructional approaches described and the detailed lessons provided, these individuals share their expertise on how to differentiate instruction for the range of learners with literacy needs in the elementary grades. This is the second book in the Intensive Instruction series and it successfully achieves the high bar of providing very specific guidance for educators and administrators on how to implement evidence-based practices to effectively meet the needs of students who require intensive instruction. It is also an outstanding, comprehensive source for educational leaders and scholars about the research-to-practice knowledge on intensive interventions in literacy and should be a useful resource for preservice training.

The knowledge, practices, and lessons in this book reflect an aim to improve reading outcomes for the many students struggling to learn to read, as well as those who require research-based reading interventions to help them reach grade-level expectations in reading. This book provides guidance for teachers instructing the many students with the most severe reading difficulties who do not make adequate progress in standard reading interventions and require more intensive interventions to make sufficient growth in reading. Also provided is guidance on the specialized instruction needed to implement an intensive intervention to make significant progress. The authors focus on the ways in which teachers can intensify interventions in reading, writing, language, and multiple components of literacy for students for whom current reading interventions are not sufficient.

Get ready to learn about how to instruct elementary students with significant reading problems. Chapter 1 provides an important overview of reading instruction, highlighting how what we know about reading relates specifically to students who require intensive instruction. Chapter 2 addresses ways to support phonological and phonemic awareness for these students and provides sample lessons for integrating all of the high-leverage practices to ensure that students have the important foundation skills of phonological and phonemic awareness. Chapter 3 builds on this knowledge and addresses intensive interventions to support phonics and word recognition. The chapter recognizes as essential that all aspects of successful word reading, from fluency to comprehension, are accomplished through understanding the principles of decoding and word recognition. Chapter 4 addresses the important and often misunderstood construct of fluency. Many teachers assume that the goal of fluency is to get students to read faster. Actually, the speed at which students read is often the indicator of their instructional needs—highlighting that they may have specific word- and meaning-level challenges preventing them from reading effortlessly. Chapter 5 covers the important and often overlooked construct of oral language and how developing oral language competency contributes to reading and writing. Chapter 6 primarily addresses reading comprehension and practices that promote students' successful meaning making from text. Addressed in this chapter are both information and narrative text types, as well as multiple approaches to improving text understanding. Chapter 7 covers writing and the reciprocal relationship between reading and writing. Chapter 8 recognizes that most of our students with significant literacy needs benefit from multicomponent approaches to reading that integrate phonics, word reading, fluency, and comprehension. A description of what is known about these approaches and how they might be effectively implemented is provided.

This volume is a perfect addition to The Guilford Series on Intensive Instruction. All of the books in the series present innovative ways to improve learning outcomes for students with challenging academic and behavioral needs. As with this volume, they provide evidence-based teaching practices for learners who require differentiated instruction and include user-friendly features, such as sample lessons, classroom vignettes, and reproducible tools. Additional features include valuable case studies to better understand the application of the practices specified. These enable you to align the learning and behavior difficulties of the individuals in the book to those in your own classroom or school. I suspect that many of you will return often to this book, as I know I will, to expand my knowledge of key literacy practices and to seek out its lessons for improving instruction.

SHARON VAUGHN, PhD

Acknowledgments

We want to acknowledge all of the teachers, researchers, and students with whom we have had the pleasure of working over the years. They have provided us with the knowledge and practical applications of the information we share in this book.

Completing this book would not have been possible without the support of several individuals. We would like to thank Nicole Roderman for her outstanding assistance in preparing many of the lesson activities and intensifications in this book, as well as her attention to the numerous details that brought these chapters together. We would also like to thank Sharon Vaughn for her guidance during the preparation of this book. Her insightful feedback brought life to each of the chapters. We are also grateful to Paul Haspel for his expert editing assistance.

Contents

CHAPTER 1

Introduction to Intensive Reading Interventions

Calvin is a fourth-grade boy with a learning disability in reading. He is struggling with decoding and word recognition as well as comprehension in grade-level text. Calvin received reading intervention in third grade to address his reading difficulties along with other students who had similar difficulties. However, the other students made significant progress toward grade-level goals, while Calvin's progress was insufficient to help him start closing the gap to grade-level expectations and successful reading. Calvin's teachers are concerned his slow progress means that he will continue to fall further behind. Calvin is in need of a more intensive intervention to help him be a successful reader. What can his teachers do to plan for a more intensive reading intervention that will help Calvin?

This book is intended for teachers and administrators who serve students with significant reading difficulties in the elementary grades, including students with learning disabilities in reading. Many students struggle to learn to read, and require research-based reading interventions to help them reach grade-level expectations in reading. Most of these students will respond to effective, data-based reading intervention that is designed to meet their reading needs. Yet some students—typically, students with the most severe reading difficulties—do not make adequate progress in standard reading interventions and require more intensive interventions in order to make sufficient growth in reading. These students can also learn to read! However, they may need specialized instruction provided in an intensive intervention to make significant progress. This book is designed with these students in mind. Identifying students with intensive needs and providing sufficiently intensive interventions for them is imperative for their success in reading and future academics. Although the information that we provide in this book can be helpful to teachers working with any student who is struggling to learn to read, we present a particular focus on the ways in which teachers can intensify interventions for students for whom current reading interventions are not sufficient.

When elementary-age students struggle with learning to read, they are likely to experience further reading and learning difficulties in the upper grades (Francis, Shaywitz, Stuebing, Shaywitz, & Fletcher, 1996; McNamara, Scissons, & Gutknecth, 2011). Yet by providing intensive reading interventions in the elementary grades, educators can assist students with significant reading difficulties in accelerating their learning (Gersten et al., 2008; Torgesen et al., 2001; Vaughn, Linan-Thompson, & Hickman, 2003; Vellutino et al., 1996; Wanzek et al., 2018). The research base on effective reading interventions provides direction regarding how to adapt or intensify instruction through organizational features and/or instructional delivery that is more individualized and tailored to student needs in order to accelerate their reading (Fuchs, Fuchs, & Malone, 2017; Vaughn, Wanzek, Murray, & Roberts, 2012).

CHARACTERISTICS OF INTENSIVE READING INTERVENTIONS

What can we do to intensify reading interventions and help more students accelerate their learning? In this section, we briefly introduce several ways to intensify reading interventions at the elementary level. We describe organizational intensifications that should be considered at the outset of implementing an intensive intervention for a student. We then define several features of instructional delivery that can be used to intensify interventions in daily lessons and activities. These instructional delivery features provide a framework of intensification that we use in each of the subsequent chapters describing the implementation of intensive instruction in each area of reading intervention. Figure 1.1 provides a visual decision-making process for intensifying interventions for students who are not making sufficient progress in validated reading interventions. Below we provide an introduction to each of the intensifications categories.

Organizational Intensifications

Two common ways to intensify reading interventions are to provide students with more time in intervention and/or instruction in a smaller group. Students with reading difficulties who receive more time dedicated to effective instruction in their area of need increase their reading success (Denton, Fletcher, Anthony, & Francis, 2006; Torgesen et al., 2001; Vaughn, Linan-Thompson, & Hickman, 2003). There are several ways to increase the amount of time during which students can receive reading intervention. For instance, the length of the intervention session can be increased (e.g., from 45 minutes to 60 minutes), or the number of sessions per week can be increased for students (e.g., from three times per week to daily intervention, or from one session per day to two sessions per day). When this time in intervention is increased, the intervention is intensified by using the additional time to provide additional instruction and practice. Of course, students with significant reading difficulties may also need a longer duration in the intervention to achieve grade-level expectations.

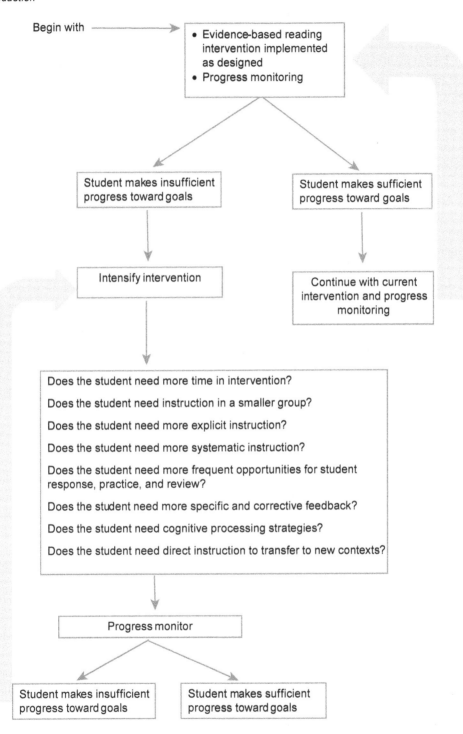

Begin with

- Evidence-based reading intervention implemented as designed
- Progress monitoring

Student makes insufficient progress toward goals

Student makes sufficient progress toward goals

Intensify intervention

Continue with current intervention and progress monitoring

Does the student need more time in intervention?

Does the student need instruction in a smaller group?

Does the student need more explicit instruction?

Does the student need more systematic instruction?

Does the student need more frequent opportunities for student response, practice, and review?

Does the student need more specific and corrective feedback?

Does the student need cognitive processing strategies?

Does the student need direct instruction to transfer to new contexts?

Progress monitor

Student makes insufficient progress toward goals

Student makes sufficient progress toward goals

FIGURE 1.1. Intensive intervention decision-making process.

The research also suggests that decreasing the size of the instructional group for intervention can intensify instruction and accelerate student learning (Hong & Hong, 2009; Lou et al., 1996; Vaughn, Linan-Thompson, Kouzekanani, et al., 2003). For example, while a less intensive reading intervention may be provided to a group of five students with reading difficulties, a student who does not respond adequately to this instruction may accelerate his or her learning if the instructional group is reduced to three students. The smaller group intensifies the intervention by allowing for more homogeneity, so that the teacher can better target specific student needs. In addition, a student receiving intervention in a smaller group may increase his or her practice opportunities, and may receive more frequent feedback on his or her performance from the teacher.

An important characteristic of effective reading interventions is data-based decision-making (Gersten et al., 2008). Student progress is monitored frequently during an intensive intervention to allow (1) identification of student needs that may be further targeted in the intervention, and (2) examination of overall progress in the intervention, to determine whether the student is adequately accelerating his or her learning toward the goals. Decades of research demonstrate that teachers who monitor whether their instruction is effective for students can achieve significantly higher levels of student learning (Conte & Hintze, 2000; Fuchs, Fuchs, Hamlett, & Allinder, 1991; Stecker, Fuchs, & Fuchs, 2005; Stecker, Lembke, & Foegen, 2008). Progress monitoring measures are sensitive to small changes in student reading achievement, allowing for frequent administration (e.g., weekly) and for decision-making within weeks rather than months or years. This ongoing decision-making helps teachers to adjust or intensify interventions to allow students to accelerate their achievement and meet learning goals.

Instructional Delivery Intensifications

Reading interventions can also be intensified in the way they are delivered by teachers. Initial and ongoing assessment provides key information on the reading components that a particular student requires in intervention instruction (e.g., phonological awareness, reading comprehension), but a student with intensive needs may require very detailed delivery of that instruction in order to accelerate learning in the area(s) of need and overall reading achievement. In this book, we describe intensive instruction that is explicit and systematic; includes frequent opportunities for student response, practice, and review; provides specific and corrective feedback; embeds cognitive processes; and teaches for transfer to other contexts. These instructional delivery areas are dynamic in that they can be used to further intensify interventions as needed for a specific student. For example, an intensive intervention lesson can be delivered in a more explicit way (e.g., providing more overt instruction or modeling of the skill or task) to help one student, or a group of students, and can be delivered in an even more explicit way to intensify the intervention further for another student or group of students. To provide teachers and administrators with the tools to adjust instructional delivery to meet student needs, we first describe intensive, research-based instruction for targeted reading components in each chapter and provide sample activities addressing the key components of instruction. We then provide examples of ways to further intensify each activity for students who continue to struggle with the master concepts despite the initial intensive efforts. Students with intensive intervention needs can accelerate their reading achievement and learn to read, but they require a knowledgeable teacher who can adapt the delivery of instruction on a daily basis to meet their needs. Below we describe each of the instructional delivery categories that we use to intensify reading interventions.

Explicit Instruction

Lessons can be intensified by increasing the explicitness of instruction. Explicit instruction refers to providing overt instruction for new reading practices or tasks. Students with learning difficulties can improve their outcomes when they are provided with explicit instruction showing them how to perform the reading practices (Gersten et al., 2008; Swanson, 2000). When teachers directly present and model new practices step-by-step for students, they are using explicit instruction. Lessons can be intensified by including additional models for students, or by presenting the material in more overt or concrete ways to help students better understand how to perform the new reading practice. For example, though many students may be able to learn to identify the main idea of a passage by learning how to identify the most important aspects of the passage, a student in need of more explicit instruction may need concrete ways to identify the important aspects (e.g., going through the passage explicitly to see which character is discussed most prominently). Explicit instruction is used during initial instruction of new practices or strategies.

Systematic Instruction

Lessons can also be intensified by making the instruction more systematic. Systematic instruction refers to teaching complex practices in small, manageable steps. When students with intensive needs receive instruction that is both explicit and systematic, they can accelerate their learning (Fletcher, Lyon, Fuchs, & Barnes, 2007; Swanson, Hoskyn, & Lee, 1999; Torgesen, 2002). Some students may require a task or practice to be broken into smaller steps in order to make learning the task manageable for them. This systematic approach can include providing supports or scaffolds for students when they are initially learning a task, to control the level of difficulty as they learn the process. As students gain facility, these supports can be gradually removed in a step-by-step fashion to allow students to master the task or practice independently. Thus, we can increase the intensity of the intervention for students by breaking a task or practice into smaller steps, further sequencing the instruction from easier to more difficult, providing step-by-step strategies for students to follow, and/or providing temporary supports for students to successfully complete the task or practice. For example, the main idea instruction mentioned above may be more systematic by providing students with a three-step strategy for identifying the main idea and then teaching one step at a time to mastery.

Frequent Opportunities for Student Response

Student engagement and practice are key to learning new and challenging tasks or practices. Another way to increase the intensity of an intervention is to provide additional opportunities for students to get deliberate practice with the tasks or practices they are trying to master. Increasing responses for students who have intensive intervention needs also provides teachers with additional opportunities to monitor student learning and understanding in order to make appropriate adjustments to the level of explicit and systematic instruction that students may need.

Specific and Corrective Feedback

Students require specific feedback on their practice attempts to master new tasks or practices effectively and efficiently. Specific and corrective feedback allows students to identify successful practice attempts, or to quickly correct misunderstandings before inaccurate learning occurs. Feedback is one of the most powerful tools teachers have to assist students in maintaining a high success rate in their practice attempts, leading to accelerated learning (Hattie & Timperley, 2007). Feedback is most valuable when it is specific and precise regarding what students have done correctly and what students need to do differently to complete the task successfully. Teachers can intensify reading lessons by increasing the specificity and amount of feedback that a student receives.

Cognitive Processing Strategies

Students with intensive reading intervention needs may have difficulties with some of the cognitive processes that relate to learning to read. For example, a student's self-regulation or executive functioning may affect his or her attention, memory, or implementation of new reading practices (Jacob & Parkinson, 2015; Robertson, 2000; Swanson, Zheng, & Jerman, 2009). Although teaching these processes in isolation has not been found to be fruitful, reading interventions can be intensified if cognitive processing strategies are embedded within the reading instruction. In this way, students can learn to manage the processes within the academic tasks where they need to be applied. These intensifications can be done by embedding instruction to help students (1) set learning goals in reading, (2) monitor progress toward those goals, (3) provide themselves with feedback as they complete tasks, (4) link effort and practice to learning and progressing in their reading ability, (5) talk themselves through tasks or strategies, and through persisting with tasks and inhibiting distractions, and (6) implement strategies to assist with memory load (e.g., graphic organizers, mnemonics).

Teaching for Transfer

Students with intensive intervention needs may learn many new tasks and practices using the intensifications mentioned above. They may, however, have particular difficulty transferring learning from one task to another (Gersten, Fuchs, Williams, & Baker,

2001). For example, a student may master identifying an individual sound in a word when it is at the beginning of the word (e.g., "What is the first sound in *fan*?"), but may have difficulty transferring that knowledge to identifying an individual sound in a word when it is at the end of the word (e.g., "What is the last sound in *off*?"). Alternatively, a student may master identifying the main idea in a narrative reading, but may have difficulty transferring that knowledge to identifying the main idea in an informational text. Thus, planning to teach specifically for transfer is a way to intensify reading interventions and accelerate learning. Students with intensive intervention needs will need explicit and systematic instruction in new tasks and practices, with plenty of response and feedback opportunities in a variety of contexts. If teachers notice particular difficulty with students successfully performing a task in one context but not remembering how to perform the task at other times, then intensifying the intervention through planned transfer instruction and practice may be warranted.

IDENTIFYING STUDENTS
FOR INTENSIVE READING INTERVENTIONS

Students with intensive reading intervention needs in the elementary grades may demonstrate insufficient response to generally effective, evidence-based reading instruction provided in the grade-level classroom, as well as small-group reading intervention. Many schools implement a response-to-intervention (RTI) or multi-tiered system of support (MTSS) to match the intensity of instruction to student learning needs (Zirkel & Thomas, 2010). RTI and MTSS models ensure that core classroom reading instruction uses evidence-based techniques that are proven to help students learn to read effectively and efficiently. Sometimes this classroom instruction is referred to as Tier 1 instruction. If a student does not respond sufficiently to this effective classroom instruction, the student is provided with supplemental reading intervention. The intervention is provided in addition to the classroom instruction, typically in a small group, and continues to use evidence-based practices, but allows the student more targeted instruction in any area(s) of difficulty in order to accelerate the student's learning. Sometimes this supplemental intervention is referred to as Tier 2 instruction. Nearly all students will be able to get on track with reading through evidence-based core classroom instruction and supplemental intervention. If many students in a grade level are struggling with meeting reading expectations after receiving core or supplemental instruction, the problem is likely to be in the validity of the instruction or the fidelity of the implementation, and not a sign of a need for very intensive interventions for many students. Thus, if the core and supplemental instruction are well implemented, using evidence-based practices, there will likely be only a few students who may continue to struggle with reading despite this effective instruction. These are students with intensive reading intervention needs. Intensive reading interventions are sometimes referred to as Tier 3 interventions. Students with intensive needs may also have reading disabilities, including dyslexia.

Student reading achievement can be monitored throughout the RTI/MTSS process to determine which students have intensive needs. In the elementary grades, screening measures are often given to all students three times per year (fall, winter, spring) to monitor student reading growth in core classroom instruction. Of course, informal measures given frequently by teachers as part of the reading instruction can also provide valuable information about student needs. Screening measures should allow a standardized, objective, and quick (a few minutes) check on each student's overall reading performance. These measures should have established grade-level benchmarks to help educators and administrators determine whether a student is on track in his or her reading development, or whether the student may need intervention.

Students who are identified as needing intervention can then be monitored more frequently (weekly or biweekly) with standardized, objective, quick measures to determine whether the prescribed intervention results in the student accelerating his or her learning toward grade-level goals. Again, informal measures given as part of the intervention instruction can also provide teachers with valuable information about student reading strengths and weaknesses. When these progress monitoring measures indicate that a student is not making sufficient progress to meet reading goals, a change in intervention is needed. Simple changes to instruction (e.g., content emphasis, practice opportunities) may be made to accelerate learning. Nonetheless, when a student continues to demonstrate slow progress over time in a generally effective intervention, despite most students succeeding with the instruction, he or she may have intensive needs. Students with intensive needs may demonstrate difficulties in only one area of reading (e.g., fluency), or they may demonstrate difficulties in multiple areas of reading (e.g., word recognition, fluency, and comprehension).

In the upper-elementary grades, some students may not have responded adequately to previous interventions in earlier grades, but may not have yet received intensive intervention to meet their needs. These students may show reading growth that is several years behind their current grade level. Assuming that a lack of access to targeted, evidence-based instruction is not the cause of their problems, these students are likely in need of intensive intervention in order to accelerate their learning and close the large gap with their grade-level expectations. Using a combination of student data and evidence-based instruction will help educators identify students who are in need of intensive interventions.

DATA-BASED INDIVIDUALIZATION PROCESS

Once a student is identified as needing intensive intervention, the intervention needs to be planned to meet the student's specific needs. A data-based individualization process can assist with this planning and implementation. First, the available data for the student should be examined to identify possible hypotheses for the student's continuing difficulties. Any additional data (e.g., a diagnostic assessment) that are needed to generate these hypotheses can also be collected. Some schools implement instructional decision-making teams of educators to regularly discuss student data and generate hypotheses for students in need of intensive interventions. These teams, sometimes called RTI or MTSS teams, can include general educators, special educators, administrators, reading specialists, speech/language pathologists, school psychologists, and so on. Data that may be helpful in generating hypotheses about student difficulties include the student's previous and current instructional context (e.g., What instruction or intervention has been implemented?; For how much time is the student receiving intervention?; In what size instructional group has the student received instruction?), and informal and formal data demonstrating the types of problems the student exhibits during reading (e.g., fluency, reading irregular words in text, segmenting sounds in words), as well as any student strengths (e.g., decoding regular words, reading text when teacher prompts/reminds student of the strategies). The team can then use these data to make hypotheses regarding the student's continued difficulties. For example, a team may hypothesize that the student requires more explicit instruction and practice in irregular word reading. Based on this hypothesis, a recommendation to intensify the lesson with a greater amount of time spent in irregular word instruction, more explicit instruction in learning the words, and increased opportunities to practice irregular words in isolation and in text can be planned in the intervention.

Once a hypothesis and general plan for intensification are made, the teacher who will implement the intensive intervention can plan to incorporate the recommended intensifications in the daily lessons. In the example above, the teacher would examine the validated, evidence-based reading intervention program and then plan the intensifications (spending more time on irregular word instruction and identifying ways to make the instruction more explicit and places to increase the response opportunities for the student to practice irregular words in isolation and in text). The teacher will implement these intensifications each day of the intervention while continuing to monitor the student's progress in reading. The teacher may make simple adjustments to these intensifications, based on the progress that the student demonstrates during daily lessons and in the progress monitoring data. After several weeks of instruction (e.g., 6–8 weeks), the team may revisit the student's data to determine whether the intensified intervention is working. If the student is showing accelerated learning with a trend toward the reading goal, the team may recommend that the intervention continue as is. In this case, it appears that the hypothesis was validated and that the intervention is working for the student. If the student is showing accelerated learning, but not at a rate that will allow him or her to meet the reading goal, the team may make further suggestions for intensifications within the current hypothesis, or they may generate additional hypotheses using the data. The intervention is then further intensified, according to these hypotheses, and implemented. If the student is not showing accelerated learning, the team may use the additional data available (or may collect further data) to generate a new or additional hypothesis, as it appears that the current hypothesis and intervention are not providing the student with what he or she needs to accelerate his or her learning.

Figure 1.2 provides data from our student, Calvin, who required three changes in intensification before accelerating learning adequately toward his goal. An initial instructional plan for Calvin's intensive intervention was planned based on his needs.

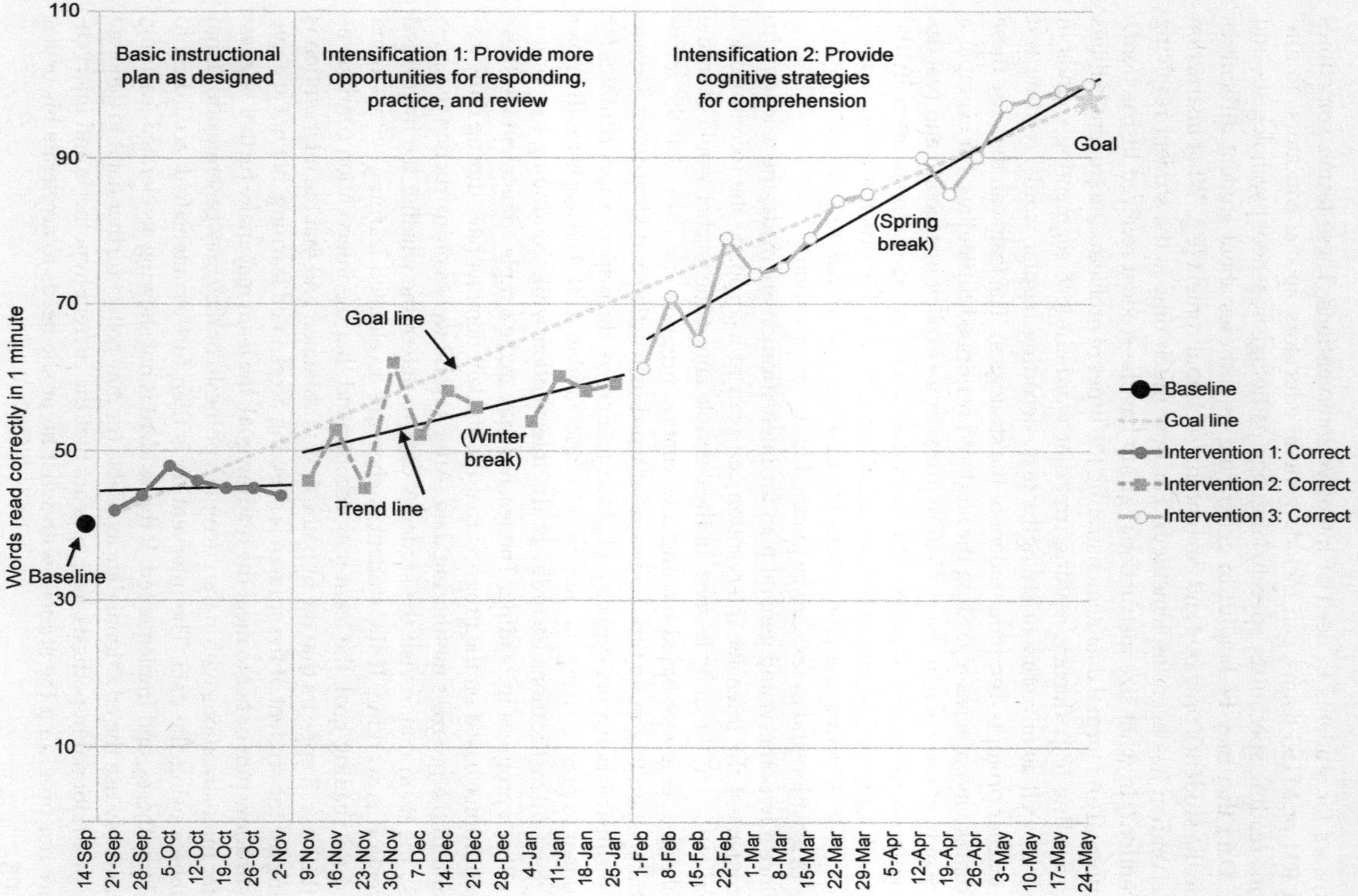

FIGURE 1.2. Calvin's progress monitoring graph.

When his data demonstrated learning below his goal line, the intervention was further intensified by including more frequent opportunities for response and practice in the area of fluency instruction. As this intervention change was implemented, student progress monitoring continued and showed some accelerated learning, but again not at a rate that would allow Calvin to meet his goal. Thus, the intervention was again intensified by including cognitive processing strategies embedded in the reading intervention. At this point, progress monitoring data demonstrated accelerated learning toward the goal. Nevertheless, Calvin's teachers will continue to monitor his progress and will provide additional intensifications if needed later. We discuss Calvin's data, decision-making, and intensifications further in Chapter 8.

THE CHAPTERS IN THIS BOOK

In the following chapters, we provide information on the content and delivery of intensive interventions in each of the components of reading with which students may demonstrate intensive needs. To help educators make important decisions regarding intensive intervention, each chapter first provides an overview of the research on instruction in the identified reading component, and of the essential elements of intensive intervention for students struggling in the component. We then provide specific examples of activities utilizing the research-based instruction discussed in the chapter. Intensifying interventions is a dynamic process of determining a specific student's needs for learning (e.g., some students require more intense feedback than others do). Thus, for each activity we provide examples of further intensifying the activity to meet particular student needs, using the intensification categories introduced in this first chapter.

CHAPTER 2

Intensive Interventions to Support Phonological and Phonemic Awareness

One October, we were screening kindergarten children to determine who might need more explicit early instruction. To check his first sound awareness, I (SA) asked Damien to tell me the first sound in his name. He replied with his whole name, "Damien." Then I asked him to spell his name and although he wrote it very painstakingly, he could tell me the letters as he wrote them, in the correct order. Next, to see whether he could segment the sounds in a short word, I asked him to tell me the sounds in *dog* and he replied, "Woof, woof?" Then I told him we would play a game and I would say a word in a funny broken-up way and he would say the whole word. I modeled: "If I say /mmm/ /ilk/, you would say the whole word, *milk*. Your turn: /f/ /ive/." He looked at me and said, "I don't know." When I gave him another example with bigger chunks of language like *cup . . . cake,* he could correctly respond with "cupcake." When I showed him the word *dog,* he could count the letters. I learned that while Damien had learned some letters in preschool, and could blend words to form compound words, he had not yet learned about the relation of sounds in speech and how they map to letters. He would need explicit instruction to make this critical connection and to master phonemic awareness.

Intensive phonological awareness instruction supports student understanding and awareness of the systematic structure of spoken language. Phonological awareness refers to the ability to hear and work with the parts of words and language. For example, it includes the ability to count the words in a sentence, to segment words into syllables, to orally blend syllables in order to pronounce words, and to hear the onset (the initial consonant sound in a word) and the rime (the vowel and sounds that follow) in a spoken word. Phonological awareness also includes the ability to hear and produce rhyming words. Phonemic awareness, a subset of skills within phonological awareness, refers to the more discrete, and therefore difficult, skills needed to identify and manipulate individual sounds within spoken words. Researchers emphasize that phonemic awareness allows children not only to consciously attend to spoken language and meanings but also to identify and manipulate phonemes that change the meanings (e.g., Stanovich, 1986; Uhry, 1999). Students can hear the difference between "Mom said 'stop'" and "Mom said 'hop,'" and can also identify the phoneme that makes the difference (*st* vs. *h*).

WHAT DOES THE RESEARCH SAY ABOUT PHONOLOGICAL AND PHONEMIC AWARENESS INSTRUCTION?

Phonemic awareness instruction is such an important part of early literacy because research has consistently documented a strong predictive relation between young children's phonemic awareness and their early reading development for alphabetic languages (e.g., Ehri et al., 2001; National Center for Family Literacy [NCFL], 2009). Specifically, the National Early Literacy Panel (NELP, 2009) examined a total of 69 studies and found a moderately predictive correlation between preschool phonological skill and school-age word reading; findings from 29 studies found an even stronger correlation to comprehension. To underscore the importance of this research, phonemic awareness is foundational for *all* aspects of reading and writing, most directly by impacting word recognition and spelling acquisition. In turn, automatic and fluent word reading is needed in order for one to read with comprehension (e.g., Perfetti, 2011). Generally, there is agreement that phonological awareness develops within and across stages of reading development as students learn to access more print (e.g., Ehri, 2000). Thus, phonological awareness training is largely for younger readers, whereas older readers who still need this training benefit more if it is directly connected with their phonics instruction.

Initial stages of phonological development begin as early as children are exposed to and hear adults talking; it grows exponentially as children learn to talk. It may be difficult to understand toddlers' language; certain phonemes are easier for them to articulate. By age 4, most children have improved their articulation and become increasingly intelligible, making it easier for them to match the sounds they hear with the sounds in words that they speak. They begin to hear and distinguish words within sentences. Some children may also become aware of alliteration and rhyme, particularly when engaged in shared book reading or verbal play with parents and caregivers. In turn, their ability to engage in phonemic matching prepares them to begin to form letter–sound representations in their memory, a process known as fast mapping (e.g., Ehri, 2000, 2002). The kindergartener in our vignette at the start of this chapter, Damien, needed help to understand that the letters he had learned represented sounds in the language he spoke and in language all around him.

Next, children begin to recognize and produce sounds. To master this stage, Damien would need explicit and systematic instruction to understand—for example, that changing a sound changes the meaning of a word (e.g., *can* vs. *man*, or *man* vs. *men*).

School-age students learn to blend and segment syllables and then onset–rimes (e.g., *c* and *an* makes *can*). With explicit instruction, over time students increase their ability to pay attention, think about, remember, and manipulate the sounds (or phonemes) in words. Gradually, they can relate phonemes to letters (letter–sound correspondence, or the alphabetic principle). They learn to blend and segment individual sounds in order to decode (or sound a word out; e.g., /mmm/ /aaa/ /nnn/ makes *man*) and to encode (or spell; e.g., the sounds in *man* are /mmm/ /aaa/ /nnn/). Ehri (2000) referred to this correlation between reading and spelling as skills that represent two sides of the same coin.

Students are expected to master the ability to manipulate phonemes within larger units of language, such as syllables and morphemes, fairly early in their elementary education. In fact, many state standards emphasize that by the end of kindergarten, students should have mastered the ability to rhyme, to correctly pronounce consonant and vowel sounds, and to blend and segment the initial, medial vowel, and final sounds in three-phoneme words. At the end of first grade, students are expected to blend, segment, and manipulate single-syllable words at the level of individual phonemes or sounds.

Fortunately, researchers have demonstrated the positive effects of explicit and systematic phonological awareness instruction, particularly for younger students like Damien (e.g., NCFL, 2009; National Reading Panel & National Institute of Child Health and Human Development, 2000). The National Reading Panel evaluated over 50 experimental studies and found that systematic instruction in phonological and phonemic awareness was highly effective with students across grades and age levels in terms of improving phonemic skills, word reading, and comprehension. Phonemic awareness instruction was most effective when it was systematically linked to letter-sound instruction. A more recent review, conducted by the Institute of Education Sciences, also reported that there is strong evidence for the efficacy of training students to orally blend and segment sounds, and link the sounds to print (Foorman et al., 2016). The effects of intensive interventions that combine phonemic awareness and phonics components have been beneficial even for adults with reading difficulties (Eden et al., 2004).

There are several reasons why some students may struggle to hear, pronounce, and manipulate sounds in spoken language, and may require even more intensive interventions. First, for many children with language and speech delays, the sounds they are able to produce may not match the sounds they hear in a word, or they may struggle with other aspects of language that can delay their phonological development and RTIs (e.g., Al Otaiba, Puranik, Ziolkowski, & Curran, 2009; Catts, 1991; Snowling, Duff, Nash, & Hulme, 2016). Second, phonological processing involves working memory and attention, and therefore may be challenging for students with poor self-regulation, limited working memory, or attention deficits (e.g., Adams & Gathercole, 1995). Third, some students enter school with very limited exposure to books, and may also have limited oral vocabularies (e.g., Hart & Risley, 1995). Fourth, some students speak a first language other than English, and some of the English language's alphabetic structural aspects may not transfer to their first language (e.g., Branum-Martin, Tao, Garnaat, Bunta, & Francis, 2012). Finally, some students struggle because they have phonological processing deficits, the primary cause of specific reading disabilities, including dyslexia (Catts,

1989). Sometimes these deficits appear unexpected; at other times, there is a family history for dyslexia or other specific learning disabilities. In summary, for any of these reasons, some students may respond more slowly to generally effective interventions (e.g., Al Otaiba & Fuchs, 2002; Lam & McMaster, 2014); the implication is that explicit and systematic instruction is necessary, but may not be sufficiently intensive to meet all students' needs.

WHAT ARE THE CRITICAL ELEMENTS OF PHONOLOGICAL AND PHONEMIC AWARENESS INSTRUCTION?

Given the research base, the critical elements for instruction in phonological awareness and phonemic awareness include pronouncing, blending, segmenting, and manipulating sounds. Because it is easier to hear and pronounce larger chunks of language, such as words or syllables, than individual phonemes, the sequence for teaching these elements will generally reflect this sound structure of the English language. In other words, researchers suggest that the scope and sequence within these elements begin with instruction targeting larger linguistic units (words and syllables) and progress toward phonemic units (onset–rime and individual phonemes; e.g., Chard & Dickson, 1999; Foorman et al., 2016; NCFL, 2009; Snider, 1995). Figure 2.1 provides a sequence from largest to smallest units with examples. If students with intensive needs have mastered earlier skills, their intensive interventions should focus on skills that the student has not yet mastered. Let's examine each critical element of phonological and phonemic awareness, along with ways to provide intensive instruction in these elements.

Sound Pronunciation

Learning the sounds of language involves mastery of the phonological rules of the English language's structure. Thus, an integral part of intensive reading intervention for students who do not yet have the correct pronunciation of sounds includes systematically introducing sounds and selecting appropriate linguistic and phonological targets. Correct sound pronunciation will further assist students in their development of oral language (described further in Chapter 5) as well as word reading and spelling (described further in Chapter 3). Researchers caution that students with reading disabilities often produce more speech errors and struggle more to repeat complex sentences and phrases than their peers, even through adulthood (Catts, 1989). The goal is for students to learn to correctly pronounce all 44 phonemes that will later be represented by 26 letters, and a total of 15 vowel sounds that can be represented by only five vowel letters (see the "Resources" section at the end of this chapter for a helpful PowerPoint slide presentation with audio of the sounds).

Students learn to correctly produce these sounds by hearing others speak and by forming memories of these pronunciations. For some students, this learning process will develop easily, but others with more intensive needs will require very explicit instruction: modeling, guided practice, and independent practice.

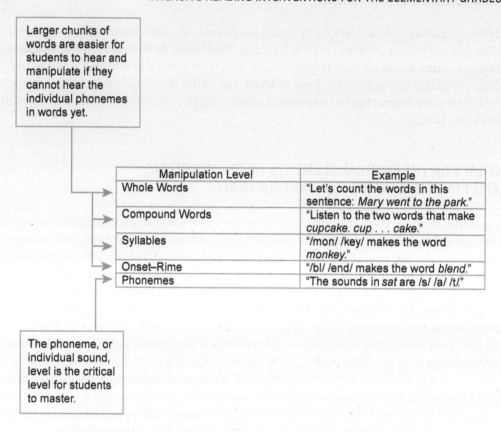

Larger chunks of words are easier for students to hear and manipulate if they cannot hear the individual phonemes in words yet.

Manipulation Level	Example
Whole Words	"Let's count the words in this sentence: *Mary went to the park*."
Compound Words	"Listen to the two words that make *cupcake. cup . . . cake*."
Syllables	"/mon/ /key/ makes the word *monkey*."
Onset–Rime	"/bl/ /end/ makes the word *blend*."
Phonemes	"The sounds in *sat* are /s/ /a/ /t/."

The phoneme, or individual sound, level is the critical level for students to master.

FIGURE 2.1. Sequence of manipulation levels in phonological awareness.

To correctly articulate syllables, students need to pronounce vowel and consonant sounds. To articulate vowels, they coordinate movement involving their tongue, jaw, and lips—hence, researchers such as Moats (2010) have categorized vowels by the position of the tongue in the mouth and by the position of the lips. Long vowels are considered tense vowels, as they are longer in duration (e.g., *no*), whereas short vowels are considered lax because they are shorter in duration (e.g., *hop*). Similarly, intensive interventions may include helping students feel and hear how sounds are produced. For example, some consonants, known as stop sounds (e.g., *b, t, k, g*) are pronounced briefly. Students may incorrectly add a schwa (e.g., a sound like /ah/ or /uh/) to consonant sounds, particularly for stop sounds. For example, they may say "duh" for the letter sound /d/. By contrast, some consonants are continuous, as they can be held or hummed (i.e., /nnn/, /mmm/). Figure 2.2 provides a list of continuous and stop sounds.

Generally, in order to provide a systematic intervention, teaching from easiest to most difficult, it is important to consider whether consonants in words selected for intervention are pronounced in a voiced or voiceless manner, meaning that they are produced at the same place in the mouth, but they differ in voicing, something that can confuse children. Thus, in early intervention, it is important to consider the sequence or

Continuous sounds	All vowels	/f/	/h/	/l/	/m/	/n/	/r/	/s/	/v/	/y/	/z/
Stop sounds		/b/	/c/	/d/	/g/	/j/	/k/	/p/	/q/	/t/	/w/	

FIGURE 2.2. Letters that represent continuous sounds versus stop sounds.

order for instruction, and to not teach these sound pairs at the same time: /p/ and /d/, /v/ and /f/, /t/ and /d/, /s/ and /z/, /k/ and /g/, /sh/ and /zh/, or /ch/ and /j/. The voiced consonants are taught before voiceless consonants.

Blending and Segmenting

Blending is defined as coarticulating sounds to pronounce a word. As previously noted, blending can involve larger or smaller chunks of sound. By contrast, segmenting is defined as pronouncing sounds within words, phrases, or sentences. Ultimately, students need to blend and segment individual phonemes, but a scope and sequence for intervention includes larger chunks of language as needed.

Phonological Blending and Segmenting with Larger Chunks of Language

As students master correct sound production, intensive instruction can target the phonological structure of language, with the first level being words in a sentence. This factor is important because, as we speak in conversation, many of our words blur together, and so students may not be aware of individual words as units of language. Consider a toddler listening to her parents' music and distorting the words. A precious example from our family was a 3-year-old boisterously singing, "Save a whale, save a whale, save a whale" instead of the lyrics intended by Enya, which were "Sail away, sail away, sail away." Young children need explicit instruction in order to understand that words can be identified, counted, and segmented, or spoken alone. Intensive activities for school-age students without this awareness could involve modeling and practice clapping, tapping, or counting each word in a sentence. These could involve sentences in a simple song, nursery rhyme, or story. Following modeling and guided practice, immediate corrective feedback is important to ensure that the student pronounces the words correctly and in order. As students master this word level of phonological structure, they build their sensitivity and will be ready to learn more about subword levels of phonology within a partial alphabetic phase.

The subsequent level for intervention includes identifying or counting, blending, and segmenting compound words and syllables. Instruction begins with familiar words. For example, when teachers say, "I can say the whole word, *goldfish*, or I can say the chunks in the word, *gold* and *fish*," they are introducing students to segmenting. By contrast, if teachers model by saying, "Listen, I am going to say two words that can make a new word: *gold*, and *fish*, makes *goldfish*," they are modeling blending. The next step in systematic intervention would involve guided practice identifying, segmenting, and blending syllables in common words and even in the students' names (e.g., *Tom . . . my*). Eventually, students would be prompted to practice blending and segmenting chunks of sounds—for example, "See whether you can name the friend I am thinking of: *Nat . . . a . . . lie*. Yes, you are right, I was thinking of *Natalie*." If needed, to make the intervention even more supported, teachers might provide pictures, or might introduce an instructional routine involving clapping the syllables or tapping on a desk for each chunk—for example, "Hmm, let's clap your name and Natalie's name. Whose name has more claps?" Teachers might also teach students to tap on their desk, or on their arm, as they count syllables in familiar multisyllabic words, such as *mother, father, sister, brother*, or select words from a shared book reading, such as *caterpillar, hungry, Monday, Tuesday*. Next, teachers might model saying the syllables with a pause in between, and might ask students to guess the word by blending the sounds (e.g., "/Fri/ . . . /day/; What day am I thinking of?").

Even older students can benefit from explicit phonological awareness intervention, particularly when the intervention links to their word reading or spelling instruction. For example, for a student who is working on multisyllabic words but does not yet have strong phonological awareness, the teacher might select a two-syllable word like *review*. The teacher could emphasize the two syllables in the word, and could then have the student count or clap and identify the two chunks or syllables in the word. The teacher might teach several related words such as *view, reviewing, preview*, and *previewing*. The segmenting of these words would then be directly connected with word reading (e.g., "Let's read those word parts in this word") or spelling instruction (e.g., "The first chunk was /re/. What letters spell /re/?") the student is receiving. Similarly, a connection between the phonological awareness instruction and the meaning of the word can be made with explicit instruction on the meaning of the prefix *re-* (e.g., something is happening again). If a student struggles to be aware of, or to hear, the syllables in a word, the teacher might suggest that the student gently place a hand under his or her chin, so the student can feel each time he or she articulates a syllable.

As students master the ability to correctly pronounce sounds, and as they learn to blend and segment syllables, they benefit from learning how to segment or split off the initial sound (in the example of *dog*, the /d/) from the remainder of a one-syllable word (/og/), known as the rime, and including the middle vowel and ending sound. Thus, alliteration, or awareness of the first sound in a word, will support their understanding of blending and segmenting onsets and rimes. Intervention would focus on identifying the initial sound in a word, something that requires segmenting the onset from the rest of the syllable (e.g., in the word *sat*, the onset is /s/, and the rime is /at/) and then moving to blending and segmenting onsets and rimes.

One reason that segmenting an initial sound from the rime is challenging, and thus requires careful selection of targeted words for intervention, is because sounds in words are coarticulated or blurred. In addition, as we segment sounds in words, consonants like the /d/ in *dog* are difficult to pronounce in their truest form without adding additional sounds (e.g., /d/ may be pronounced as "duh," with an added schwa sound). In particular, the vowels (often medial sounds) in words are most challenging to hear and differentiate for students. Thus, a sequence for intervention should consider whether the initial sound is a stop sound or a continuous sound. It is easier to segment a stop sound from the rime—for example, the first sound in *dog* is /d/. By contrast, however, it is easier to blend continuous sounds, as when /sss/ and /ammm/ make the word *Sam*. Further, given the working memory load associated with phonological tasks, intervention can be made more concrete by allowing students to use pictures or objects. The teacher might model how to sort pictures into piles that start with the same onset sound(s), or into piles with the same rime endings, something that would be easier than expecting students to generate words on their own. It is critical to select a variety of words for student practice, so that students can master identifying the first sound in a word, as well as blending and segmenting onsets and rimes in words. Although most students become sensitive to onsets and rimes as early as preschool, even older students who need intensive reading interventions may need phonological awareness instruction in onset–rime, as it connects to their word reading and spelling instruction.

Phonemic-Level Blending and Segmenting

Blending, segmenting, and manipulating each individual phoneme in a word represents the most challenging linguistic level. For beginning readers who need intensive intervention, it is important to plan explicit and systematic instruction that builds from less to more complexity. Short familiar words, such as *mom, dad, dog,* or *cat,* would be good target words for segmenting each sound in a word. For blending, target words should initially include continuous sounds, such as *mom,* because these sounds can be stretched without distorting the sounds, making the blending task easier. Another feature related to complexity is the concreteness of the word—Can it be represented by a picture or object to reduce working memory load? To make a blending task easier, a teacher might show a picture of a mom and a dad and ask the student to say the word with the sounds /m/ /o/ /m/, or for a segmenting task, a teacher might show a picture of a dog while asking students to say each sound in the word *dog*. These words also reflect the feature we mentioned earlier—that segmenting is easier when introducing target words with stop consonant sounds.

There are a few methods that can make phonemic awareness intervention even more concrete. For example, a teacher can utilize colored tiles or blocks, and Elkonin boxes (Elkonin, 1971). Elkonin boxes are blank boxes drawn on paper to represent individual sounds (see Figure 2.3). The teacher and student can move or point to a tile for each sound heard in the word, slide the tiles together as sounds are blended into a word, or indicate which tile represents a change in sound between two words—for example, "Let's change *pan* to *can*. Which tile needs to change? That's right, /p/ is the first sound in *pan,* and it needs to change to /c/ to make *can*." As students gain mastery with

FIGURE 2.3. Example of an Elkonin box with cubes for a three-phoneme word.

hearing and manipulating phonemes in words, explicit instruction can progress with letter tiles, with the consequence being that thereafter, phonemic intervention activities will focus on decodable words that follow the phonetic rules.

Recognizing student errors, identifying possible sources for student confusion, and providing supportive corrective feedback in intensive phonological awareness interventions requires knowledge and expertise about phonological development and the phases of reading development. This process may require very careful listening in order to discern whether a student is developing correct sound pronunciation and developing a broader oral vocabulary (see Chapter 5), as well as developing the ability to hear and manipulate individual sounds in words. In addition, a knowledgeable teacher will help students transfer phonemic skills into the reading and spelling of words (see Chapter 3).

Shared Book Reading to Support Phonological and Phonemic Awareness

The purpose for teaching phonological and phonemic awareness is to support students' ability to acquire phonics and word recognition, and ultimately to read for understanding. Thus, students need to explicitly see and hear the connection between their phonological practice and as they participate in book reading. Next, we describe a few texts as exemplars for supporting intensive practice.

Many children's books incorporate rhyming words; we imagine that many of you reading this book are familiar with the rhyming books written by authors including Margaret Wise Brown (e.g., *Goodnight Moon*), Dr. Seuss (e.g., *The Cat in the Hat*), and Bill Martin (*Brown Bear, Brown Bear*; *Chicka Chicka Boom Boom*). Many picture books feature common nursery rhymes or songs that also feature rimes and rhymes (e.g., Raffi). A knowledgeable teacher will explicitly emphasize onset–rime, using the books as a concrete model for instruction about identifying the rime in words, generating lists of rhyming words, and substituting various initial sounds to change the meaning of words. Similarly, there are many books that emphasize alliteration—for example, Audrey Wood's *Silly Sally*. Any of these texts can be used to generate word lists for blending, segmenting, or manipulating phonemes. Of course, teachers will also select books based upon students' interests.

HOW DO I MONITOR PROGRESS IN PHONOLOGICAL AND PHONEMIC AWARENESS?

Given that phonological awareness is the strongest predictor of early reading problems, screening and monitoring student progress should help teachers make decisions about the sequence of intervention, planning lessons that include appropriate words and skills, identifying and correcting errors in learning, and pacing intervention. There are a number of standardized measures that assess skills encompassing phonological and phonemic awareness levels; notably, these have age- and grade-based norms that range into adulthood. Below we identify formal and informal progress monitoring techniques that intervention teachers can use to monitor students' learning and make instructional decisions. Both sources of data can help teachers determine who, like Damien, needs more explicit instruction in phonological awareness and also plan which particular skills to target. In Damien's case, his teacher could follow up on my initial testing, which indicated he knew many letters and could blend two words to form a compound word, but that he could not identify the initial sound in a word and could not blend or segment at an onset–rime level. Instructional next steps would be to provide more explicit instruction in identifying initial sounds in words, and then systematically move on to phonemic blending and segmenting. Damien likely needs more modeling and practice opportunities than he is currently receiving in phonological awareness. His teacher would also want to select an appropriate and sensitive progress monitoring tool to help determine whether he was mastering these skills with the more intensive instruction, or whether he requires additional instructional changes.

Formal Measures

A well-researched approach to monitoring overall reading progress is curriculum-based measurement (CBM; e.g., Deno, 1985; Hosp, Hosp, & Howell, 2016). CBMs typically include multiple forms of an assessment of similar difficulty, so that teachers can track progress for students across the school year. Test developers provide benchmarks, or a score, that is associated with future risk or future success. Teachers can track progress toward grade level, and can evaluate the success of an intervention based on student progress toward a goal.

There are many standardized commercially available brief CBMs of phonological awareness, such as phonemic segmentation, or initial sound awareness. A phonemic segmentation task includes an array of words to be pronounced by a teacher, followed by the student saying each sound (segmenting) in the word. There are also several CBMs that assess first-sound fluency; some provide several pictures and ask a student to name the first sound in the word. Others ask the student to point to the picture that starts with a particular sound.

Informal Measures

There are also several informal techniques that a teacher may employ to provide additional information to guide a student's intensive intervention in phonological awareness. One informal way in which a teacher can track student ability to correctly produce sounds is to listen and monitor the sounds a student produces during intervention. A monitoring list for tracking sound production could be in alphabetic order, could follow the order in a curriculum, or could follow a scope and sequence from easier to more difficult sounds, as we described earlier in the chapter. Teachers can also take note when students do not master phonological awareness skills following generally effective instruction, record errors that students make while looking for patterns, or note if students are not able to successfully complete an end-of-unit assessment. Having information about the specific pattern of errors can assist the teacher in planning intervention to teach the most appropriate skills and to provide an intensive level of support that ensures mastery of those skills.

INSTRUCTIONAL ACTIVITIES FOR PHONOLOGICAL AND PHONEMIC AWARENESS

Introducing Correct Sound Pronunciation and Initial Sound Identification

Objectives

The student will be able to pronounce the most common sounds in English. The student will be able to match words with the same initial sound and identify the sound.

Materials

Word list and picture cards.

Children's books.

Mirror.

Procedures

MODEL

1. Tell the student the new sound (e.g., /f/). For example: "Listen, I can say /fff/, like the first sound in *father, fantastic, fun.* Say /fff/ with me." Ask the student to repeat the sound. Check for correct pronunciation.

2. Show the student picture cards with objects or animals that start with the new sound. Name each picture for the student, emphasizing the first sound. For example: *"Fox. Fffox* starts with /fff/." Have the student repeat the name of the picture and the first sound. For example: "What is this picture? [fox] What is the first sound in *fox?* /fff/."

SUPPORTED PRACTICE

1. Practice the new sound (e.g., /fff/) and select several picture cards with first sounds that the student has already learned for review (e.g., if the student knows the sounds for /s/, /m/, /t/, then some picture cards could include *sand, map, tent*). Name each picture for the student, to ensure that he or she knows what each picture represents. Ask the student to give a thumbs-up when he or she sees a picture that starts with /f/. Then have the student say the name of each picture and say the first sound.

2. Put the picture cards together and play a game of Go Fish. Teach the rules for the game. For example: "I am looking for something that starts with /fff/, like my *fish.* Do you have a picture that starts with /fff/?"

Review

Incorporate the new sound into supported practice activities for several lessons along with familiar, previously taught sounds.

Examples of Activity Intensifications

DOES THE STUDENT NEED MORE SYSTEMATIC INSTRUCTION?

- Ensure that the student can correctly articulate the sound. Initially, do not simultaneously introduce sounds that are easily confused auditorially (e.g., /f/ and /v/).

- Demonstrate placement of the mouth and tongue in pronouncing the correct sound for a new sound. For example: "I can feel my top teeth tickle my bottom lip when I say /fff/. Can you?"

- Hold a mirror so the student can see his or her own mouth placement, and provide feedback on mouth placement to produce the correct sound.

- Consider whether the student has lost his or her front teeth or has an articulation error, and praise approximations of the correct sound pronunciation. For example: "You are working hard to learn the /f/ sound. You have almost got it right."

- Provide a key word or visual, such as a picture, to help the student remember the correct sound of the phoneme (e.g., /f/ as in *father*). Consider a cognate if a student is an English language learner (e.g., *lion/león* for Spanish), or explicitly teach that this is a new sound if it is not a sound in the native language (e.g., there are no /v/ or /p/ sounds in Arabic).

DOES THE STUDENT NEED MORE FREQUENT OPPORTUNITIES
FOR STUDENT RESPONSE, PRACTICE, AND REVIEW?

- Practice the new sound for 2–3 days before adding a new sound.

- Ensure that the new sound features prominently and frequently in cumulative review lists that are practiced daily. If possible, vary the picture cards for each sound (e.g., not only *fish*, but also *fox, feather, fan*).

- When reading a story to the student, have him or her use a thumbs-up each time he or she hears the new sound.

- Provide a peer-pair or small-group activity such as Go Fish for child center time to allow additional practice.

Counting the Words in Sentences

Objective

The student will be able to count the words in sentences.

Materials

Children's books.

Blank cards or sticky notes.

DVD, video, or other source for music.

Procedures

MODEL

1. Select a brief sentence (one to five words) from a nursery rhyme or a brief stanza from a poem or song that the student is familiar with. Play the song or rhyme and demonstrate how to clap for each word. For example: "Listen as I clap each time I say a word in this song we learned. Row, row, row your boat." Model clapping for each word said as the student says the line with you.

2. Next, model counting the words. For example: "Listen as I count the words in this song we learned. Row, row, row your boat." Model holding one finger for each word. Say: "I heard five words."

SUPPORTED PRACTICE

1. Select another stanza from the song "Row, Row, Row Your Boat." Have the student practice clapping each word in the stanza. Then have the student hold up a finger for each word. Ask the student how many words he or she counted. Then ask the student to identify the first word in the stanza. Repeat the model with several stanzas.

2. Select a book with a nursery rhyme. Read a three- to five-word section aloud and ask the student to repeat the sentence and count the words. Have the student identify the first or last word.

Review

Include opportunities to count words throughout the day.

Examples of Activity Intensifications

DOES THE STUDENT NEED MORE EXPLICIT INSTRUCTION?

- If a student is having difficulty differentiating each word, orally separate the words in the sentence more explicitly, pausing for a few seconds between each word to help the student hear. Over time, shorten the pauses until the student can count the words in a sentence spoken at a normal rate.

- Model tapping as each word is pronounced for emphasis.

- Use a sticky note to represent each word, and think aloud as you model counting each word.

- Provide blank cards for the student, one for each word. Have the student repeat the given sentence, pointing to a card for each word.

Blending Syllables in a Word

Objective

The student will be able to blend the syllables in a two- to three-syllable word.

Materials

Children's picture books.

Picture cards.

Sticky notes.

Procedures

MODEL

1. Select pictures of several two-syllable words that are familiar to the student. Initially include several compound words. Then introduce additional two- to three-syllable words.
2. Lay the pictures out and say the word of each picture (e.g., *cupcake, birthday, pancake, bathtub, Monday, Tuesday, cookie*). Ask the student to repeat each word.
3. Select a word (e.g., *pancake*) and model blending of each syllable. For example: "I'll say the parts of the word, and then I'll say the whole word. Listen, *pan . . . cake* makes *pancake* [point to the picture]. Say *pancake* with me."

SUPPORTED PRACTICE

Select another word and say the parts for the student. For example: "I'm going to say the parts of a word. You tell me what word I am saying: *cup . . . cake*." Repeat with several words until the student demonstrates mastery blending the two- and three-syllable words.

Review

When multisyllabic words come up during the day, point out the process of blending the syllables together to the student while making a connection to the reading activity.

Examples of Activity Intensifications

DOES THE STUDENT NEED MORE EXPLICIT INSTRUCTION?

- Provide sticky notes to represent each syllable of the word. Then say the syllables in the word and have the student point to each sticky note while saying each syllable, followed by saying the word in its entirety and moving the sticky notes together to represent blending.
- Model some errors and ask the student whether you are correct. For example: "The parts of *backpack* are *pack . . . back*. Is that right?"

DOES THE STUDENT NEED MORE SPECIFIC AND CORRECTIVE FEEDBACK?

- During student practice, if a student is just repeating the syllables, begin with correction of the error, and then guide the process of blending the syllables. For example:

"The parts of the word are *Mon . . . day.*" Then ask the student to blend with you. For example: "Let's say the parts together and then say the whole word."

- During student practice, if a student says the syllables but then says a different word (e.g., for *cup . . . cake,* the student says "birthday cake"), correct the error. For example, "I heard you say the parts of the word, *cup . . . cake.* When you put that together, do you hear 'cupcake' or 'birthday cake?'" Then ask the student to repeat.

- During student practice, praise some responses (e.g., "You looked at the pictures to help yourself remember it was a cupcake"), and some self-corrections (e.g., "That was a nice job catching a mistake and saying the right word").

Segmenting Syllables in a Word

Objective

The student will be able to segment the syllables in a word.

Materials

The book *Thumbtacks, Earwax, Lipstick, Dipstick: What Is a Compound Word?* by Brian Cleary.
Picture cards.
Whiteboard and dry-erase markers.
Blank tiles or cubes.

Procedures

MODEL

1. Select several two-syllable words that are familiar to the student. Include several compound words as well as high-frequency two-syllable words. Say each word as you point to picture cards. Check for correct pronunciation. The following word list could be used for modeling: *cupcake, birthday, bluebird, lipstick, cowboy, happy.*

2. Say each syllable with a pause between each. For example: "I can say the whole word *cupcake,* or I can say the parts in the word—*cup* [pause] *cake.*"

3. On the whiteboard, draw a long line to represent *cupcake,* and then draw two lines underneath to represent *cup* and *cake.*

4. Model how to "stretch" a word into its parts using tiles. For example: Put two tiles close together and say "cupcake," and then move each tile apart and say "cup . . . cake."

SUPPORTED PRACTICE

1. Select both previously learned and additional compound, two-syllable, and three-syllable (or longer) familiar words. Say each word. Ask the student to say the whole word and say the parts.

2. Select several familiar words. Ask the student to say and show the whole word with tiles, and then to show and tell the parts by moving the tiles apart.

Review

When multisyllabic words come up during the day, point out the process of saying the word, followed by saying each syllable to the student. Model and ask the student to clap the syllables in his or her name, the names of peers, the days of the week, or objects in the classroom.

Examples of Activity Intensifications

DOES THE STUDENT NEED COGNITIVE PROCESSING STRATEGIES?

- To reduce the working memory load, provide a picture card of the word, or draw the image on a whiteboard. Teach the student that looking at the picture can help him or her remember.
- Do not get "stuck" at this level! Balance encouraging the student that practice leads to success with leading the student to try to segment onset and rime, which in some cases could be easier.

Does the Student Need Direct Instruction for Transfer to New Contexts?

- Select pictures from a book featuring compound words, such as Brian Cleary's *Thumbtacks, Earwax, Lipstick, Dipstick: What Is a Compound Word?*
- Ask the student to identify rhyming words in children's books.

Blending Onsets and Rimes

Objective

The student will be able to blend the onset and rime in a three- to four-phoneme word.

Materials

Picture cards.

Elkonin boxes.

Blank tiles or cubes.

MODEL

1. Select several words that are familiar and that contain sounds the student already can pronounce. Initially, it is helpful to focus on words from one rime or word family. Consider rimes that are high frequency in primary-grade texts (e.g., *at, it, ot, in,*

ip, an, ug, ame, ice, ink). Initially model words that begin with a continuous sound; gradually introduce words like *bat* with stop sounds. If, for example, the focus is on the rime *at*, the following word list could be used for modeling of three-phoneme words: *mat, sat, rat, chat*.

2. Model blending by saying the onset and rime with a short pause in between. For example: "I can say the parts of the word, /rrr/ . . . /at/, and I can say the whole word, *rat*."

3. Repeat the model with other words and other word families.

SUPPORTED PRACTICE

1. Have the student repeat each onset and rime, and then say the whole word.

2. Encourage the student to use the tiles in the Elkonin box to represent blending the onset and rime to say the whole word.

3. Repeat the model for each new word.

Review

Continue to point out and model opportunities to practice blending onsets and rimes within read-alouds and additional teachable reading moments.

Examples of Activity Intensifications

DOES THE STUDENT NEED MORE EXPLICIT INSTRUCTION?

• Show the student how to move the tiles in the Elkonin box to represent blending. Say the onset and rime with a short pause in between. For example: "I can say the parts of the word, /mmm/ . . . /at/, and I can say the whole word, *mat*. Watch and listen as I move the tiles to show I can say the parts or the whole word."

• Put a set of picture cards in front of the student. Tell the student you will say the word parts for one of the pictures, and ask the student to identify the correct picture card. Then ask the student to say the parts with you, and then to say the whole word.

Segmenting Onsets and Rimes

Objectives

The student will be able to segment onsets and rimes in one-syllable words. The student will be able to sort, match, and identify words that rhyme.

Materials

Elkonin boxes.

Blank tiles or cubes.

Picture cards.

Children's books featuring rhyming words.

Letter tiles.

Procedures

MODEL

1. Select several words that are familiar and that contain sounds the student already can pronounce. Initially, it is helpful to focus on words that end with the same rime and that begin with stop sounds. For example, if the focus is on the rime *at* and the student already knows the sounds of the following onsets, the following word list could be used for modeling words with three phonemes: *cat, pat, bat.*

2. Say all of the words, and model parts that the words have in common. For example: "I notice all of these words end in *at.*" Pronounce the words and emphasize the ending to help the student hear the ending sound.

3. Model segmenting by saying the entire word and segmenting the onset and rime, with a brief pause between each sound segment. For example: "I can say the whole word, *cat* . . . or I can say the first part of the word and the rest. Listen, /c/ . . . /at/." Repeat this model for each word.

4. Repeat the model with another word family.

SUPPORTED PRACTICE

1. Select picture cards showing words with a common rime, or word family. Say the name of each picture card and have the student identify the similar ending sound. Have the student say the name of each picture and segment it into onset and rime.

2. Mix in picture cards from previously learned onset and rime combinations. Have the student say the name of the picture and segment it into onset and rime. Then have the student sort or match cards with the same rimes.

3. If the student knows how to play Go Fish, incorporate a game of Go Fish that features rhyming words at center time for peer-pair practice.

Review

When reading aloud books that include rhyming words, invite the student to repeat the word, followed by the onset and rime.

Examples of Activity Intensifications

DOES THE STUDENT NEED MORE SYSTEMATIC INSTRUCTION?

Use letter tiles to represent the rime being used (e.g., *at*) within the Elkonin box. For example: "This part says /at/." Then help the student move other letter tiles into the onset position. Emphasize the rime remaining the same, although the first sound tile is changing.

DOES THE STUDENT NEED MORE SPECIFIC AND CORRECTIVE FEEDBACK?

- During student practice, praise some responses by reminding the student that his or her success is due to practicing with the tiles.
- When the student makes an error, begin with correction. Then guide the student to correctly blend the onsets and rimes using Elkonin boxes.

Blending Phonemes

Objective

The student will be able to blend phonemes in words.

Materials

Picture cards.

Blank tiles or cubes.

Elkonin boxes.

Letter tiles.

Procedures

MODEL

1. Display pictures of three-phoneme words, initially introducing words with continuous sounds that are familiar vocabulary for the student. Lay the pictures out and say the word for each picture. Ask the student to repeat each word. An example of a word list for instruction could include *mom, nap, fish, lip, run, fun.*

2. Explain the use of blank tiles and explain how they will be used to blend each individual phoneme in each word to say the whole word. For example: "I will show you how each tile stands for each sound we hear in a word. Then I'll blend the sounds together to make a word."

3. Select a word that is represented on one of the picture cards. Say the sounds in the word and model blending the sounds together into the word using the tiles. For example: Place three blank tiles on the table and say, "I'm going to say each sound as I move a tile. Listen, /mmm/ /ooo/ /mmm/ [point to a blank tile for each sound]. That word is *mom* [slide finger under all three tiles to show the word being blended]." Repeat the model, stretching the sounds together while pointing to the tiles, so that the student can begin to hear the blended word and say the whole word, sliding your finger under the tiles to represent the blended word (e.g., /mmmm/ /oooo/ /mmm/ makes *mom*).

4. Have the student say the model with you—the sounds, followed by the whole word—while pointing to the tiles.

5. Repeat the model with several words. Begin with consonant–vowel–consonant (CVC) words that have continuous sounds, and progress to words with stop sounds as the student gains facility. As the student masters blending three-phoneme, or CVC words, then four-phoneme (stop) and then five-phoneme (street) words can be modeled and practiced to mastery.

SUPPORTED PRACTICE

1. Select several familiar words with three phonemes. Ask the student to say each word and correct any errors in pronunciation. Then have the student practice saying each sound and then practice saying the whole word.

2. Repeat with several words.

Review

Briefly incorporate this process with or without the tiles when the student comes in contact with new or reviewed words throughout the day.

Examples of Activity Intensifications

DOES THE STUDENT NEED DIRECT INSTRUCTION FOR TRANSFER
TO NEW CONTEXTS?

- Incorporate the use of tiles and blending sounds when orally introducing new content words to the student across subject areas.
- Have the student use a finger to point and drag blank tiles, as if underlining the difficult word while blending the sounds.
- Show the student how to blend letter tiles, and how to blend in order to read a word.

DOES THE STUDENT NEED MORE FREQUENT OPPORTUNITIES
FOR STUDENT RESPONSE, PRACTICE, AND REVIEW?

- After the first model, provide an additional model following the same sequence, but allow the student to echo each step back to you. Provide immediate and corrective feedback.
- Have the student repeat the stretched sounds before saying the blended word, followed by repeating the stretched phonemes for a decreased amount of time (e.g., /caaaat/ /caaat/ /caat/ /cat/ makes *cat*).
- Ensure that the student has frequent opportunities to practice.

Segmenting Phonemes

Objective

The student will be able to segment phonemes in a word with three to four phonemes.

Materials

Picture cards.

Elkonin boxes.

Blank tiles.

Letter tiles.

Procedures

MODEL

1. Display a picture of a three-phoneme word with three tiles lined up side-by-side below the picture. Initially introduce words beginning with a stop sound. The following word list could be used to model: *can, cake, bike, dad, dog.*

2. Model the use of tiles for segmenting the phonemes of a word. For example: "Each tile represents a sound we hear in the word. Listen, I can say the whole word, *can,* or I can say each sound in the word. I will drag a tile down for each sound I hear— /c/ /a/ /n/."

3. Once all the tiles are dragged down, point below each tile while saying the corresponding phoneme. For example: Point to the first tile, /c/, point to the second tile, /a/, point to the last tile, /n/. "The sounds in *can* are /c/ /a/ /n/."

4. Repeat Steps 1–3 with several different words.

SUPPORTED PRACTICE

1. Have the student select a new picture card and state what it is.

2. Have the student say the sounds in the word and drag a blank tile down for each sound as modeled above.

3. Once all of the tiles have been dragged down with the corresponding phoneme, the student should say the word.

4. Repeat Steps 1–3 with several words.

5. Play a practice game, asking the student to guess what word you are thinking of as you provide two to three phonemes for him or her to blend. For example: "Guess what animal I am thinking of—/g/ /oa/ /t/?"

Review

Briefly incorporate this process, with or without the tiles, when the student comes in contact with new or reviewed words throughout the day. If tiles aren't available, the student can tap out each phoneme with his or her thumb, starting with the pointer finger followed by the middle finger and so on. If the student has progressed and is able to segment and blend, alternate asking the student to demonstrate how to segment *and* blend the same word.

Examples of Activity Intensifications

DOES THE STUDENT NEED MORE SPECIFIC AND CORRECTIVE FEEDBACK?

- During student practice, praise the student for self-corrections and for using the segmentation with tiles strategies correctly.
- If the student is having difficulty segmenting phonemes, correct the error and use the tiles to help represent the error being made. Then remodel the correct segmentation while dragging down the corresponding tiles. For example: When trying to segment, if the student says "/mmmaaaa/ /p/," drag down the first two tiles to demonstrate saying "/mmmaaa/" followed by the /p/. Then remodel the correct segmentation, dragging down each tile per phoneme.
- If the student is segmenting larger parts of the word and not individual phonemes, help represent the individual phonemes by tapping for each phoneme before introducing the tiles.

DOES THE STUDENT NEED DIRECT INSTRUCTION FOR TRANSFER TO NEW CONTEXTS?

- When words of the same format (e.g., three phonemes) are presented in other subject areas throughout the day, incorporate the segmenting process for the student to strengthen his or her phoneme-segmenting skills.
- Point out that blending and segmenting are related. For example: "I heard you say each sound and blend them together. Now, can you take them apart?"
- Ask the student to segment words that are read aloud to him or her throughout the day, even when the student is transitioning around the school and is in contact with words that would apply.
- As the student is learning new letter sounds in phonics and word recognition, add letters to the blank tiles so the student can see the connection between the sounds in a word and the letters that go with those sounds.

RESOURCES

The Meadows Center for Preventing Educational Risk: Phonological Awareness PowerPoint presentation with audio.

http://resources.buildingrti.utexas.org/modules/Phonological_Awareness_Research-Based_Practices/multiscreen.html

This is a link to a slide presentation that demonstrates the correct formation and pronunciation of consonant and vowel sounds.

National Center on Intensive Intervention

www.intensiveintervention.org

This website provides tools for identifying reliable and valid progress monitoring assessments for phonemic and phonological awareness. Sample intensive phonological lessons are also available for instructional support.

Foorman, B., Beyler, N., Borradaile, K., Coyne, M., Denton, C. A., Dimino, J., et al. (2016). *Foundational skills to support reading for understanding in kindergarten through 3rd grade* (2016-4008). Washington, DC: National Center for Education Evaluation and Regional Assistance, Institute of Education Sciences, U.S. Department of Education.

This practice guide provides practical, research-based recommendations for developing foundational skills in the early elementary grades for reading success.

Gillon, G. T. (2017). *Phonological awareness: From research to practice* (2nd ed.). New York: Guilford Press.

Gillon discusses evidence-based strategies to enhance and improve phonological awareness in students ages 3–17 with a range of needs. Assessments, instructional strategies, and case studies are provided to best assist teachers.

Hosp, M. K., Hosp, J. L., & Howell, K. W. (2016). *The ABCs of CBM: A practical guide to curriculum-based measurement* (2nd ed.). New York: Guilford Press.

This book describes how to screen and monitor progress for a range of reading, writing, and math skills. The authors also provide tools for data-based decision-making.

Moats, L. C. (2010). *Speech to print: Language essentials for teachers* (2nd ed.). Baltimore: Brookes.

This book provides key research-based information to build teacher knowledge of the structure of the English language and knowledge of how to deliver explicit, targeted instruction in written and spoken language.

CHAPTER 3

Intensive Interventions to Support Phonics and Word Recognition

"When my teacher explained how the letters in the books make the same sounds and the words I already say, I realized I could read and didn't know it!"

—Sierra, age 9

Intensive phonics and word recognition instruction assists students in gaining mastery of the letter and sound structure of the English language. With careful instruction students gain knowledge of the predictable relationships and patterns between letters and sounds that allow them to change print into language for understanding. Students with intensive reading needs require detailed instruction in understanding how spoken sounds map onto print and how to use letter-sound knowledge to read (decode) and spell (encode) words.

WHAT DOES THE RESEARCH SAY ABOUT PHONICS AND WORD RECOGNITION INSTRUCTION?

Successful student understanding of text begins with the ability to change print into meaningful language. The *simple view of reading* (Gough & Tunmer, 1986; Hoover & Gough, 1990) identifies word recognition as a complex skill that is necessary for reading comprehension. Word recognition refers to the ability to decode and read printed words regardless of context. Automatic or fluent word reading is essential for comprehension because it minimizes the need to focus on lower-level processes, such as decoding words, allowing readers to devote resources to higher-level comprehension processes (Perfetti, 2011). The simple view notes that automatic decoding of printed words is specific to the task of reading print, even though other skills like comprehension are shared in both written and oral language. Research on the simple view provides evidence that readers' word-reading automaticity can account for significant variance in readers' ultimate reading comprehension (Catts, Hogan, & Adlof, 2005; Johnston & Kirby, 2006; Joshi & Aaron, 2000; Savage, 2006). In other words, if you cannot read the print, it will not be possible to comprehend the print.

Beginning readers' acquisition of word recognition skill has been described in four phases, labeled as prealphabetic, partial alphabetic, full alphabetic, and consolidated alphabetic (Ehri, 1995). These phases describe a process of print learning that progresses from a basic understanding that print can communicate language to the ability to read print with words that have complex units.

The prealphabetic phase is the earliest phase where a young child may understand that print can be translated into language, but the child does not yet understand that there are letter-sound connections that allow him or her to read the print. It is in the partial alphabetic phase that early readers begin to understand the connection between letters and reading words. These readers, however, do not have an extensive knowledge of the alphabetic system, or a strategy for using the system to accurately identify unknown words. Instead, these readers use only some of the letters or sounds in a word to try to read or spell the word. Many students with significant reading difficulties, regardless of their age, demonstrate word recognition abilities in the partial alphabetic phase, using only partial representations of words to attempt to read. The full alphabetic and consolidated alphabetic phases represent continued advances in students' word recognition growth. In the full alphabetic phase, students have complete connections between letters and sounds that they can use to read and spell words. By contrast, Ehri's (1995) theory of reading development describes the consolidated phase as being able to consolidate letter-sound knowledge into larger units, such as syllables, allowing the student to read larger words and commit more words to memory.

Elementary students with intensive reading intervention needs may be in the early phases of word recognition, and often lack mastery of critical elements of phonics and word recognition, and of how to apply this knowledge to reading text (Blachman, 2013; Leach, Scarborough, & Rescorla, 2003; Vellutino, Fletcher, Snowling, & Scanlon, 2004). A large amount of research has been conducted on the benefits of explicit instruction in phonics and word recognition. At a basic level, interventions that include instruction in letter–sound correspondences, blending of letter sounds to read words, the use of word patterns to read and spell families of words, and irregular word patterns can improve students' word recognition abilities (Foorman, Francis, Fletcher, Schatschneider, & Mehta, 1998; Joseph, 2000; O'Shaughnessy & Swanson, 2000). As students advance in phonics and word recognition abilities, it is also important that they master effective strategies for reading and spelling multisyllabic words (Archer, Gleason, & Vachon, 2003; Bhattacharya & Ehri, 2004). Providing step-by-step instruction for identifying syllables and thinking of larger words in chunks is important for struggling readers to continue advancing in complex text (Diliberto, Beattie, Flowers, & Algozzine, 2008; Toste, Capin, Vaughn, Roberts, & Kearns, 2017). Intensive reading interventions that include phonics and word recognition instruction have been found to be beneficial to both lower-elementary students (Wanzek et al., 2018) and upper-elementary students (Wanzek, Wexler, Vaughn, & Ciullo, 2010).

WHAT ARE THE CRITICAL ELEMENTS OF PHONICS AND WORD RECOGNITION INSTRUCTION?

From the research base described above, it is not surprising that the critical elements in intensive phonics and word recognition instruction for elementary students include teaching letter–sound correspondences, blending of letters to read words, use of word patterns and families to read and spell words, irregular words, and strategies for reading multisyllabic words. Let us examine each critical element of phonics and word recognition and ways to provide intensive instruction in these elements.

Letter–Sound Correspondences

Teaching letter–sound correspondences provides the building block for decoding and reading a variety of words. Thus, one part of an intensive reading intervention includes systematically introducing the most common letter–sound correspondences. The goal is for students to gain automatic knowledge of these sound patterns so that they can then apply them to word reading. Instruction begins with the individual letter–sound correspondences (e.g., the sound of the letter *a*, or the sound of the letter *m*). When students have mastered those sounds and can readily apply them to reading words, the most common letter combinations found in words (e.g., the sound of /ea/ as in *meat*, or the sound of /th/ as in *thin*) can be introduced. Students in the upper-elementary grades who have mastered individual letter sounds and letter combinations should also be taught the sounds for the common affixes (e.g., the sound /re/ in the word, *redo*, or the sound /tion/ in the word, *action*).

Many students can handle learning one new sound per day, with daily review of previously taught sounds. The pace of instruction, however, should be adjusted depending on student needs. For example, if a student is unable to remember newly learned sounds in the review, that may be a sign that one new sound a day is too much for the student.

The sequence of sound introduction is also an important consideration for intensive intervention. First, instruction should focus on the most common sounds, letter combinations, and affixes. The goal is to teach for transfer to word reading, so students need to know sounds that will be useful to them in reading many words. Second, there are a few guidelines to consider for the most systematic instruction in letter–sound correspondences. Beginning readers should initially be taught sounds that will allow them to transfer their knowledge quickly to reading words. For example, if they are taught /a/, /m/ as the first two letter–sound correspondences, they can already read the word *am*. In addition, letters that have similar but different sounds (e.g., /e/, /i/) should be separated by many days of instruction. These letter sounds can be confused easily by students, so it is important to provide the most systematic, step-by-step instruction, ensuring that students have solidly mastered one of the sounds before being introduced to a similar one. There are many ways to sequence sound introduction—we provide one example of a sequence in Figure 3.1.

Explicit instruction in new sounds includes modeling the sound for the student, and ensuring that the student pronounces the sound correctly and is associating the sound with the correct letter(s). In addition, previously taught sounds should be reviewed frequently by asking the student to say the sound for each letter, letter combination, or affix.

Decoding and Encoding

Explicit instruction in how to use newly learned sounds to read (decode) words is another critical element of phonics and word recognition instruction. In every lesson, students should practice reading words with new and previously introduced sounds. Beginning-level readers will need modeling of how to use the letter–sound correspondences they have learned to sound out printed words orally in order to determine the word. Students say the sounds in the word and then blend the sounds together to read the word (e.g., /s/ /a/ /t/ makes *sat*). As students master sounding out words orally, systematic instruction can progress to having students whisper the sounds, mouth the sounds but not say them, and then finally sound them out in their head. Following teacher modeling of sounding out a few words with the new sound, students need to practice reading many words with the new sound as well as previously introduced sounds. Systematic instruction can also include prompting students to say the letter sounds and blend them to read the word, or prompting the student to find and say the new letter combination before figuring out the whole word.

It is important to select a variety of words each day for student practice. Because students are applying their sound knowledge, they can use the sounding-out strategy to figure out any regular word, and do not need to memorize particular words. Thus, word lists for practice should include different words for students to practice, using their sound knowledge. All of the words should be regular words—meaning that the sounds in the word make their most common sound, and the student has already been taught that sound. Students should not be asked to sound out words with irregular sounds or sounds that they have not yet been taught, as they cannot successfully apply

1. *a* (at)	6. *r* (rat)	11. *g* (got)	16. *b* (bed)	21. *j* (jam)	26. *x* (box)
2. *m* (mom)	7. *f* (fun)	12. *u* (up)	17. *k* (kick)	22. *p* (pup)	
3. *t* (top)	8. *d* (did)	13. *h* (hot)	18. *w* (win)	23. *y* (yell)	
4. *i* (it)	9. *o* (on)	14. *c* (can)	19. *e* (Ed)	24. *z* (zip)	
5. *s* (sat)	10. *l* (let)	15. *n* (not)	20. *v* (vet)	25. *q* (quit)	

FIGURE 3.1. Sample letter-sound introduction sequence.

their sound knowledge to those words. For example, if students know the most common sounds of *a, m, t, s, i, f, d, g, o, l, h*, and *r*, an appropriate word list for modeling and/or student practice might include words such as *am, sit, hot, sat*, or *rot*. An inappropriate word list that would be confusing to these students would include words like *goat* (*oa* makes a different sound than the sounds they have learned so far), *his* (the *s* does not make its most common sound), or *most* (the *o* does not make its most common sound). In intensive interventions, the examples chosen for modeling and student practice are important for maintaining student success and progress without confusion.

As students gain facility in decoding words, they should also receive explicit instruction and practice in using their sound knowledge to spell or encode words. The process for explicitly teaching spelling is the reverse of the reading work. First, teachers should model and provide guidance for saying the sounds they hear in the word (applying their segmenting skills from phonological awareness), and then writing the letters that go with each sound. Across a week of lessons, both reading and spelling of words with new sounds can be practiced. Students who know the sound system of English well can see letters in a word and know the sounds to read the word, as well as hear words and know the sounds and letters to spell the word.

Upper-elementary students who have mastered reading and spelling one- and two-syllable words with letter sounds and common letter combinations will need explicit instruction in a strategy to decode multisyllabic words. Mastering the early phonics skills for decoding and encoding does not guarantee that a student will be able to read or spell the more complex words seen in third- to fifth-grade-level text. The strategy of sounding out words sound-by-sound is a beginning reading strategy that does not work well with larger, multisyllabic words. Rather, students need a specific strategy for decoding unknown multisyllabic words. If students can remember three or four steps to follow when they come to an unknown large word in text, they will be more successful with upper-elementary-grade-level text. For example, students may be taught to:

1. Find the prefixes.
2. Find the suffixes.
3. Find other sounds, word parts, or base words in the rest of the word.
4. Read the word using each part.

The strategy for multisyllabic words should allow students to look for word parts they know and put those word parts together to determine the word, rather than sounding out the word sound-by-sound. Students with intensive reading needs can benefit from having a generalizable strategy that they can successfully use to read many multisyllabic words.

Instruction in multisyllabic word-reading strategies can be made more explicit and systematic for intensive intervention by overtly modeling each step and asking students to overtly demonstrate each step. For example, when students are first learning to identify the affixes in a word, the teacher and the students can underline the affixes they find to overtly demonstrate and provide a visual of the step. Similarly, they can underline or circle other sounds or base words they find in the word. These overt steps can be removed as students become more automatic with each step, until they are able to complete the steps mentally and automatically.

Spelling instruction for multisyllabic words should follow a similar pattern of having students identify larger chunks rather than individual sounds of a word. If students can say the syllables they hear in the word, they can then spell each syllable using the sounds they know.

Irregular Word Instruction

Unfortunately, there are also many words in the English language that do not follow common letter-sound patterns. Many of these words are frequently used in print, even in beginning-level text. Therefore, it is necessary for students to become facile with reading a large bank of words that cannot be decoded simply by using the most common letter-sound patterns.

Explicit instruction in irregular words should be provided to students with intensive intervention needs on a daily basis. These words require much review and practice. Intervention teachers need to introduce new irregular words regularly by telling the student the word and explaining that the word cannot be read with only its sounds. Sometimes, teachers refer to these words as "funny words" or "rule breakers." In order for students to begin to master the reading of a new irregular word, they need to make some connections to the letter sequence and/or sounds in the word. Students can repeat the word after it is modeled, and then spell the word while looking at the letters, or write the word while saying the letters, followed by saying the word again. If there are letter sounds in the word that do follow regular patterns, then it may also be helpful to point out those sounds in order to help students remember the word.

After the initial introduction of the word, students will need immediate practice in remembering and reading the word. Teachers can ask students to read each new irregular word in a random order until the students' command of the words is firm. In addition, it is important to frequently review irregular words in order to allow students to obtain mastery. Newly introduced words should be practiced daily for several days and periodically reviewed in future lessons to maintain mastery. In addition to the regular introduction of new irregular words and frequent practice of previously introduced words, students should be practicing these words in the text that they are reading daily.

Systematic irregular word instruction includes selecting new words for students to learn from the text the students are reading, or from lists of frequently used words in print (e.g., Dolch Word List, n.d.). Many students can learn new irregular words each day, allowing them to build up larger banks of known words quickly. Depending on student level, two to seven words can be introduced each day. If students cannot remember the words that are being introduced, then fewer new words should be introduced each day, and review of previously learned words should be increased. In some cases, students may need new irregular words introduced and modeled for two consecutive lessons before placing them in review lists. Any time students make an error reading an irregular word, the word should be retaught.

Sight-Word Reading

As students gain skill in accurately reading words, they will need to begin gaining fluency in reading the words. *Sight-word reading* refers to the facility with which students recognize the letters and sounds of words and can read them rapidly. Over time, students need to add both regular and irregular words to their sight-reading ability. Intervention teachers can provide explicit practice in developing fluency of word recognition in a variety of ways. Providing this practice with individual words will allow students with intensive needs to master the recognition of words in isolation, and to transfer that recognition to fluently reading those words in text. Teachers can provide this practice by structuring activities for reading previously taught words multiple times within and across lessons. These activities can include timing students to see how many words they can read in a specific time frame, and then allowing them to practice multiple times to see whether they can improve the number of words they can read within the time limit. Games that allow students to read words multiple times and encourage quick recognition of the words will also facilitate this practice and help students begin to automatically apply the word-reading skills they have learned.

Selecting Connected Text for Reading

Students need to read connected text that allows them to apply the phonics and word recognition knowledge they are acquiring every day. The only purpose of teaching phonics and word recognition is to help students better read and understand text. Thus, students need to see explicitly the connection between their word-reading practice and the act of reading text each day. Students who are at a beginning reading level may need simple sentences containing only regular words with sounds they have learned and irregular words that have been taught. Even a student who only knows the sounds for *a, m, t, s,* and the irregular word *I,* can read the simple text "I sat" to begin making the connection between word-reading strategies and reading text. As students gain facility with more sounds and irregular words, teachers can select text that allows them to practice the skills they have learned for reading text. The complexity of the text builds as students learn more and more about letter-sound patterns and increase their bank of irregular words and sight words. Text reading should always include discussion of students' understanding of the text to ensure that students explicitly make the connection between reading and understanding text.

For beginning readers who need intensive intervention, regardless of their actual grade level, it is important not to ask them to read words that they do not have the skills to read. Students should know that the skills they are learning will help them to read text. Asking them to read words that have letter-sound patterns, or irregular words that they have not learned, will lead struggling students to start guessing at words, and to consider that the phonics and word recognition knowledge they are gaining does not help them with text. Systematic instruction for students with intensive reading needs requires step-by-step phonics and word recognition instruction and step-by-step integration in text reading, allowing students to focus on applying the knowledge they are learning. If a text does contain a word that students cannot read, simply provide the word for the students.

Error correction and feedback during text reading requires a knowledgeable teacher. When a student makes an error on a regular word for which he or she knows the sounds, error correction should involve the teacher facilitating the student saying the correct sounds and decoding the word with the sounds. When a student makes an error on an irregular word that has been previously introduced, error correction should involve the teacher reteaching the word by telling the student the word and asking the student to say the word, spell it, and say it again. In both cases, it is helpful to then have the student reread the sentence. A knowledgeable teacher can quickly identify student errors as regular or irregular words, and apply the most efficient error correction to assist the student in his or her learning.

HOW DO I MONITOR PROGRESS IN PHONICS AND WORD RECOGNITION?

Monitoring student progress in phonics and word recognition can help teachers to make decisions about pacing the introduction of new skills or words, planning for appropriate practice opportunities in letter sounds and words, and identifying misconceptions in learning. Below we identify formal and informal progress monitoring techniques that intervention teachers can use to objectively monitor students' learning and make instructional decisions.

Letter–Sound Correspondence

There are commercially available measures of letter-sound knowledge, such as letter-sound fluency or assessments of specific phonics skills, to diagnose areas of need. These measures have the advantage of providing information on expected or benchmark scores to assist teachers in monitoring student progress toward specific grade-level goals.

Teachers can also gain some information for planning intervention lessons with informal measures. One way in which teachers can keep track of the letter sounds that students have mastered is to develop a simple tracking system for marking the letter sounds that students say correctly/incorrectly during the review portion of the lesson. Similarly, teachers can periodically provide a list of letter sounds to students and ask them to say the sound of each letter (letter combination, affix) to check on their knowledge. These informal measures of student letter–sound knowledge can assist teachers in determining which sounds need to be introduced or retaught, and which sounds students have mastered.

Alphabetic Principle

Formal measures of the alphabetic principle with normative comparison data are available to determine student strengths and weaknesses and gaps related to grade-level expectations. Often, these measures require students to read carefully selected nonsense words to ensure that students' ability to use letter-sound knowledge to read words is measured, rather than measuring the number of words students have memorized. Progress monitoring measures in alphabetic principle can be scored by the number of sounds read correctly to provide a measure sensitive to small gains in phonics knowledge. Similarly, spelling measures can be scored for the number of correct letter sequences written.

Teachers can also informally monitor the progress of student decoding or encoding abilities by developing systems to mark errors during decoding or encoding practice within lessons. It is important not only to mark words where an error was made but also to mark what aspect of the word contained the error. For example, if a student reads the word *made* as *mad*, the teacher can note the misread word and also mark the vowel as the aspect that was mispronounced. Obtaining information on where students are making errors in words can allow the teacher to identify patterns of errors (e.g., misreading or misspelling a word due to the vowel, or due to a blend in the word). This additional error pattern information can assist the intervention teacher in planning instruction.

Word Reading

Students who are reading many regular and irregular words by sight may be monitored in word reading. Formal measures of word reading or identification typically provide students with a list of grade-level words and ask them to read the words. Some of the measures include a time limit to provide information on a student's fluency of word reading. These fluency measures can be administered quickly, and are sensitive to student growth in word reading. Although error patterns are not commonly a part of the scoring on these measures, teachers can examine the errors that students made to provide additional instructional information.

A simple, informal way to monitor progress in word reading is to keep track of each student's first reading of words during sight-word practice. The teacher can identify the number of words that students are able to read without assistance, as well as examining error patterns in the words that students miss. A few errors that teachers may want to look for include (1) what words the student does not know or attempt and may need to be retaught; (2) whether the student makes errors with a particular type of word, either regular or irregular, that might suggest that the student is having difficulty with either using the regular word strategy or remembering irregular words that have been taught; (3) whether the student is making particular errors related to phonics skills that have been introduced (e.g., difficulty with vowels, difficulty with words that have the sound, difficulty with multisyllabic words); or (4) whether the student is largely accurate with word reading but has difficulty decoding the word quickly. A sample recording sheet for keeping track of student word-reading errors is provided in Figure 3.2. The phonics

Word in print (+ for insertion)	Word student read (– for omission)	Graphophonetic Errors								Comprehension Errors		
		Irregular word	Beginning sound	Ending sound	Long/short vowel	Silent-e rule	Consonant blend	Letter combinations	Other:	Semantic	Syntactic	Other:
took	take							X				
Park	Bark		X									
Ran	Run				X							
Get	Got				X							
Far	Fast			X				X				
Couldn't	Could			X								
Anyway	All the way	X		X								
Came	Comes					X						
Covered	Cover			X								
Off	Of	X		X								
Once	One			X								
Gave	Gav					X						
being	be			X				X				

FIGURE 3.2. Example of an error analysis recording sheet.

error columns can be adjusted to meet student reading levels (e.g., multisyllabic words, prefixes, affixes).

Spelling

Formal measures of spelling progress typically provide a list of grade-level words for students to write, and can sometimes be timed. Scoring often includes both the number of words spelled correctly and the number of correct letter sequences written in each word. The number of correct letter sequences provides a sensitive measure of students' progress in their use of newly learned phonics elements. Spelling progress monitoring can be administered to multiple students at a time.

Teachers can informally examine student progress in spelling of regular or irregular words by asking students to write a list of words and examining the number of words that students are able to write correctly. As with word reading, error patterns in spelling, including the types of words commonly missed or specific phonic elements that students consistently misspelled, can also be examined to help guide instruction for a student who is not making sufficient progress.

INSTRUCTIONAL ACTIVITIES FOR PHONICS AND WORD RECOGNITION

Introducing and Reviewing Letter Sounds

Objective

The student will be able to say the sounds of letters, letter combinations, or affixes.

Materials

Dry-erase board, chart paper, or chalkboard.

Writing utensils.

Procedures

MODEL

1. Write the letter(s) for the new sound (e.g., /sh/). Tell the student the sound for the letter(s). For example: "The letters *sh* say /sh/." Point to the letter(s) and have the student repeat the sound. Check for correct pronunciation.

2. Erase the letters on the board. Have the student say the new sound (e.g., /sh/). Tell the student the letters that match the sound. For example: "When you hear the sound /sh/, it is spelled *sh*." Say the sound and then write the letter(s) that match the sound. Erase the letter(s), have the student say the sound, and write the letters for the sound.

SUPPORTED PRACTICE

1. Select several sounds that the student has already learned for review. Write the letter(s) for the new sound, mixed with review sounds in random order so that the student does not memorize an order. Point to each letter, letter combination, or affix, and have the student say the correct sound. Have the student practice the new sound several times during the activity. For example: If the new sound is /sh/ and the student already knows the most common sound of each letter, along with the letter combinations *th*, *er*, and *ing*, the following list could be used for practice: *a, sh, ing, n, e, th, p, er, i, d, h.*

2. Have the student practice writing the correct letters for the sounds used in Step 1. Say a sound (e.g., /a/), and have the student write the letter(s) to match the sound. Have the student practice the new sound several times during the activity.

Review

Incorporate the new sound into supported practice lists for several lessons.

Examples of Activity Intensifications

DOES THE STUDENT NEED MORE SYSTEMATIC INSTRUCTION?

- Ensure that letter sounds that can be easily confused due to similar written features (e.g., /b/ and /d/) or similar sound features (e.g., /e/ and /i/, /f/ and /v/) are not introduced in lessons that are close in proximity. Ensure that the student has fully mastered one of the similar sounds and can apply it to reading or spelling words without support before introducing the second sound.

- Demonstrate the placement of the mouth and tongue in pronouncing the correct sound for a new letter, letter combination, or affix.

- Provide a visual image or keyword to help the student remember the correct sound of the letter, letter combination, or affix (e.g., *sh* says /sh/ as in *ship*).

DOES THE STUDENT NEED MORE FREQUENT OPPORTUNITIES
FOR STUDENT RESPONSE, PRACTICE, AND REVIEW?

- Practice the new sound for 2 consecutive days before adding a new sound.

- If a sound is challenging for a student to articulate due to speech or language delays, continue to model and reinforce approximations to production of the correct sound.

- Ensure that the new sound is incorporated in review lists for many lessons to allow the student to have daily practice with newly introduced sounds.

Modeling and Practicing Decoding and Encoding

Objective

The student will be able to read and spell regular words with known sound patterns.

Materials

Dry-erase board, chart paper, or chalkboard.
Writing utensils.

Procedures

MODEL (DECODING)

1. Select several words that incorporate the newly learned sound. All of the words should include only sounds that the student already knows, and should be "regu-lar" words where all of the letters make the sounds that the student has learned. For example: If the new sound is /sh/ and the student already knows the most common sound of each letter, the letter combinations *th*, *er*, and *ing*, and the vowel–consonant–final *e* (VC*e*) rule, the following word list could be used for modeling: *ship, wish, shut, shame, dash, crash.*

2. Point to the letter combination in the first word and say its sound. For example: "I know this says /sh/." Then model sounding out the entire word and blending it together. For example: "/sh/ /i/ /p/ makes *ship*." Have the student repeat the sounding out and say the word with you. Repeat this model for each word.

SUPPORTED PRACTICE (DECODING)

1. Select several words that incorporate sounds the student has learned, including the new sound. All of the words should include only sounds that the student already knows, and should be "regular" words where all of the letters make the sounds that the student has learned. Most of the words should allow practice in either the newly learned sound or recently learned sounds (review). Select words that are in the student's vocabulary (i.e., the student knows the meaning of the word) whenever possible. Briefly explain the meaning of any words with which the student is unfamiliar. For example: If the new sound is /sh/ and the student has recently learned *th, er,* and *ing,* the following word list could be used for supported practice: *shed, shrimp, fish, her, sing, brush, shack, drop, bring, that, dish, fifth, shake, thing, fresh, ash, perk, swing, splash, shop, crane.*

2. For the first few words, point to each letter combination in the word and have the student say the sound. For example: "What sound is this?" /sh/. Then have the student sound out the word and say the whole word. For example: "Say the sounds in the word"; /sh/ /e/ /d/. "What word?"; *shed.* For the rest of the words, prompt the student to sound out the word and say the word. If the student has learned to sound out the words silently, prompt him or her to sound out the word on his or her own, pause for 2–3 seconds, and then ask the student to state the word.

MODEL (ENCODING)

1. Select several words that incorporate the newly learned sound. All of the words should include only sounds that the student already knows, and should be "regular" words where all of the letters make the sounds that the student has learned. For example: If the new sound is /sh/ and the student already knows the most common sound of each letter, the letter combinations *th, er,* and *ing,* and the VC*e* rule, the following word list could be used for modeling: *wish, shut, shame, crash.*

2. Say each word and its sounds, orally. For example: "The word is *ship*; /sh/ /i/ /p/." Then say the sounds individually while writing the matching letters on the board for the student. For example: "/sh/" [write *sh*], "/i/" [write *i*], "/p/" [write *p*]. Then read the written word to the student (*ship*). Repeat the model with each word.

SUPPORTED PRACTICE (ENCODING)

1. Select several words that incorporate sounds that the student has learned, including the new sound. All of the words should include only sounds that the student already knows, and should be "regular" words where all of the letters make the sounds that

the student has learned. Most of the words should allow practice in either the newly learned sound or recently learned sounds. Select words that are in the student's vocabulary (i.e., the student knows the meaning of the word) whenever possible. Briefly explain the meaning of any words with which the student is unfamiliar. For example: If the new sound is /sh/ and the student has recently learned *th, er,* and *ing,* the following word list could be used for supported practice: *shed, shrimp, fish, sing, brush, drop, ash, shop, crane.*

2. Say the first word aloud and ask the student to say the sounds in the word. For example: "The word is *shed.* What are the sounds in *shed*?" /sh/ /e/ /d/. Then have the student say the sounds again and write the letters to match the sound. For example: "What is the first sound?" /sh/; "What letters make the /sh/ sound?" *sh;* "What is the second sound?" /e/; "What letter makes the /e/ sound?" *e;* "What is the next sound?" /d/; "What letter makes the /d/ sound?" *d.*

3. After the student has written the word, have him or her read the word. Repeat this process for the first few words in the list. For the rest of the words, prompt the student to say the sounds and write the letters that match each sound.

Review

Words with the new sound (e.g., /sh/) should be included in the supported practice lists for reading or spelling for several lessons.

Examples of Activity Intensifications

DOES THE STUDENT NEED MORE EXPLICIT INSTRUCTION?

- In the decoding instruction, highlight or underline the letter combination in the words that are modeled or are in the first few words of the practice list.

- Add letter tiles—to move while saying the sounds of the word to be decoded, and to demonstrate putting the word back together with the sounds.

- Think aloud during modeling of the encoding instruction to demonstrate how you think about which letters match the sounds in the word. For example: "/sh/; I know that is our new sound. There are two letters that make up that sound. They are *s, h* so I will write *sh.*"

DOES THE STUDENT NEED MORE SPECIFIC AND CORRECTIVE FEEDBACK?

- During student practice, affirm some responses by reminding the student that his or her knowledge of letter sounds and sounding out are how he or she knew the word. For example: "That is correct. You used the sounds you knew to sound out and read the word."

- When the student makes an error, begin with correction of the error, and then guide him or her through the steps of the process with questioning to result in a correctly read or spelled word. For example: If a student says "peck" for the word *perk,* the error to be corrected is the letter combination *er*. Start by correcting the error: *"Er* says /er/ [point]; What does *er* say? /er/." Then guide the student through the process for reading the word. "What is the first sound? [point] /p/"; "What is the next sound? [point] /er/"; "What is the last sound? [point] /k/." Now point and say each sound without stopping in between: "/perrrrk/; What word? *perk.*"

Introducing and Reviewing Irregular Words

Objective

The student will be able to read and spell irregular words.

Materials

Dry-erase board, chart paper, or chalkboard.
Writing utensils.

Procedures

MODEL (READING)

1. Select three to seven words that have one or more sounds that do not follow sound patterns that the student knows. Selected words should be of high frequency in grade-level print materials. High-frequency word lists (e.g., Dolch Word List, n.d.; Fry & Kress, 2006), as well as text the student is reading, can be used to select appropriate words for instruction.
2. Introduce each word by writing the word and telling the student the word. Have the student read the word, say or write the letters in the word, and read the word again.
3. Have the student read each newly introduced word several times (varying the order of presentation).

SUPPORTED PRACTICE (READING)

1. Select several previously learned irregular words as well as the newly introduced words for practice. Continue to vary the order of presentation of words. Ensure that the student has multiple opportunities to read words, particularly the new words and words the student has struggled to remember.
2. If the student has difficulty remembering the word, use the modeling procedure above to reteach the word.

MODEL (SPELLING)

1. Select three to five words that have one or more sounds that do not follow sound patterns that the student knows. Selected words should be of high frequency in grade-

level print materials. High-frequency word lists, as well as text that the student is reading, can be used to select appropriate words for instruction.

2. Introduce each word by writing the word and telling the student the word. Have the student read the word, say or write the letters in the word, and read the word again.

3. Have the student read the word and say or write the letters in the word again without looking at the word.

SUPPORTED PRACTICE (SPELLING)

1. Select several previously learned irregular words as well as the newly introduced words for practice. Say each word in random order. Have the student repeat the word and say the letters in the word while writing the word.

2. If the student has difficulty remembering the word, use the modeling procedure above to reteach the word.

Review

Newly introduced words should be included in the supported practice lists for reading or spelling for several lessons.

Examples of Activity Intensifications

DOES THE STUDENT NEED COGNITIVE PROCESSING STRATEGIES?

- Prior to text reading, use a think-aloud to model applying irregular word knowledge to the upcoming text. For example: "I am learning a lot of irregular words and they are difficult to remember. I just practiced several words. Let me see whether I can find them in the text today and keep track of the words I remember. I know I can do this."

- Have the student keep track of his or her progress in learning and remembering irregular words. For example, the student can graph the number of irregular words read correctly during the review portion of a lesson.

- Encourage the student to identify words he or she missed, and to want to practice more to help the student monitor his or her word reading and connect practice with success.

DOES THE STUDENT NEED DIRECT INSTRUCTION FOR TRANSFER TO NEW CONTEXTS?

- Prior to text reading, provide additional practice with reading newly introduced regular and irregular words mixed together. Remind the student to look for sounds he or she knows or words he or she has memorized as irregular words.

- Select words for the word list practice from the text the student will read. Remind the student that the words he or she just practiced will be in that day's text. Ask the student to find those words in the text prior to reading.

- When appropriate for the student's level, select words for the word list practice that are a part of the text the student is reading in the core classroom instruction, or that are a part of the content-area reading requirements. Remind the student that the words he or she just practiced will be in the classroom text reading, or read excerpts from the text that contain the new words together as a preview for the upcoming classroom instruction.

Strategy for Teaching Multisyllabic Words

Objective

The student will be able to read and spell multisyllabic words.

Materials

Dry-erase board, chart paper, or chalkboard.

Writing utensils.

Chart with the multisyllabic reading or spelling strategy steps listed.

Procedures

MODEL (READING)

1. Select several multisyllabic words that incorporate the newly learned affix (see the "Introducing and Reviewing Letter Sounds" activity). All of the words should include only sounds, base words, and affixes that the student already knows. Select words that are in the student's vocabulary (i.e., the student knows the meaning of the word) whenever possible. Multisyllabic word reading can also be combined with vocabulary instruction (see Chapter 5) for words that the student is unfamiliar with. For example: If the new affix is *dis* and the student already knows the most common sound of each letter and letter combinations, and knows the most common sound of the affixes *un-, -est, -le, re-, de-, -al, -ful,* and *-ly,* the following word list could be used for modeling: *disclaim, discount, distract, distrustful, disable, disturbingly.*

2. Teach the student a step-by-step strategy for reading multisyllabic words. The following four steps could be used:

   a. Find the prefixes.
   b. Find the suffixes.
   c. Find other sounds, word parts, or base words in the rest of the word.
   d. Read the word using each part.

3. Model the use of the strategy with the first word (e.g., *disclaim*). For example: "First, I'm going to find the prefixes. Prefixes are at the beginning of the word. I see *dis.* I'm

going to circle *dis*. Second, I find the suffixes. Suffixes are at the end of the word. I don't see any suffixes. Some words have no suffixes. Third, I'm going to identify the sounds and word parts for the rest of the word. I'm underlining the rest of the word and that part is *claim*. I know that because I see the /ai/ sound. Fourth, I'm going to read the word using the parts I found—*dis* and *claim*. The word is *disclaim*."

4. Model with the other words and include student questions throughout each step. For example: "Do you see any prefixes?"; "Do you see any suffixes?"; "What known sounds or word parts do you see in the rest of the word?"; "Let's put the word parts together and read the word."

SUPPORTED PRACTICE (READING)

1. Select several multisyllabic words that incorporate sounds and affixes the student has learned, including the new sound. All of the words should include only sounds and word parts the student already knows. Most of the words should allow practice in either the newly learned sound or recently learned sounds (review). Select words that are in the student's vocabulary (i.e., the student knows the meaning of the word) whenever possible. Multisyllabic word reading can also be combined with vocabulary instruction (see Chapter 5) for words the student is unfamiliar with. For example: If the new sound is /dis/ and the student has recently learned the affixes *-ly*, *-ful*, and *-al*, the following word list could be used for supported practice: *admit, admittedly, disorder, playful, furnish, disinfect, discreetly, practical, practically, disgusted, quickly, quicker, display, displayed, sandal, painful, dispute, disputed*.

2. Have the student circle or underline the affixes for word parts for each step of the strategy. For example: "Find the prefixes and circle them." Then have the student put the word parts together to say the whole word. After the student has read each word, go back to the list of words and have the student read each word.

3. As the student gains facility in the steps and in applying them to read words, he or she can complete each step in his or her head rather than overtly circling or underlining the word parts.

MODEL (SPELLING)

1. Select several multisyllabic words that incorporate the newly learned affix (see the "Introducing and Reviewing Letter Sounds" activity). All of the words should include only sounds, base words, and affixes that the student already knows. Select words that are in the student's vocabulary (i.e., the student knows the meaning of the word) whenever possible. Multisyllabic word reading can also be combined with vocabulary instruction (see Chapter 5) for words that the student is unfamiliar with. For example: If the new affix is *dis* and the student already knows the most common sound of each letter and letter combinations, and knows the most common sound of the affixes *un-*, *-est*, *-le*, *re-*, *de-*, *-al*, *-ful*, and *-ly*, the following word list could be used for modeling: *disclaim, discount, distract, distrustful, disable, disturbingly*.

2. Teach the student a step-by-step strategy for spelling multisyllabic words. For example, the following three steps could be used:

   a. Say the syllables.
   b. Sound out each syllable and write it.
   c. Read the syllables together to check.

3. Model the use of the strategy with the first word (e.g., *disclaim*). For example: "First I'm going to say the syllables *dis* and *claim*. I'm going to draw a line for each syllable [draw two lines on the board]. Second, I'm going to say the first syllable—*dis*. That's a prefix I know. So, I'll write it on the first line. Now, I'm going to say the second syllable—*claim*. I'll sound it out and write the letters I hear on the second line: /c/ [write *c*], /l/ [write *l*], /ai/ [write *ai*], /m/ [write *m*]. I have written all of the syllables. Third, I will read what I wrote to see whether I have the right word: *dis* . . . *claim*; makes *disclaim*. That's the right word. Now I'll write the whole word."

4. Model with the other words and include student questions throughout each step: "What are the syllables?"; "What is the first syllable?"; "What are the sounds in the second syllable?"; "Let's read the word we wrote."

SUPPORTED PRACTICE (SPELLING)

1. Select several multisyllabic words that incorporate sounds and affixes the student has learned, including the new sound. All of the words should include only sounds and word parts that the student already knows. Most of the words should allow practice in either the newly learned sound or recently learned sounds (review). Select words that are in the student's vocabulary (i.e., the student knows the meaning of the word) whenever possible. Multisyllabic word reading can also be combined with vocabulary instruction (see Chapter 5) for words that the student is unfamiliar with. For example: If the new sound is /dis/ and the student has recently learned -*ly*, -*ful*, and -*al*, the following word list could be used for supported practice: *disorder, playful, disinfect, discreetly, practical, display, sandal, painful*.

2. Say the first word aloud and ask for the first step in the strategy. Have the student say the syllables in the word. For example: "What are the syllables in *disorder*?" *dis, or, der*. Have the student draw a line for each syllable. Ask the student to identify the second step in the strategy. Have the student say and sound out each syllable while writing the spelling for each syllable on the lines. For example: "What is the first syllable?" *dis*; "What letters spell /dis/?" *dis*; "What is the second syllable?" *or*; "What letters spell /or/?" *or*; "What is the third syllable?" *der*; "What sounds do you hear in the syllable *der*?" /d/ /er/; "What letters spell /d/ and /er/?" *der*.

3. Ask the student for the third step in the strategy. Then have the student read the syllables that he or she wrote to say the whole word. If the student has the correct word, have him or her write the whole word.

4. Repeat this process for each word in the list. As the student gains facility in the steps and in applying them to spell words, he or she can complete each step when writing the word, rather than drawing the lines and writing the syllables separately first.

Review

Newly introduced words should be included in the supported practice lists for reading or spelling for several lessons.

Examples of Activity Intensifications

DOES THE STUDENT NEED MORE SYSTEMATIC INSTRUCTION?

- Teach the steps of the reading or spelling strategy one step at a time. For example, teach the first step of spelling multisyllabic words, saying the word in syllables and drawing a line for each syllable. Introduce Step 2 of the strategy only after the student has mastered the first step.

- During initial instruction, use only words with affixes added to a known or regular base word. For example, *dis*orderly, *playful*, *uneventful*. Once the student has identified the affixes, he or she will then know the rest of the word. For example: If the student identifies the known affixes *dis* and *-ly*, and knows or can sound out *order*, he or she can read *disorderly*. Once the student has mastered multisyllabic words with known base words, instruction can systematically continue with multisyllabic words containing word parts rather than base words (e.g., *vegetable, preclude, complement*).

- Use syllable cards to allow the student to "see" and move the word parts in a multisyllabic word as he or she reads it (see below). Have the student complete the steps of the multisyllabic word-reading strategy using the syllable cards.

- Teach the multisyllabic spelling strategy using syllable cards with the word parts already written first. Have the student say the syllable and find each syllable card to build the word.

| dis | in | fect |

DOES THE STUDENT NEED DIRECT INSTRUCTION FOR TRANSFER
TO NEW CONTEXTS?

- Before text reading, ask the student to preview the text, looking for multisyllabic words. Have the student read the words that he or she identifies.

- Provide the student with sentences that have multisyllabic word choices differing only in an affix. Have the student read the sentences and determine the correct word for the sentence *Elena's dog was showing his [playful, played] tricks*.

- Provide the student with a written essay. Select two multisyllabic words that can be used in the essay. Ask the student to read the essay and find places to revise the essay using the two words you selected. Remind the student to use the strategy to spell the words correctly in his or her revision.

Sight-Word Practice

Objective

The student will be able to read words accurately and fluently.

Materials

Word cards.

Timer.

Procedures

Note: There are no modeling procedures for this activity because the focus is on practicing to build automaticity in reading mastered words.

1. Write mastered regular words (words with sounds the student has mastered) and irregular words (words the student has learned in irregular word instruction) on word cards. Show the student each word card and have him or her read it. Review any words the student reads incorrectly.

2. Set a timer for 1 minute. Tell the student that he or she will read the words, saying the word as soon as he or she knows it, until the timer goes off. As the student reads, place words read correctly into one pile, and words read incorrectly into a second pile. Stop when the timer goes off.

3. Count the number of words the student read correctly in 1 minute. Have the student graph the number correct.

4. Review the words the student read incorrectly.

5. Set the timer for 1 minute again. Remind the student to read the words, saying the word as soon as he or she knows it, until the timer goes off. Let the student know the goal is to read more words correctly. As the student reads, again place the correct words into one pile, and words read incorrectly into a second pile.

6. Count the number of words the student read correctly in 1 minute. Have the student graph his or her second attempt at the reading, comparing the number read correctly to the first try.

7. Review the words the student read incorrectly.

8. Repeat the 1-minute word reading a third time, using the same procedures.

9. Review any words the student read incorrectly.

10. Count the number of words the student read correctly in 1 minute. Have the student graph his or her third attempt at the reading, comparing the number read correctly to the first and second attempts.

Review

Include any words read incorrectly in the sight-word practice daily until the student demonstrates mastery. Review mastered words by including them periodically.

Examples of Activity Intensifications

DOES THE STUDENT NEED COGNITIVE PROCESSING STRATEGIES?

* Have the student set a goal for the number of words read correctly in 1 minute. As the student graphs his or her words read correctly, discuss the student's goal and the progress toward that goal. If the student needs scaffolding to set an appropriate goal, give the student several choices for a goal and have him or her select his or her goal.

* When reviewing the words a student read incorrectly, ask the student to identify the strategy they should use to read the word (e.g., use the known sounds to read the word, spell the letters to remember the known word).

DOES THE STUDENT NEED MORE FREQUENT OPPORTUNITIES
FOR STUDENT RESPONSE, PRACTICE, AND REVIEW?

* Increase the amount of time for reading words (e.g., 2 minutes instead of 1 minute).

* Have the student read any words read incorrectly to fluency before completing the second or third timing.

RESOURCES

National Center on Intensive Intervention
www.intensiveintervention.org

   This website provides tools for identifying reliable and valid progress monitoring assessments for phonics and word recognition. Sample intensive phonics lessons are also available for instructional support.

Foorman, B., Beyler, N., Borradaile, K., Coyne, M., Denton, C. A., Dimino, J., et al. (2016). *Foundational skills to support reading for understanding in kindergarten through 3rd grade* (NCEE 2016-4008). Washington, DC: National Center for Education Evaluation and Regional Assistance, Institute of Education Sciences, U.S. Department of Education.

   This practice guide provides practical, research-based recommendations for developing foundational skills in the early elementary grades for reading success.

Wanzek, J., Harbor, A., & Vaughn, S. (2010). *Word recognition and fluency: Effective upper-elementary interventions for students with reading difficulties.* Austin, TX: Meadows Center for Preventing Educational Risk. Available at *www.meadowscenter.org/library/resource/word-recognition-and-fluency-effective-upper-elementary-interventions-for-s.*

This book provides intervention lessons in phonics and word recognition from beginning-level skills to on-grade-level upper-elementary skills.

Wasowicz, J., Apel, K., Masterson, J. J., & Whitney, A. (2004). *SPELL-links to reading and writing.* Evanston, IL: Learning by Design.

This book provides sequenced lessons teaching early phonics skills with an encoding emphasis.

Moats, L. C. (2010). *Speech to print: Language essentials for teachers* (2nd ed.). Baltimore: Brookes.

This book provides key, research-based information to build teacher knowledge of the structure of the English language and how to deliver explicit, targeted instruction in written and spoken language.

CHAPTER 4

Intensive Interventions
to Support Fluency

If you have ever worked with a student who has a significant reading difficulty, you have likely heard the struggle many students have turning written language into a fluent, smooth oral language. Many students with intensive reading needs struggle to master reading fluency, and their teachers struggle to help them make adequate progress in this important area of reading. Although there is still much to be learned about how students process written language and become fluent readers, there are important ways we can help dysfluent readers make great strides in their reading development.

Reading fluency is the ability to read text with high accuracy, a quick rate, and appropriate expression (National Reading Panel & National Institute of Child Health and Human Development, 2000). Intensive fluency instruction provides students with a passageway from knowledge of phonics and word recognition to the comprehension of text. Students need to be not only accurate but also rapid in their word recognition as they read text, in order to focus on gaining meaning from the text.

WHAT DOES THE RESEARCH SAY ABOUT READING FLUENCY?

Early research identified two primary causes of reading disability: phonological deficits (detailed in Chapters 2 and 3 on phonological awareness and phonics and word recognition, respectively) and/or deficits in the fluency or automaticity aspects of reading (Torgesen, Wagner, Rashotte, Burgess, & Hecht, 1997; Wolf & Bowers, 1999). As we noted in earlier chapters, intensive interventions that target students' phonological deficits have proven very effective (Wanzek et al., 2018). Affecting change in the area of fluency, however, has proven to be a challenging task. For example, several studies have found significant effects for increasing phonological skills (Lovett, Steinbach, & Frijters, 2000;

Torgesen et al., 2001; Vadasy, Sanders, & Peyton, 2005), but fluency outcomes were not significantly affected by the interventions employed. These studies did not emphasize fluency instruction, but rather note that progress in word recognition ability did not significantly affect reading fluency. Thus, we recommend including instruction specifically on fluency development as part of intensive reading interventions.

Samuels's (1979, 2006) theory of automaticity in reading has assisted many researchers in better understanding fluency. Samuels posited that automatic word recognition is necessary to free up the cognitive resources for a reader to focus on text meaning. In other words, students who read accurately but laboriously must spend much of their effort on decoding words, and may be unable to focus their attention on the meaning of the text. Generally, students who can read text fluently are better overall readers and comprehenders (Good, Simmons, & Kame'enui, 2001; Klauda & Guthrie, 2008). Students with faster decoding speeds tend to demonstrate more appropriate expression in their reading and have higher levels of comprehension (Schwanenflugel, Hamilton, Wisenbaker, Kuhn, & Stahl, 2004). Additionally, fluent readers tend to read more print, and to find reading more enjoyable, than less fluent readers who must put forth a great deal of effort to read. This difference can lead to Matthew effects, wherein good readers improve their reading skills more quickly as a result of their increased contact with written language, while poor readers tend to lag further and further behind (Stanovich, 2009).

As the automaticity theory might suggest, reading fluency is highly correlated with elementary students' reading comprehension (Kim, Petscher, Schatschneider, & Foorman, 2010; Silverman, Speece, Harring, & Ritchey, 2013). In the earliest stages of reading development, students' word-reading fluency and listening comprehension best predict their reading comprehension of the simple text typically encountered by beginning readers (Kim & Wagner, 2015). In fact, for early readers, word recognition automaticity or efficiency may be a key component of reading fluency and comprehension (Schwanenflugel et al., 2006). However, as students develop their reading through the elementary grades, text-reading fluency becomes an important factor in their reading comprehension beyond simple word-reading fluency.

Research examining ways to improve student fluency has found explicitly teaching fluency to be valuable (Fuchs, Fuchs, Mathes, & Simmons, 1997; Hasbrouck, Ihnot, & Rogers, 1999). This instruction has been carried out successfully in a variety of ways. Modeling fluent reading by reading aloud as well as practicing fluent reading with repeated readings, including timed readings, are successful strategies for increasing fluency on the practiced text (Chard, Vaughn, & Tyler, 2002; Therrien, 2004; Vadasy & Sanders, 2009). Students can make the highest gains in fluency and comprehension when they can practice reading the passage at least three to four times (Therrien, 2004). Incorporating goal setting and feedback on progress toward goals can further increase reading fluency outcomes for students (Conte & Hintze, 2000; Morgan & Sideridis, 2006). As noted earlier, fluent readers tend to read more text. Practice reading a wide range of texts, sometimes called wide reading, may increase students' fluency (as well as vocabulary and comprehension) due to the increased exposure to print. In fact, in a study comparing repeated reading of text and continuous reading of text with upper-elementary students, both types of text-reading practice led to significant increases in fluency, word reading, and comprehension (O'Connor, White, & Swanson, 2007). Yet there were no differences in outcomes between the students who participated in the repeated reading and the students who participated in the continuous reading. Thus, structuring opportunities for students with reading difficulties to practice reading a wide range of texts may also serve to help students improve their reading ability.

WHAT ARE THE CRITICAL ELEMENTS OF READING FLUENCY INSTRUCTION?

Fluency instruction generally involves providing students with systematic practice of the word- and text-reading methods that they have been learning, to allow them to reach an efficient or automatic level with these practices. Students need to have a high level of accuracy with a text (e.g., 95% or higher) in order to work on their rate of reading, even with support. If students are unable to read the words in the text, they will not be able to focus on the meaning of the text, and are likely to become frustrated. As noted earlier, research supports structured practice activities that include modeling of fluent reading and repeated reading of text with goal setting and feedback. Wide reading may also improve students' fluency. The key to intensive fluency instruction is structured, purposeful reading fluency activities that have a specific goal for the student. The fact that students are reading text does not mean that they are engaged in fluency practice. We discuss the implementation of intensive instruction in each of the research-based areas of reading fluency instruction.

Modeling

Models of fluent reading can provide a standard of the accuracy, rate, and expression expected for fluent reading. Students can then practice and work toward achieving the modeled standard. When teachers read aloud passages or books, they provide a model of fluent reading. When one is modeling fluent reading, it is important to point out the key characteristics of fluent reading to students to make the instruction explicit and overt. Students can then home in on what to listen for and what elements to practice in their own reading. For example, while modeling fluent reading with a read-aloud, a teacher may point out that his or her reading sounds as if he or she is talking or telling a story. The teacher may identify places where he or she pauses or shows expression based on the words in the passage. It may also be useful to provide a non-example (i.e., dysfluent reading) to help students better understand the concept of *fluent*. The teacher may read a passage fluently, pointing out the key characteristics of fluent reading, and then reread the same passage in a dysfluent way, pointing out the lack of key characteristics of fluent reading (e.g., "It does not sound as if I'm talking"; "I sound like a robot"; "I am not pausing between sentences"). Importantly, reading *fast* is not a key characteristic of fluent reading—that is, it is possible to read a passage too fast and make the read-aloud not understandable. Students who have intensive intervention needs should not be encouraged to think of fluent reading as fast reading, because they may lose sight of the true purpose of fluent reading—the ability to read accurately with automaticity and expression, and to focus on the meaning of the passage.

Students who have intensive intervention needs in the area of fluency will need multiple opportunities to practice fluent reading paired with the models. For example, a teacher may demonstrate fluent reading with a short passage and then allow students to practice reading the same passage fluently, sounding like the teacher. In addition to read-alouds, techniques such as echo reading or duet reading provide modeling and student practice. In echo reading, the teacher models fluent reading of a short segment of a story or passage while the student follows along. The student then reads the same segment of the story or passage that was modeled, practicing fluent reading. The teacher then continues the story or passage by modeling the next short segment, followed again by the student mimicking (echoing) the teacher's reading. Duet reading involves the teacher and student reading a passage together. Duet reading can occur with simultaneous reading, as the teacher reads just a bit more fluently than the student's current level and the student works to keep up with the teacher's reading, thus practicing reading more fluently. Alternatively, duet reading can occur when the teacher and student take turns reading each word (e.g., for the sentence *The car sped down the road*, the teacher reads "The," the student reads "car," the teacher reads "sped," the student reads "down," etc.) as quickly as the student can.

In all reading fluency activities involving modeling and practicing of fluency, it is important that the passage is long enough to allow the student to focus on reading the passage fluently, and not just memorizing the words and phrases the teacher used. Consequently, older readers will likely need a longer passage for this practice than younger readers, as the memory capabilities of older students are generally stronger.

As students practice reading passages with the fluent levels that the teacher modeled, it is essential to provide specific feedback on the key characteristics of fluent reading. In other words, what characteristics (minimal pauses between words, pauses between sentences or other punctuation, expression that matches the punctuation) are students demonstrating (affirmative feedback), and what characteristics can the students continue to work on (corrective feedback)?

Although we have referred mainly to teacher modeling of fluent reading in this section, modeling can also occur through audio recordings of fluent reading, and through peer readers who are more fluent than the student who is practicing. But for students who require intensive intervention in fluency, the teacher will likely need to point out the key characteristics of the model in order to provide more explicit instruction and help students understand what they should listen for and practice in their own reading. In addition, these students will need specific affirmative and corrective feedback during student practice.

Repeated Reading

Repeated reading is a fluency practice consisting of multiple readings of the same passage until a fluent level is reached. There are multiple ways to implement repeated reading. First, a short passage at the student's reading level is selected for reading. This may be a passage that the student has previously read, or a new passage at the student's reading level, including regular word types and irregular words the student has learned. To provide the most systematic instruction, it may also be beneficial to ensure that the text has many frequently used words. A text with high-frequency words allows students to practice fluency with words that they will see not only in this text but likely in many other texts, so that they can better transfer and improve their reading fluency across texts. Second, the purpose for reading is set. Setting a purpose can include cues about reading at a quick rate and reading for understanding. It may also include the repeated reading task, such as reading the passage a certain number of times to try to improve fluency and comprehension, or reading the passage until a preset fluency level is obtained (e.g., 90 words correct in 1 minute).

As noted earlier, the research suggests that repeated reading should include at least three to four readings of the passage to achieve the highest gains in fluency and comprehension. For students in need of intensive interventions, affirmative and corrective feedback from the teacher in between each of the readings can help to improve the fluency of each additional reading. In between each reading, students can receive affirmative and corrective feedback to improve subsequent readings. This feedback may include specific cues related to the student's rate of reading, instruction on specific word errors made by the student, and/or comments on the student's performance related to the goal—for example, "You read 75 words per minute on that reading. Let's see whether you can get closer to our goal of 90 words correct per minute in the next reading." Teachers may also do quick check-ins on student understanding of what is being read. Repeated reading of a passage can also be combined with the fluency practice of modeling. Teachers may model reading the passage using the practices described earlier, followed by a repeated reading activity with the passage.

We noted in the research section that upper-elementary students may benefit equally from repeated reading or sustained reading activities for the same amount of time—that is, students may read longer passages for a set amount of time, time that might be similar to reading a shorter passage three to four times. The key components of reading fluency practice should still be applied to the sustained reading, including cueing students to read at a quick rate and focus on understanding the text, as well as providing affirmative and corrective feedback on student reading fluency.

Goal Setting

As discussed in Chapter 1, setting goals is one cognitive processing strategy that can be embedded in an intensive intervention. When students work toward a goal in their fluency practice, they can make greater gains. Goals can be set by the teacher and shared with the student prior to the fluency practice. For younger students, it may be most motivating to set a goal that the student can likely reach within the fluency session. For older students, goals can be either session goals or longer-term goals that a student works toward over multiple sessions. Working toward a specific reading achievement goal (e.g., reading 120 words correctly in 1 minute) can be more powerful for improving reading fluency than a task goal (e.g., read this passage three times).

Charting student progress toward goals can assist students in monitoring their gains, another cognitive processing strategy. For example, as students engage in repeated reading, they can graph how many words they read correctly after each reading. Figure 4.1 provides a sample graph. The students can then visually see their gains with each reading. If students are working toward a specific reading fluency goal, they can see their progress toward that goal. Teachers can reinforce these gains with affirmative feedback—for example, "On the first read you had 10 errors, but you improved already on your second read with only five errors. Fewer errors means you can understand the passage better." Teachers may also incorporate feedback that will help students continue to make gains—for example, "Now, on the third read let's see whether you can make even fewer errors. Let's take a minute to practice the words you missed last time. Remember to look at all the letters in the word to read it." Over time, it may also be beneficial to have students start to set their own reading fluency goals. It is likely that they will need instruction and practice in how to set reasonable yet challenging goals to improve their reading fluency. Table 4.1 provides grade-level reading fluency guidelines.

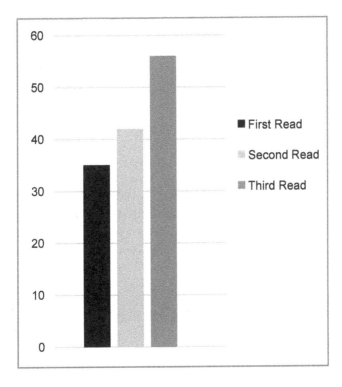

FIGURE 4.1. Sample reading fluency chart.

TABLE 4.1. Grade-Level Goals for Oral Reading Fluency

Grade	Fall WCPM	Winter WCPM	Spring WCPM
1	na	29	60
2	50	84	100
3	83	97	112
4	94	120	133
5	121	133	146

Note. Source of norms: Hasbrouck and Tindal (2017). WCPM, words read correctly per minute; na, not applicable.

Opportunities for Wide Reading

Intensive interventions for students with significant reading difficulties must include daily opportunities for students to read a variety of texts and apply the reading practices they are learning. It is not surprising that the more students successfully practice with text, the better their fluency becomes. Access to a variety of texts, particularly with instructional support, may improve many aspects of reading ability, including language and vocabulary development. In an intensive intervention, repeated reading and wide reading can both be incorporated in instruction.

Of course, supplemental intensive interventions provide only one opportunity for wide reading, and occur for only a limited period of the students' school day. In addition to providing many opportunities for text reading during intervention, providing students with appropriate text-reading opportunities outside of intervention, including during classroom instruction or outside of school, can help to increase the amount of practice students participate in each week. When students are reading text without teacher assistance, the text needs to be at their independent level (i.e., students can read all or nearly all of the words without assistance). For students with significant reading difficulties, it may be best to have them read orally to another adult, such as a parent. If student reading abilities indicate facility with silent, independent reading of text, then the text-reading activity should include a reading check-in, such as a short comprehension task related to the text that is read. This activity will help students stay focused on the purpose of reading for understanding when reading, and will assist teachers or adult helpers in determining whether the student successfully read the text. Obviously, student reading fluency can only improve if students are actually reading the text.

HOW DO I MONITOR PROGRESS IN READING FLUENCY?

Monitoring student progress in oral reading fluency can provide teachers with a broad measure of student reading ability once students can read short, connected text passages. A variety of oral reading fluency measures are available for grades 1–5. These measures typically require the student to orally read a grade-level passage for 1 minute.

Student errors are marked, and the number of words read correctly per minute is calculated as the score. Errors often include omitted or mispronounced words, as well as taking longer than a specified amount of time (e.g., 3 seconds) to read a word. Standardized and normed measures of oral reading fluency provide grade-level benchmarks to compare student scores and progress. These measures allow teachers to identify whether students are making progress toward grade-level or individualized education plan (IEP) reading fluency goals. If students demonstrate insufficient response toward these goals, the oral reading fluency measure, along with observations during fluency instruction, can provide the teacher with information regarding how to adjust instruction. For example, if a student makes no errors in the reading but is still obtaining a low fluency score, the student is having a rate issue that needs to be emphasized in instruction. Perhaps there are even particular types of words or phrases where students demonstrate slow reading (e.g., multisyllabic words, content, or more technical words or phrases). If a student has many errors in his or her reading and that is contributing to the low score, there may be accuracy issues, such as those discussed in Chapter 3 related to phonics and word recognition. Some students may have both rate and accuracy issues that need to be addressed in instruction.

For students who are working on beginning reading skills, teachers may also be interested in a student's fluency in letter sounds, decoding, or word reading. As noted in Chapter 3, several formal progress monitoring measures are available to monitor these beginning reading skills. It may be difficult for students to master reading connected text if they are not fluent with beginning reading skills. Therefore, monitoring progress not only in the accuracy but also the automaticity of beginning reading skills may provide valuable information regarding students' early progress toward reading fluency.

INSTRUCTIONAL ACTIVITIES FOR FLUENCY

Note: Text for fluency practice should be familiar to the student in that there are few words or sound patterns that the student has not mastered. If there are a few unknown words—including words that are difficult to pronounce, character names, or words with unknown meanings in the selected text—introduce and familiarize the student with these words before the activity begins.

Echo Reading

Objective

The student will be able to fluently read selected text.

Materials

Copy of selected text for the teacher and the student.

Optional: reading pointer.

Procedures

MODEL

1. Before reading, instruct the student to listen closely to how the text is read while following along as the text is read aloud. Be sure to read this text by demonstrating expected fluency with appropriate tone and pacing.

2. Read a portion of the selected text aloud while the student follows along. A student with tracking needs can point, using a pointer or finger as the text is read.

3. After reading the text aloud, point out specific areas where words were stressed or emphasized, and/or where tone was changed. This can be done through questioning the student, as well as explicitly pointing out fluency characteristics that were used. For example: If the text read "The drive home was so long. It felt like forever!", questioning could include "What did you notice about how I read this sentence?" [answers related to rate, accuracy, or expression], or "Did you hear how I read the word *forever*?" [it was louder or emphasized because of the exclamation mark], allowing the student the opportunity to identify fluency characteristics.

4. Continue this process with the remaining text.

SUPPORTED PRACTICE

1. Instruct the student that now you will read the text again, but the student will be repeating back the text, echoing exactly how it sounds read aloud. The length of text read aloud/echoed will vary based on selected text and student need. For some students, it will be best to model one sentence at a time, whereas other students may be able to read three to five sentences. The range should be long enough for the student to focus on reading fluency, rather than memorization.

2. Read a portion of text, demonstrating fluency with appropriate tone and pacing.

3. Instruct the student to read the same portion of text, trying to sound as identical as possible to the original reading. If errors occur, provide corrective feedback immediately and remodel the portion of text aloud. Then have the student try again. Repeat until the student reads the text fluently.

4. Continue throughout the entire selection of text.

Review

Incorporate echo reading into reading instruction across areas throughout the day. If a student reads aloud without fluency, read text as it is expected to be read, and have the student echo. This can be applied to different subject areas, as well as to signs around the school.

Examples of Activity Intensifications

DOES THE STUDENT NEED MORE FREQUENT OPPORTUNITIES FOR STUDENT RESPONSE, PRACTICE, AND REVIEW?

- Shrink the portion of text that is expected to be echoed. This process can be demonstrated with sentence strips to paragraphs. If a student is having difficulty fluently echoing two sentences, begin by modeling one and have the student echo. Repeat the process while increasing the range of sentences included, to ensure that the student is not memorizing text but rather is reading the text.

- Demonstrate the first part of the sentence being read fluently, and have the student echo—then demonstrate the second part of a sentence being read fluently, and have the student echo. Then model reading aloud both parts of the sentence fluently, and have the student echo back the process.

DOES THE STUDENT NEED MORE SPECIFIC AND CORRECTIVE FEEDBACK?

If the student is having difficulty incorporating characteristics of fluency across the echo reading process, have the student focus on one component of reading fluency (e.g., attending to punctuation) that can be set as a goal before each echo reading. If errors are made, provide immediate and corrective feedback with a model of a correct reading. Repeat until fluent. Once fluent, incorporate a new fluency skill to have as a goal in addition to the previous.

Duet Reading

Objective

The student will be able to increase reading fluency.

Materials

Copy of selected text for the teacher and the student.

Practice sentence strips with prewritten sentences that the student will be able to decode.

Optional: sound-recording device, headphones.

Procedures

MODEL

1. Present a sentence strip with a prewritten sentence to the student. These will be used to practice the concept of duet reading before transferring the skill to longer text, as well as giving the student confidence in completing the activity. Discuss how you will be reading the sentence aloud while the student is expected to simultaneously

read the sentence aloud, matching the tone and inflection of your voice. *Note: If the student makes an error, stops, or loses his or her place on the sentence strip, stop. Provide immediate corrective feedback for errors, and let the student regroup before starting from where you left off.*

2. Once sentence strips are read, instruct the student that this will be done with a longer text, but that the same rules apply.

SUPPORTED PRACTICE

1. Read aloud selected text while the student simultaneously reads aloud, following the above procedure. At the end of reading, provide corrective feedback on any student errors, and praise characteristics of fluent reading that were demonstrated.

2. Repeat this procedure with the same reading if more practice is needed, as well as with additional texts.

Note: This activity can also be done with prerecorded text where the student can listen with a headphone in one ear and one without, so the student can hear him- or herself read and match the reader. If using prerecorded text, continue to provide feedback and correction procedures while pausing the recording.

Review

To continue improving fluency skills, explicitly point out moments of modeled fluent reading, and include open discussion on strategies that can be used to increase words read correctly per minute and other fluency goals. A student with fluency needs can be paired with a student who already has skills in fluency, to gain more exposure as well as to practice modeling back the strategies observed in the partner.

Examples of Activity Intensifications

DOES THE STUDENT NEED MORE FREQUENT OPPORTUNITIES
FOR STUDENT RESPONSE, PRACTICE, AND REVIEW?

Use a variation of duet reading that allows for more frequent opportunities to respond. Read the text aloud, but every couple of words, omit a word or two, allowing the student to take the lead. When doing so, continue to provide immediate and corrective feedback to any errors made.

DOES THE STUDENT NEED DIRECT INSTRUCTION FOR TRANSFER
TO NEW CONTEXTS?

Incorporate text and passages across subjects and types of reading. This will allow the student to learn and be able to differentiate between and among the expectations of different reading tones, as well as to transfer and apply his or her fluency skills.

Repeated Reading (Variation 1)

Objective

The student will be able to increase reading fluency.

Materials

Selected reading.

Different color highlighter for each reading (four readings, four different colored highlighters).

Timer.

Procedures

MODEL

1. Select a text containing both regular and irregular high-frequency words based on the individual reading needs of the student.

2. With the student, set a purpose for the repeated reading model, focusing on a component of reading with fluency. For example: "I am going to try to read 80 words correct in a minute." An additional focus could include the number of errors in the reading. For example: "My goal is to make less than six errors."

3. Model reading a short passage aloud for the first time while setting the timer for 1 minute. When the timer goes off, mark the last word read with a highlighter. Determine how many words were read. *Note: If focusing on words read correctly per minute, it is helpful to use a reading where the amount of words is counted and displayed after each line.*

4. Provide corrective feedback on the first reading—on both components that did and components that did not demonstrate fluent reading.

5. Indicate to the student that when completing this process, he or she will repeat the reading and make a mark after the last word read, again using a different colored highlighter. *Note: Ideally, this mark would be after the first mark. If fewer words are read in consecutive readings, a different level or selection of text may be used, or the goal may be altered.*

SUPPORTED PRACTICE

1. Provide the student with leveled text different from the modeled text.

2. Set a goal specific to student needs. This goal can include words read correctly per minute, focus on a specific component of fluency, or specify the number of errors in the reading. Remind the student that he or she has 1 minute to read the text, and when the timer goes off, to stop reading. The student should make a mark, using a highlighter, after the first reading. Determine how many words were read correctly.

3. Provide corrective feedback on the student's first reading. This can also be an opportunity for the student to self-monitor and assess his or her own reading skills, if able.

4. Reset the timer and have the student reread the text, marking where he or she finishes when the timer goes off, using a different colored highlighter.

5. Repeat this process for at least three to four total readings, continuing to provide corrective feedback as well as acknowledging strengths between each reading. Focus on student growth between each reading.

Review

When the student is reading throughout the day, even outside of formal reading instruction, focus on the student reading more fluently. The specific goal from this activity can be used and referenced throughout the day, to bring awareness to the student's reading fluency progress. This can be applied when reading in different subject areas. Be sure to focus on words read correctly per minute, rather than reading speed. Take different opportunities throughout the day to model your focus on your own reading fluency, again to bring the student's awareness to improving his or her own fluency.

Examples of Activity Intensifications

DOES THE STUDENT NEED COGNITIVE PROCESSING STRATEGIES?

A graphic organizer, such as a checklist listing different components of fluent reading in child-friendly language, can be created for the student to use and reference before and between readings. This checklist can also help the student set fluency reading goals. The student can graph his or her progress, allowing for visual guidance in creating goals while moving through the reading process.

DOES THE STUDENT NEED MORE EXPLICIT INSTRUCTION?

Prior to repeated readings and the modeling process, provide examples and non-examples of fluent reading. Non-examples should include characteristics and errors the student has been making to help the student recognize it in his or her own reading. Additionally, student readings can be recorded so the student can hear and analyze his or her own reading and determine whether the readings sounded fluent or not.

Repeated Reading (Variation 2)

Objective

The student will be able to increase and improve reading fluency.

Materials

Copy of selected text for the teacher and the student.

Progress graph.

Writing utensils.

Colored pencils/markers.

Timer.

Procedures

MODEL

1. Present the text to the student. Any words that are above the student's decoding level can be precorrected for the student prior to reading if necessary.

2. Instruct the student that he or she will be following along while you read the text aloud until the timer goes off. *Note: If there is a specific fluency goal that your student is working on, be sure to incorporate that goal into your reading so you are able to point out how and when it is used, acting as a precorrect before the student reads.*

3. Read the text aloud, demonstrating appropriate fluency skills.

4. Instruct the student that he or she will be joining you in reading the same text aloud for 1 minute.

SUPPORTED PRACTICE

1. When the student is reading with you, his or her tone should match your tone, similar to the duet reading process.

2. Provide feedback on the student's strengths during reading, as well as corrective feedback on the student's reading.

3. Inform the student that he or she will now read the text independently. When the timer goes off, the student should stop and make a mark after the last word read, using a colored pencil or marker.

4. Continue to provide immediate and corrective feedback after each reading, as well as calculating how many words were read correctly per minute.

5. Have the student graph/chart the number of words read per minute.

6. Allow the student to complete at least two more readings of the same text while graphing/charting his or her progress after each reading. Provide praise for growth made in reading.

Review

Incorporate repeated reading into new texts and subjects, as well as a transition to new reading levels.

Examples of Activity Intensifications

DOES THE STUDENT NEED MORE SYSTEMATIC INSTRUCTION?

If the student is having difficulty increasing the length of reading or meeting the goal, select a shorter text (this can be as short as a sentence or two). Then set a new fluency-related goal and have the student read the sentence(s). The goal can include phrasing or pacing. Apply the repeated reading process to this new selection of text. Eventually, you can build the text by adding a sentence to slowly build the fluency of reading multiple sentences, without memorization.

DOES THE STUDENT NEED MORE EXPLICIT INSTRUCTION?

Prior to reading, review components of fluent reading with the student, providing a short example of each. For example, if a student's needs relate to attending to punctuation when reading, provide an example sentence containing varied punctuation, and model how it is expected to be read. If a student has a comprehension need, model reading a few sentences, followed by self-monitoring for meaning and possibly paraphrasing the text that was read. Incorporate examples and models of each component reviewed.

Phrasing

Objective

The student will be able to increase reading fluency.

Materials

Whiteboard.

Dry-erase markers.

Selected text (printed on computer paper).

Transparency slip (paper protector slips can also be used).

Procedures

MODEL

1. Introduce fluent reading with a prewritten sentence displayed on the whiteboard to be read fluently as an example of expected reading.

2. Direct the student to follow along and listen to how you read the sentence aloud. While reading the sentence aloud, point to each word read, reading it fluently the first time. Be sure to explain what made the first reading fluent.

3. Then read the sentence word-by-word, demonstrating a non-example of fluent reading. *Note: Younger students may enjoy the nonfluent reading being compared to robot reading.*

4. Ask the student whether the first reading was fluent, and have a brief discussion about why it was. This is an opportunity to review characteristics of fluent reading that have been introduced and check for understanding.

5. Instruct the student that you will be rereading the sentence the same way as you did the first time, but this time you will be scooping the words as you read it. You should draw a scooped line below each word read. In this example, that will be after every word.

Example: The cat ran all the way home.

6. Erase the scoops and have student follow along while you reread fluently, and scoop, demonstrating the difference between fluent and nonfluent reading.

Example: The cat ran all the way home.

7. Create selected student text on transparency slips for both you and the student to scoop with dry-erase markers. Model scooping as you read the first two to three sentences of the text while the student follows along. Include examples and non-examples of fluent reading. When a non-example is given with more scoops, model how that example is an indicator to go back and reread, as well as rescooping the sentence.

SUPPORTED PRACTICE

1. Have the student pick up where you left off in the selected text, reading aloud and scooping sentences.

2. If the student is not scooping correctly, remodel on the sentence he or she just read. Provide corrective feedback throughout the passage reading.

Review

Have the student complete the passage. Once done, the student can read the entire text as a whole, using the scoop marks to guide him or her to more fluent reading. The scooping can be transferred to any context when reading takes place. When there are not opportunities to write the scoops, the student can use a pointer finger to draw them in the air.

Examples of Activity Intensifications

DOES THE STUDENT NEED MORE FREQUENT OPPORTUNITIES
FOR STUDENT RESPONSE, PRACTICE, AND REVIEW?

- During the modeling process, have the student echo back each example modeled while scooping. Incorporating both examples and non-examples will further help the student discriminate between fluent and nonfluent reading.

- Include more single-sentence examples to model, then slowly work up to a passage. This can be done by working on single sentences in one session, and then two to three sentences in the next, followed by a paragraph.

- Provide the student with a recording of typed text, or read the text aloud to the student fluently. Have the student scoop while it is read aloud. Then have the student reread the text, using the scoop marks he or she made.

DOES THE STUDENT NEED MORE SPECIFIC AND CORRECTIVE FEEDBACK?

- Incorporate more examples and non-examples of fluent and nonfluent reading, based on the student's errors, to allow for further discrimination of what makes fluent phrasing.

- Have the student create a fluency-based goal prior to reading (based on previous practice), or after reading the first couple of sentences (based on repeated errors) that can be referred back throughout the process. This goal setting will allow for more focused and specific corrective feedback.

RESOURCES

Oregon Reading First Center

http://oregonreadingfirst.uoregon.edu/inst_addtl_tools.html

This resource provides user-friendly fluency passage forms across different levels. There are also procedure forms, summary spreadsheets, and strategy graphic organizers.

Florida Assessments for Instruction in Reading (FAIR) Search Tool for Links to Instructional Materials

www.fcrr.org/FAIR/index.shtm

FAIR provides a search engine for different fluency and reading-based activities with video models of instruction in each lesson and activity.

Intervention Central

www.interventioncentral.org/teacher-resources/graph-maker-free-online

This resource provides a graph maker where students and teachers are able to set goals and track their progress.

The Meadows Center for Preventing Educational Risk: Library search *www.meadowscenter. org/library/search-results/search&keywords=fluency&category=+++reading-instruction-resources&&elementary*

The Meadows Center provides a library of different educational resources, including journal articles and book chapters related to reading fluency instruction and research.

Hasbrouck, J., & Tindal, G. (2017). *An update to compiled ORF norms* (Technical Report No. 1702). Eugene: Research and Teaching, University of Oregon. Available at *www.readingrockets.org/ article/fluency-norms-chart-2017-update.*

Reading Rockets is a literacy initiative providing resources to teachers, parents, and students. This link includes an oral reading fluency-normed chart to reference in student goal setting, progress monitoring, and comparing progress throughout the year.

CHAPTER 5

Intensive Interventions to Support Oral Language

The purpose of oral language is to communicate, and the elements of oral language include the content, form, and use of language (e.g., Bloom & Lahey, 1978). Learning oral language follows a relatively predictable developmental process. However, when students experience language delays or disorders, or even when they lack exposure to oral language, or have limited background knowledge, it can influence reading and writing development. Elements of oral language are related to reading and writing, and the strength of these relations may change as students mature and have more experiences reading a variety of texts (e.g., Kim & Wagner, 2015; Storch & Whitehurst, 2002). Having a limited vocabulary often makes it harder for children to read with understanding and to express their ideas through written expression. In his cleverly written book aimed to make science more accessible, *Thing Explainer: Complicated Stuff in Simple Words*, former NASA roboticist Randall Munroe (2015) set out to explain hard stuff in simple language. In fact, he used only 1,000 words, along with drawings and blueprints, to explain how things work and where they come from. Simple examples include *wood writing sticks* or pencils and *water writing sticks* or pens; more complicated examples include machines (e.g., *boxes that make clothes smell better* or your washer and dryer), and the periodic table or *the pieces everything is made of*. Teachers might use his book as a scaffold for using words students know to learn new ones and to build conceptual knowledge. Knowledge about how oral language develops, and about how it relates to reading and writing, informs the scope and sequence for instruction, and for intensifying interventions.

WHAT DOES THE RESEARCH SAY
ABOUT ORAL LANGUAGE DEVELOPMENT AND INSTRUCTION?

Content

Language content includes vocabulary or semantics, and also involves knowledge of the world, background information, and experiences with classifying words, using objects, memories of events, and connections among these elements. The rules about language content include word meanings, as well as how words can be combined into phrases and sentences, and, as students learn to read, how punctuation represents those rules and changes the meaning of the sentence. As an extreme example of how a missing comma changes the meaning of a sentence, consider *I enjoy cooking my family and my pets* rather than *I enjoy cooking, my family, and my pets.*

The breadth of students' knowledge of vocabulary is known as their oral lexicon, or their knowledge of the meanings of words. The lexicon functions as a sort of mental filing cabinet, and is measured by the breadth or number of words stored. Research suggests that by the end of first grade, students should know at least 4,000 words, and that they need to learn about 3,000 words per year going forward (Biemiller, 1999). Beyond third grade, students build their vocabulary mainly through reading (Cunningham & Stanovich, 1998). Another aspect of the lexicon is the depth of understandings for words, and how these words may connect to background knowledge, experiences, and other words within the lexicon. The overlap of experience with words and with world knowledge influences how a young child uses a word to represent meaning. Consider a young child who learns the word *dog,* and then later learns that there are different breeds, such as poodles or Maltipoos, that are part of the category of dogs. This example reflects that developing semantics, or word learning, is a developmental process.

Other aspects about the development of language content include the relations among words, such as synonyms, antonyms, homonyms, or phrases, including idioms and metaphors. Homonyms are words that are spelled the same, but have different meanings. For example, a *date* could be a specific day of the year, fruit from a date tree, or going out with a companion. An example of an idiom, such as *It's raining cats and dogs,* indicates that it is raining hard, not that it is raining pets. Metaphors, like idioms, are figures of speech that are not to be taken literally (e.g., *clear as mud* refers to something that is complex rather than clear).

Form

Language form refers to aspects of language that include (1) phonology, or the sound system for a language; (2) morphology, or the structure of words; and (3) syntax, or grammatical order of words within sentences. Each of these language forms involves learning the rules of a language, something that of course supports reading development. Phonology includes rules about how phonemes, or speech sounds, combine to form words, how syllables within words are pronounced with intonation or stress, and even how words combine in sentences. Specifically, phonological awareness and how it develops is a chapter to itself (see Chapter 2).

Morphology includes rules for how words may be formed through combining units of meaning, something that influences reading comprehension (Carlisle, 1995) and predicts reading comprehension performance (e.g., Bowers, Kirby, & Deacon, 2010; Goodwin & Ahn, 2013). Knowledge and awareness of morphemes can also help students flexibly decode academic language found in science and social studies texts, language that frequently includes prefixes and suffixes. For example, some morphemes, known as unbound morphemes, mean something on their own, such as *cook*. By contrast, bound morphemes have meaning only when attached to other words, such as the *-ing* in *cooking*. Bound morphemes include endings that change the number of nouns (e.g., *s* as in *too many cooks*), change the tense of a verb (e.g., *-ed* in *cooked*), or indicate possession (e.g., *the cook's spoon*). Morphology is acquired as children learn to speak—they learn to use parts of speech including verbs (e.g., *going*), nouns (e.g., *friend*), pronouns (e.g., *she*), articles (e.g., *a, the*), prepositions (e.g., *in, under*), conjunctions (e.g., *and, but*), adjectives (e.g., *sweet*), and adverbs (e.g., *slowly*). Later, children learn about derivational morphology, or how the change in a word's structure can change its grammatical use (e.g., *run* is a verb and *runner* is a noun). They also learn about prefixes and suffixes. A humorous example of confusion or incomplete awareness about morphemes stemmed from a young boy's multiple experiences with construction and building with Legos, which led him to call the directions not *instructions,* but *constructions.*

Researchers (e.g., Carlisle, 1988; Fowler & Liberman, 1995; Soifer, 1999) caution that instruction about morphology should follow a scope and sequence of easiest to more difficult. For example, it is easier for students to hear and produce words in which there is no phonological change (e.g., *view, review,* and *preview*) than words that have a phonological change (e.g., *courage* vs. *courageous*). Explicit and systematic instruction is needed to face more challenging demands, such as when students are reading words that change not only in phonology but also in spelling, or orthography (e.g., *deep/depth*). Because the English language borrows words from many other languages, upper-elementary students benefit from instruction about the origins of words (e.g., Anglo-Saxon, Latin, Greek, Arabic, or French).

Syntax, or grammar, includes rules for combining words into sentences, so that sentences have an understandable meaning. Generally speaking, in the English language, sentences follow a subject, verb, object order—for example, *The girl ran; The boy ran.* In the early stages of syntactic development, children speak in simple noun and verb phrases, and then can begin to manipulate words in a sentence into a question—for example, *Who is running?*—or to indicate a negative—*I'm not running*—or an imperative sentence—*I want it now!* Children benefit from instruction to combine sentences—for example, *The girl and the boy ran*—to introduce them to different sentence structures, and to scaffold increasing the length and complexity of spoken sentences (Brown, 1978; Justice & Ezell, 2008). The length and complexity of sentences are related to the difficulty, or readability, of texts. Understanding of spoken and written language is enhanced when the context is familiar, or when there are explicit context clues. For example, children living in the southern United States might have less experience with snow, winter sports, or generally cold winter contexts than children living in the northern Midwest.

Use

Language use, or pragmatics, includes rules about intent to communicate, the codes or styles about communication in various contexts or with various audiences, and the social rules for conversation and written language. Some communication is verbal, and some may include gestures, body language, and tone. There is also a cultural element to pragmatics. The intent to communicate begins with a baby's cries to communicate hunger and other needs, and then may involve preverbal communication through pointing or reaching. At or around 1 year of age, most typically developing children begin to talk in one-word phrases, often combined with gestures. Ideally, when their needs are met and they have a secure attachment to their caregivers, they begin to learn about social interactions. The toddler years, however, can be a time of frustration when children cannot communicate their emotions, do not understand turn taking, or do not get what they want. As children develop more self-regulation and observe conversation in various social situations, they can benefit from modeling and direct instruction about how they communicate to friends, family, or teachers. Speakers of dialect may also benefit from learning to code shift or switch from home vernacular or colloquial speech to the more standard language of the classroom and to academic language (e.g., Craig, Connor, & Washington, 2003; Terry, Connor, Petscher, & Conlin, 2012). Many children need explicit instruction about social expectations for communication in school settings (e.g., to show what you know, to listen to the teacher, to volunteer or raise a hand to answer a question). These expectations differ from those on the playground. Then, as children gain more experience with reading, they may need instruction about text structures, to benefit from understanding that an author helps readers to understand the sequence of a story by using words such as *first, next,* and *last,* or to understand that words like *because* and *if–then* relate to cause and effect. Similarly, students may need explicit instruction to understand that there are differences in genres, so an author who is writing a narrative story might use different styles than an author who is writing an informational text.

In summary, the importance of each of these elements of language development relates to its influence not only on oral language but also on reading and writing, something that in turn influences educational and employment opportunities. There are several reasons why children may experience limited language. One reason stems from poverty and associated limited exposure to language and early literacy. A classic study by Hart and Risley (1995) found that by age 3, children living in poverty knew far fewer words than did children from professional families. They estimated the gap in exposure to be 3 million words; moreover, researchers documented that children living in poverty grew their vocabulary at a much slower rate, and rates of growth strongly predicted standardized language scores of content and form at third grade (Hart & Risley, 2003).

A second reason for limited oral language is related to speech and language delays, or reading disabilities. Students who have language delays, or who have weaker language comprehension, experience slower development of the content, form, and use of language. Students with reading disabilities also struggle with language. In particular, syntactic difficulties are a signature challenge for students with specific language impairments (Kamhi & Catts, 2012)—this challenge impedes comprehension and written expression.

A third reason could be other disabilities, including autism spectrum disorder. Children with autism spectrum disorder struggle in particular with pragmatics. They may not understand humor, sarcasm, figurative language, or even the basics of reading another person's body language or tone.

WHAT ARE THE CRITICAL ELEMENTS OF ORAL LANGUAGE INSTRUCTION?

With the research base described above, the critical elements in oral language instruction for elementary students include content (vocabulary or semantic breadth and depth), form (morphological and syntactic awareness), and use (pragmatics). Let's examine each of these critical elements and ways to provide intensive instruction, starting with vocabulary, keeping in mind that there is relatively more research for intervention in this element than exists for form or use.

Explicit Vocabulary Instruction

Prominent vocabulary researchers Beck, McKeown, and Kucan (2002) emphasize the importance of explicit and systematic vocabulary instruction or semantic knowledge. They also caution that it is not possible for teachers to explicitly teach every vocabulary word, and so advise that instruction should prioritize words that are useful, are relatively high frequency, and help students build connections to other words and to conceptual understanding. Other, more basic words—or other, more specialized and low-frequency words—may have less utility. Beck et al. have conducted considerable research on teaching vocabulary across the elementary grades, and recommend that several instructional components be followed. The first is to select important words based upon their prominence in a story or text—in turn, we recommend selecting text based on the text's word content. For example, therefore, in a science text about the life cycle of a butterfly, the word *caterpillar* would be important, and it might differ from the meaning of *caterpillar* in the context of a story about transportation or construction.

The next is to define the words in a child-friendly format. A few steps follow:

1. Extending students' use of the word through direct teaching.
2. Modeling of positive and negative examples.
3. Providing guided practice, including choice of word.
4. Building relationships among words.
5. Developing multiple opportunities for application and use of the word through independent practice and cumulative review.

Another approach to developing vocabulary knowledge for students with intensive needs who may struggle to learn vocabulary when reading complex content-area texts is through the use of graphic organizers. Graphic organizers can be used to activate students' prior knowledge around word meanings and explicitly draw connections among vocabulary words and concepts. One type of graphic organizer involves a semantic feature analysis, in which students analyze related concepts (e.g., suborders of bats: microbats and macrobats) by systematically comparing and contrasting them based on defining features (for bats: including their diet, how they navigate, and whether they hibernate). See Figure 5.1 for an example. This approach can also allow students to bring together concepts they are learning in an informational text (see Chapter 6 for further discussion and an example activity). Another approach involves creating semantic maps (also known as concept maps) in which the word or concept of interest—in this example, a little brown bat—is depicted in the center of a page, and relevant categories that help to describe that concept are depicted in a web (see Figure 5.2 for an example). Again, students with intensive needs are likely to require extensive modeling and practice with feedback in order to engage successfully in these activities.

Another recommendation is to support implicit vocabulary learning, including supporting students in learning new words as they read, and through building a classroom environment that is rich in academic language. For example, an upper-elementary classroom or intervention room wall might feature vocabulary from an upcoming science unit that includes both pictures and definitions. Some words might be targeted for direct instruction (such as *galaxy, Milky Way*). Other words (such as *stars, dust,* and *gas*) may be familiar, but students still may benefit from implicit vocabulary strategy instruction. A teacher might read that our galaxy is estimated to have over 11 billion stars, but that there is also dust and gas in our galaxy. Implicit instruction might help students understand how gas and dust might be different from or similar to gas and dust on Earth.

Shared book-reading strategies that teachers in elementary grades often use to support listening comprehension can also provide many opportunities for explicit vocabulary instruction (e.g., NCFL, 2009). Some evidence for the importance of explicit rather

Suborder	Species	Diet			Navigation/Finding			Hibernation	
		Insects	Fruit	Blood	Sight	Echo-location	Smell	Yes	No
Microbats	Long-eared myotis	+	–	–	+	+	–	+	–
	Little brown bat	+	–	–	+	+	–	+	–
	Tricolored bat	+	–	–	+	+	–	+	–
	Vampire bat	–	–	+	+	+	+	–	+
Megabats	Egyptian fruit bat	–	+	–	+	+	+	–	+
	Flying fox	+	+	–	+	–	+	–	+
Myotis refers to an insectivorous bat.									

FIGURE 5.1. Example of a filled-in semantic feature analysis.

FIGURE 5.2. Example of a completed semantic map (concept map).

than implicit instruction comes from a study conducted by Coyne, McCoach, and Kapp (2007), who conducted small-group read-alouds involving targeted vocabulary within the books. The more explicit read-aloud process included reading a text in which target words and their meanings were introduced, followed by *deep processing* in which students interacted with the target words in rich and varied contexts. The implicit or embedded process included providing simple definitions for the targeted words while reading the story. Significantly stronger effects were reported on measures of expressive and receptive definition tasks for the explicit condition—effects that were maintained 6 weeks after treatment ended. Another research team examined whole-group read-alouds and found that children in the explicit vocabulary read-aloud condition showed significantly greater vocabulary growth than children in a typical read-aloud condition (Baker et al., 2013).

Another read-aloud practice that has extensive research evidence is dialogic reading, which has resulted in improved vocabulary and language skills for young children, including students from economically disadvantaged families (e.g., Arnold, Lonigan, Whitehurst, & Epstein, 1994; Dale, Crain-Thoreson, Notari-Syverson, & Cole, 1996; Whitehurst et al., 1988, 1994). Dialogic reading has several instructional components:

1. Preteach essential vocabulary.
2. During reading, ask children questions that encourage their use of vocabulary.
3. Help children recall information and draw inferences.

Developers of dialogic reading created the teacher-friendly acronym CROWD to help teachers remember types of questions or prompts: Completion, Recall, Open-ended, Wh-questions, and Distancing questions (meaning questions that get away from the story, often requiring students to draw inferences, as in "How would you feel if this happened to you?"). They also created another acronym, PEER, to guide teacher extensions of child language: Prompt a response, Evaluate the response (i.e., "Was it a correct answer, but too short?"), Expand the response, and Repeat the response. Flynn (2011) wrote a helpful teacher-friendly article about how to conduct dialogic reading, something that is also helpful for training teachers and parents. Al Otaiba, Lake, Greulich, and Folsom (2012) added two extra question types to the CROWD process: Home and School (CROWD-HS). Home and school questions can build on students' background knowledge and experiences, can allow children to apply and transfer newly learned vocabulary to different settings, and can support them in making inferences. For example, when teaching the phrase *take care,* a home prompt might be "Can you think of a time someone took care of you at home?"; a school prompt might be "If a friend is crying, how can you take care of him or her?"

Explicit Morphology and Syntactic Instruction

The goal of morphological instruction is to help students acquire vocabulary, to understand how morphemes connect words in the lexicon, and ultimately, to improve reading and writing (e.g., Bowers et al., 2010). Morpheme instruction therefore overlaps with spelling and decoding, or, more globally, word study. For example, in a recent study, students in kindergarten, first grade, and second grade received small-group training in recognizing and analyzing morphological patterns, and in producing these patterns orally and in writing (Apel, Brimo, Diehm, & Apel, 2013; Apel & Diehm, 2014). Findings indicated that instruction about these patterns led to significantly greater growth in morphological awareness and early literacy outcomes relative to a control condition.

To make morphological instruction more explicit, Mountain (2005) suggests three strategies. First, when teaching the meaning of a word, teach several common derivative forms. Therefore, if teaching the word *view,* one would also teach *views, viewed, viewing,* and *viewer.* Second, when teaching a prefix or suffix, introduce it as part of a word with the most common meaning. For example, for the prefix *re-,* begin with the *re-* as meaning "again," as in *restart, review, recharge.* Then teach *re-* as meaning "back," as in *retreat* or *retract.* Third, when teaching multisyllabic words, practice breaking a multisyllabic word apart into meaningful roots and affixes, and then rebuilding it. In the word *reviewer,* for example, teach that *re-* means "again," *view* means "to look at something," and *-er* means "someone who." Therefore, a reviewer is someone who looks at something again.

In contrast to morphology, which involves rules for word meanings, syntax relates to the rules governing the use of larger chunks of language, including sentence structures and meanings of clauses. Written language is typically more dense and complex than oral language, and so it requires explicit instruction. Furthermore, different disciplines of text—for example, science texts as opposed to social studies texts—are associated with different sentence structures and text structures (Fang, 2012; Scott & Balthazar, 2013); thus, instruction must incorporate transfer to these different structures. There are several instructional strategies for syntax, and as students learn to read and write, these are often embedded in comprehension and writing instruction—areas covered in Chapters 6 and 7, respectively. For example, teachers can explicitly train students to combine sentences in oral and written language, while emphasizing awareness of the order in which words appear in a sentence (Scott & Balthazar, 2013).

Explicit Pragmatics Instruction

Pragmatics instruction supports students in understanding language use. Instructional activities from special education sources (e.g., Light & Binger, 1998) emphasize explicit instruction in oral social pragmatics, including taking turns, making eye contact, following directions, and recognizing and using appropriate tone of voice. Such instruction might include modeling, prompting, and even visual cues. Additional activities are informed by strategies used in English language instruction, including oral instruction to express feelings, to express personal needs, to seek information and help, and to establish relationships. In addition, students may need support to understand and express humor—for example, riddles, jokes, puns, and idioms, such as *It was raining cats and dogs*. Students may also benefit from instruction about how to speak to or write for different audiences. For example, they might sort cards that contain messages that would be something OK to say to a friend but not to a teacher, or to say at home but not at school.

HOW DO I MONITOR STUDENT PROGRESS IN ORAL LANGUAGE?

Monitoring student progress in oral language can assist teachers in determining students' overall growth as well as specific strengths and needs, something that in turn can help in planning for appropriate areas to focus on in instruction. There are few vocabulary measures with standardized procedures that can be given frequently for progress monitoring (see the "Resources" section for some sources). One type of curriculum-based measure of vocabulary for young students is a picture-naming task. For 1 minute, students are asked to name pictures of familiar items (e.g., book, cake, train) as quickly as possible. Teachers keep track of the number of pictures named correctly. For older students, teachers may select commercially available computer-based assessments. This type of assessment might ask students to answer a multiple- choice question identifying a definition, a synonym, or an antonym of a particular vocabulary word. Curriculum-based measures typically provide benchmarks to compare a student's scores, set goals, and assess progress. These measures can provide teachers with an indication of whether an intensive intervention is assisting a student in successfully broadening his or her language knowledge. Students who do not gain new vocabulary knowledge with their current instruction may need more direct, explicit word instruction, review, or practice using the new words.

A more informal approach to monitoring students' oral language development is to create a progress monitoring checklist or rubric. To create a rubric to monitor students' mastery of taught vocabulary words, the first step is to generate a list of words that will be targeted for instruction. Consider the tale *Goldilocks and the Three Bears*, a common story that is also available in brief video or cartoon form on the Internet. In this story, vocabulary instruction might focus on words such as *forest* or *broken,* or on phrases such as *just right* or *all gone.* These words could be directly taught in child-friendly terms using the techniques discussed in this chapter. In contrast, a word like *porridge* is less likely to be seen or read in other stories, and so it can be briefly taught by saying that *porridge* is another word for hot oatmeal or cereal.

Figure 5.3 provides an example of a rubric based on dialogic reading and vocabulary for the book *When I Feel Angry* by Cornelia Spelman. Note that the first column denotes the session/lesson number, while the next lists the vocabulary words. The teacher rates how well the student understands the word. A rating of 0 indicates that the student had no idea about the word meaning or provided an incorrect definition; 1 = knows something about the word, or provides a partially correct definition; 2 = understands and uses the word correctly, or provides a complete and correct definition (modified from Baker et al., 2013; Beck et al., 2002; Coyne et al., 2007). A teacher can ask students what the words mean before starting instruction to learn which words they already know, and which should be targeted, and then can use the rubric to determine whether students are learning the word meanings and using them appropriately.

Teachers can also informally attend to spoken language behaviors and keep notes during book reading. For example, do students make frequent false starts? Do they beat around the bush? Do they make errors of omissions of words, or errors in word order? Do they use very brief sentences, or utilize repetitive simple sentences? These observations might lead a teacher to have concern about a student's syntax.

Another informal approach is to track the accuracy and completeness of students' responses to questions during dialogic reading or other read-aloud activities. Figure 5.4

	try my hardest	angry	spoiled	figure it out
Session 1				
Session 2				
Session 3				
Session 4				

FIGURE 5.3. Vocabulary progress monitoring rubric for the book *When I Feel Angry* by Cornelia Spelman. Scoring can be completed using the following ratings: 0 = no idea about the word or incorrect definition, 1 = knows something about the word or provides a partially correct definition, 2 = understands and uses the word correctly or provides a complete and correct definition. Scoring adapted from Baker et al. (2013), Beck, McKeown, and Kucan (2002), and Coyne, McCoach, and Kapp (2007).

provides an example of a rubric for tracking responses to questions. Teachers could track student response to the CROWD-HS prompts in order to learn whether there is a particular question type that is challenging. The acronym PEER (Whitehurst et al., 1988) guides teachers' judgment about students' linguistic responses: Prompt a response by asking a CROWD question, Evaluate the response in terms of whether it is too short or incomplete, and then Expand the response by modeling a complete and correct answer. Next, encourage the child to Repeat the correct answer by rephrasing or repeating a question.

In addition to noting whether students answer questions correctly or use the targeted vocabulary, a teacher can observe and informally record whether students need more support for the following in terms of language form: answering in complete sentences, using grammar and syntax appropriately, and attending to and recognizing changes in word structure related to morphology. It is sometimes helpful for a teacher to audio- or video-record instructional sessions during read-alouds, or while a student is reading out loud, to more closely consider the student's pragmatics, including the form and use of language. Informal notes about response to oral language instruction during book reading or other instructional activities could indicate strengths (e.g., the student is paying attention to the teacher and to the book; the student is engaged; the student is taking turns and answering questions when prompted; the student can name the who, what, when, and where in the story; the student can retell the story in his or her own words). Notes could also highlight areas of improvement or outright errors (e.g., the student does not understand or misuses the targeted vocabulary word, the student seems unaware of the relation between the word *construction* and *structure*, the student is using short answers, the student is not using background knowledge, the student is sponging off another student in the group, the student is not using academic/book language and may need support in code shifting from dialect use) to help guide further instruction or intensifications in instruction

	C	R	O	W	D	HS
Session 1						
Session 2						
Session 3						
Session 4						

FIGURE 5.4. Oral language comprehension progress monitoring. CROWD-HS is the acronym for questions, including C = completion, R = recall, O = open-ended, W = wh-questions, D = distancing, and HS = home–school applications and inferences. Scoring can be completed using the following ratings: 0 = incorrect or no answer, 1 = very brief or partially correct answer (needs elaboration or needs error correction), 2 = complete and correct answer.

INSTRUCTIONAL ACTIVITIES FOR ORAL LANGUAGE

Introduction of New Vocabulary Words

Objective

The student will learn useful high-frequency words.

Materials

Preselected vocabulary word list with simple definitions.

Examples and non-examples of each word (e.g., demonstrations, pictures, videos, objects, scenarios, or sentences showing use).

Procedures

MODEL

1. Preselect words that are high frequency and high utility in language and print that are unknown to the student. Additionally, select known words that have a different meaning (e.g., a steering wheel of a car could be familiar, but the word *steer* might not be understood in the context of a steering committee, or of steering ahead toward a solution). It may also be relevant to teach some non-examples (i.e., that the "steering wheel" of an airplane is called a *yoke*).

2. Present the most familiar form of the word to the student orally and in writing. Provide a simple definition and/or key characteristics of the word to help the student get a basic understanding of the meaning of the word. For example: "Steering wheel. A *steering wheel* is a wheel that is used by a driver to control where a car, or other vehicle, goes. It's usually in a circle shape and inside the vehicle with the driver. To *steer* means to guide, to drive, or to direct, so a steering wheel lets the driver guide the car."

3. Model several examples and non-examples of the word, explaining why the example meets the characteristics or definition of the word, or why it does not. When possible, use concrete examples and non-examples such as demonstrations, pictures, or the actual object. For example: "This is a picture of a steering wheel in a car. It is used to drive the car. You can turn it to make the car go in the direction you want. This is not a steering wheel [show picture of a car tire]. It is not inside the car with the driver, and the driver cannot turn it."

    a. Make sure the examples include the key characteristics and show the variety that is a part of the word's meaning (e.g., steering wheel on a boat, car, tractor, toy car).

    b. Make sure non-examples are lacking at least one key characteristic to demonstrate the boundaries of the word's meaning (e.g., car tire, bike handles, bike tire, yoke in an airplane, a knob, a stick shift).

SUPPORTED PRACTICE

1. Present additional examples and non-examples to the student. Engage the student in identifying why each is an example (e.g., "That is a steering wheel") or not (e.g., "That is not a steering wheel") and why, using the key characteristics that have been taught.

2. Help the student to process the use of the word, or to make connections with other known words. This can include questioning, such as:

   a. "How is a steering wheel different from a handlebar?"
   b. "Have you ever seen a steering wheel? Where?"
   c. "What was it like using a steering wheel?"

Review

Provide continual review of newly introduced words. The other activities in this section provide many ways to review words, help the student acquire deeper understanding of words, and assist the student with making connections and relationships among words.

Examples of Activity Intensifications

DOES THE STUDENT NEED DIRECT INSTRUCTION TO TRANSFER
TO NEW CONTEXTS?

• Align read-aloud selections to other subject areas where vocabulary overlaps to strengthen a student's connection to vocabulary across contexts. For example: "You have learned about the meaning of a *steering wheel*. Remember, to *steer* means to guide, to drive, to direct. Our school elections are coming up. Do any of you want to be the president? We can use the word *steer* to mean 'to guide decisions we make about school,' or 'to steer a group to solving a problem.' Today in our reading, we will be learning about how one fourth grader *steered* her school to starting a recycling program."

• Preview content-area vocabulary and present with pictures or through texts with images prior to introduction in core classroom instruction. When vocabulary is repeatedly used throughout a unit, refer back to the key characteristics used during the initial introduction.

DOES THE STUDENT NEED MORE FREQUENT OPPORTUNITIES
FOR STUDENT RESPONSE, PRACTICE, AND REVIEW?

• Keep a chart of words introduced and of the lessons in which those words have been reviewed, to ensure that newly taught words are frequently reviewed initially and then occasionally reviewed throughout the school year.

• Assist the student with organizing knowledge of multiple vocabulary words by asking questions or completing activities that allow the student to identify similarities and differences between and among words. For example, as a review, provide the student with a vocabulary sort that involves sorting key characteristics for two different vocabulary words to demonstrate understanding.

- Refer to books such as *The Thing Explainer* to convey more complex ideas in simple words, images, and blueprints.

Dialogic Reading

Objectives

The student will be able to define words that are explicitly taught or implicitly trained during dialogic book reading. The student will be able to answer a variety of question types, including CROWD-HS questions about the story.

Materials

Engaging children's book (e.g., *When I Feel Angry* by Cornelia Spelman; this book is about a bunny that learns to manage her anger and problem solve).

Three to five vocabulary words or phrases to directly teach (e.g., *try my hardest, angry, spoiled, figure it out*).

One to two words to implicitly teach (*cool down*).

Sticky notes with dialogic reading questions moving from simple concrete questions to higher-level questions that involve inferencing

Progress monitoring rubric (see Figure 5.3 and 5.4).

Procedures

MODEL

1. Explicitly teach and model the definition of the vocabulary words before or during the read-aloud. For example: *"Angry* is a word that means mad. Sometimes when I am really angry I feel hot, just like the bunny."

2. Model how to learn implicitly from the story. For example: "In this picture, I can see her cooling down by taking a big breath and taking a break."

3. Read aloud a brief section of text and pause to talk about the story and ask questions that increase in difficulty—repeat a phrase from the text, and model answering a simple fill-in-the-blank completion question. For example: "In the story, the bunny said, 'When someone makes fun of me I feel _____.' I remember, or I can look back to help me remember, that she felt 'angry.'" Ask the student to show a thumbs-up when he or she hears one of the new words or phrases. Continue with another section of text and new vocabulary words and phrases.

SUPPORTED PRACTICE

Provide praise for correctly answering. For example: "Nice job giving me a thumbs-up. What word did you hear? Yes, *angry*." Ask a recall question: "Can you tell me two things in the story that made her angry?" If the student replies with a one-word answer, repeat the answer with an extension to the answer, or a longer, more complete sentence. Ask open-ended questions: "What does it mean to feel angry? We just read that she felt hot when she was angry." Ask a school question: "If a friend at school gets angry, what can you do to help him or her cool down?" Support the student in answering the questions and using the vocabulary. Follow steps to support the practice described in the acronym PEER.

Review

Incorporate the vocabulary words and phrases into conversation throughout the day. Use the dialogic reading strategies with other books.

Examples of Activity Intensifications

DOES THE STUDENT NEED MORE SPECIFIC
AND CORRECTIVE FEEDBACK?

- Praise the student for correctly using a word or phrase.
- Praise the student for figuring out the meaning of a word or phrase implicitly.
- If the student does not correctly define a word or phrase, or makes an error in answering a question, repeat the definition. If possible, reinforce the meaning or show how to find the answer to a question using pictures from the storybook.
- Use the PEER prompts to extend answers to questions that are too brief.

DOES THE STUDENT NEED MORE FREQUENT OPPORTUNITIES
FOR STUDENT RESPONSE, PRACTICE, AND REVIEW?

- Provide opportunities for the student to listen to the story again, and use the vocabulary word and phrases in a variety of contexts during the school day (e.g., make up sentences using the word, or have the student use the word in sentences).
- Place the book or an e-book in a center so the student can browse the pictures or listen independently.

DOES THE STUDENT NEED DIRECT INSTRUCTION
FOR TRANSFER?

- Use the CROWD-HS question types with videos.
- Use the CROWD-HS questions with other types of text, such as nonfiction texts.

Word Sorts and Building Categories

Objective

The student will be able to sort and categorize selected words.

Materials

List of categories.

List of previously taught words matching each category and picture cards.

Whiteboard and markers.

Timer.

Procedures

MODEL

1. Select categories familiar to the student that will be used for the model sort. Categories can include types (e.g., fruits vs. vegetables), singular versus plural, and so on. Provide a heading for each category to be used.
2. Model thinking through each of the category headings and what words will be included under that heading. For example: "Fruits are foods that have seeds."
3. Begin to go through each word while thinking aloud the process of sorting and why it would go under one category rather than another. For example: "Here is a picture of an apple. I know an apple is a round fruit that I eat and it has seeds in the middle."
4. Model several of the words and think aloud about how to sort them into the categories.
5. Also model thinking aloud of several types of words within each category.

SUPPORTED PRACTICE

1. Ask the student to indicate the heading meanings.
2. Allow the student to sort each picture into a category and explain why it belongs with that category. Provide feedback for student explanations.
3. When finished, have the student read through each column/category.
4. Encourage the student to brainstorm words that fit one category, like fruit. Write a category on the whiteboard. Set the timer and count and tally (or write out) the number of words the student can think of in 1 minute within a category.

Review

Continue to sort words into the categories, or brainstorm words within categories.

Examples of Activity Intensifications

DOES THE STUDENT NEED COGNITIVE PROCESSING STRATEGIES?

- Prior to sorting, discuss the features of words and label possible visual cues. For example: If sorting plurals versus singular words, have the student underline the ending of words to act as a visual guide when sorting between singular and plural headings.

- Have the student brainstorm a clue that aligns with the header that he or she can refer back to when sorting. For example: If sorting plurals, have the student ask, "Does this word end with an *s* or *es*?" as he or she sorts each word.

DOES THE STUDENT NEED MORE SPECIFIC AND CORRECTIVE FEEDBACK?

- Provide praise to the student for accurately categorizing a word and for increasing the number of words he or she can generate within a category.

- Carefully use the key characteristics introduced for the word or category to provide feedback. For example: "Hmm, you said a tomato is a vegetable. That is a little tricky. Does a tomato have seeds? So do you think it could be a fruit?"

- Review several of the words when the sort is complete, providing confirmation of the key characteristics the student used to correctly place the word in the category.

Synonym and Antonym Scaling

Objective

The student will be able to deepen understanding of word meanings, synonyms, and antonyms.

Materials

Whiteboard or easel poster.

Markers.

Procedures

MODEL

1. Present a blank scale (line) to the student on a whiteboard or easel.

2. Review the meanings of *synonym* and *antonym* to the student, referring back to previous instruction on this topic. Model your thinking while providing examples of each. For example: "I know a synonym means two words have the same meaning. A synonym for *end* could be *finish*. I know an antonym means the words are opposites. An antonym for *end* would be *begin*."

3. Put words at each end of the scale, modeling how they are antonyms. For example:

"I'm going to put *boiling* on one end and *freezing* on the other. I know they're opposites, so that makes them antonyms."

4. Model thinking what word would go in the middle of the scale based on meaning. For example: "I know *room temperature* is in between boiling and freezing, so I'm going to write it in the middle of the scale."

5. Begin working from the middle to one end, thinking aloud how you'd fill in half of the scale in one direction. For example: "If I'm starting at room temperature and know I need to end at freezing, the next word to describe the temperature may be *cool,* because it's getting a little colder than room temperature." Write *cool* along the scale. "Then, *chilly* would be how I would describe a temperature colder than cool." Continue writing the words on the scale as you are thinking aloud. Engage the student in describing the reason you have chosen a word. For example: "What does *chilly* mean? How does it relate to *cool*?" Ask the student to suggest words to show how he or she understands the scaling.

6. Repeat the process, going from the middle in the other direction. For example: "Now, if I'm starting at room temperature and know I need to end at boiling, the next word to describe the temperature may be *lukewarm,* because lukewarm is a little warmer than room temperature." Write *lukewarm* on the scale. "Next may be *warm*. What does *warm* mean?" Continue writing the words on the scale as you are thinking aloud until the scale is full.

7. Review the entire scale from one end to the other, while thinking aloud and cross-checking that the order of the words makes sense and appropriately shows the progression from one word to the other.

SUPPORTED PRACTICE

1. Give a new antonym/synonym pair with an additional review on what an antonym and a synonym are, as well as what each word means. After you discuss one word, write it on one end of the scale.

2. Have the student brainstorm what would be best used to describe the middle of the scale, and have him or her fill it in.

3. Ask the student to start at the middle and discuss what would be the best word to describe next working toward one direction, as modeled above. Have the student describe the chosen word or its relation to the other words.

4. Repeat in the other direction.

5. When the scale is complete, have the student read through the entire scale to double-check the progression from one word to another.

Review

When new words are introduced, prompt questioning referring to the scaling procedure, asking where certain words may fall when comparing to others.

Examples of Activity Intensifications

DOES THE STUDENT NEED MORE SYSTEMATIC INSTRUCTION?

- Provide the student with pictures or a word bank to fill in a scale. The student portion can also begin by having the student brainstorm a list of possible related words to fill the scale to create his or her own word bank.
- Cut out words that would be on the scale for the student to arrange in order.
- Include pictures or representations of words that show the progression or scaling to help the student consider words or their order of relation.

DOES THE STUDENT NEED MORE FREQUENT OPPORTUNITIES
FOR STUDENT RESPONSE, PRACTICE, AND REVIEW?

- If using a word bank, play the game *Hot or Cold?* where you select a word and the student must say whether it belongs in the right place, based on its proximity to the words on each end and middle, by saying whether it is "hot" or "cold."
- Have the student first do a word sort by category to create a word bank of related words. Then have the student use the words in the word bank in a scaling activity.

Word Parts

Objective

The student will be able to dissect words into their prefixes, roots, and suffixes to strengthen understanding of word meaning.

Materials

Three different colored markers.
Word list.

Procedures

MODEL

1. Think aloud about what is known about prefixes, root words, and suffixes. The language used in the think-aloud should mirror prior instruction on word parts.
   a. "I know a prefix is placed before the root word and can change the meaning."
   b. "I know a root word is the base word alone, without a prefix or a suffix."
   c. "I know a suffix is placed at the end of a root word and can change the meaning."
2. Present a word containing a prefix and a suffix (e.g., *disrespectful*).
3. Underline the root word in one color, followed by an explanation of what it means.

For example: While underlining, "The root word is *respect*. This means admiring someone or something. It can also mean taking care of something or being kind toward someone."

4. Underline the prefix in a different color, followed by an explanation of what it means. For example: While underlining, "The prefix is *dis*, which means the opposite of."

5. Underline the suffix in a different color, followed by an explanation of what it means. For example: While underlining, "The suffix is *ful*, which means full of."

6. Model thinking through the whole word, combining information presented about the prefix, root word, and suffix. For example: "With the prefix *dis* in front of *respect*, that would mean not having respect. Since *ful* is at the end of *disrespect*, this must mean to be full of disrespect or unkindness.

7. Repeat with several models.

SUPPORTED PRACTICE

1. Present a new word with a prefix and a suffix.

2. Have the student complete the steps outlined above, underlining the root word and discussing its meaning, followed by the prefix and the suffix.

3. Have the student put together the three word parts to come to a definition of the word.

4. Repeat with several words.

Review

As new words come up during lessons, or throughout the school day, that contain prefixes and suffixes, direct the student to identify the root word and determine the meaning based on the familiar prefixes and suffixes.

Examples of Activity Intensifications

DOES THE STUDENT NEED MORE EXPLICIT INSTRUCTION?

- Read a text from the Words Are Categorical series by Brian Cleary (2015): *Pre- and Re- and Mis- and Dis- : What Is a Prefix?* or his book *-Ful and -Less and -Er and -Ness: What Is a Suffix?* Both books directly explain prefixes or suffixes, focusing on common words and their use in a comic-like format that is child-friendly.

- Make a list of known prefixes and suffixes, with their meanings, for the student to use prior to dissecting words.

- Provide prefixes written on one set of cards, suffixes on another set, and roots on another, and have the student build words and determine meanings based on the word parts.

DOES THE STUDENT NEED MORE SYSTEMATIC INSTRUCTION?

- Review prefix + root word meaning in isolation before putting them together. Then review the meaning of the suffix followed by what it does to the meaning in the previously created word.

- Begin with focusing only on the prefixes of words, followed by focusing only on the suffixes of words. Then combine instruction for words with both, making connections to lessons on the prefixes and suffixes in isolation.

RESOURCES

myIGDIs Early Literacy Assessments

www.myigdis.com/preschool-assessments/early-literacy-assessments

This website provides an array of CBM screening and progress monitoring tools for young children, including a picture-naming task.

Baker, S., Lesaux, N., Jayanthi, M., Dimino, J., Proctor, C. P., Morris, J., et al. (2014). *Teaching academic content and literacy to English learners in elementary and middle school* (NCEE 2014-4012). Washington, DC: National Center for Educational Evaluation and Regional Assistance, Institute of Education Sciences, U.S. Department of Education. Available at *https://ies.ed.gov/ncee/wwc/PracticeGuide/19.*

This practice guide, provided by What Works Clearinghouse, includes recommendations for English learners in both reading and content instruction. Example activities are provided, as well as recommendations on aligning activities with the Common Core and state standards.

Instructional Research Group. (2015). Activities to promote word learning (second/third-grade combination class) [Video file]. In J. A. Dimino, M. Taylor, & J. Morris, *Professional learning communities facilitator's guide for What Works Clearinghouse practice guide: Teaching academic content and literacy to English learners in elementary and middle school* (REL 2015-105). Washington, DC: Regional Educational Laboratory Southwest, National Center for Education Evaluation and Regional Assistance, Institute of Education Sciences, U.S. Department of Education. Available at *https://ies.ed.gov/ncee/edlabs/regions/southwest/plc.asp.*

This video models a second-/third-grade classroom activity focusing on promoting word learning to students who range from proficient to advanced in their command of English. The end of the video description includes a link outlining the teacher's role in the activity.

Beck, I., McKeown, M. G., & Kucan, L. (2013). *Bringing words to life: Robust vocabulary instruction* (2nd ed.). New York: Guilford Press.

This book includes researched-based instruction on vocabulary, including content on a wide range of subjects and lesson topics. Sample lessons and vignettes are provided, as well as additional resources.

CHAPTER 6

Intensive Interventions to Support Language and Reading Comprehension

Crystal is a fourth-grade student who has struggled with reading throughout elementary school, and has received extensive intervention primarily focused on phonics and reading fluency. She has made great gains in these areas, and her most recent progress monitoring data indicate that her reading rate is on par with her average-performing peers. This achievement is to be celebrated! Her teachers have noticed, though, that while she reads grade-level text fairly quickly and accurately, she continues to have significant difficulty recalling what she has read, summarizing the main idea, or drawing inferences from text. Even when text is read aloud to her, she experiences these comprehension difficulties. In other words, she struggles to gain meaning from text, and is in need of more intensive support to improve her language and reading comprehension skills. Such support is critical given the increasing importance that Crystal will be able to understand and learn from many different kinds of texts as she advances through school.

Intensive instruction in language and reading comprehension supports students in gaining meaning from a wide variety of texts (including fiction and nonfiction), and for a wide variety of purposes (e.g., for enjoyment and for learning). Language and reading comprehension instruction helps students to activate relevant prior knowledge, use cognitive processes, and employ different comprehension strategies as needed, all of which can support understanding of text.

WHAT DOES THE RESEARCH SAY ABOUT LANGUAGE AND READING COMPREHENSION INSTRUCTION?

According to the simple view of reading (Gough & Tunmer, 1986), successful reading relies on word recognition skills (as discussed in Chapter 3), but also on comprehension.

Comprehension can be defined as "making sense of language" (Catts & Hogan, 2003). This basic definition holds true whether one is engaged in a conversation, watching a show, or listening to or reading a story. Even if a student has developed sufficient word recognition skills to decode text, as Crystal has, reading comprehension will not occur unless the student can also make sense of the language in that text. Thus, just as it is critical to develop word recognition skills as early as possible, it is also important to develop language comprehension skills early on, and in fact, instruction focused on language comprehension can (and should) happen at the same time that a student is learning to decode print (Kendeou, McMaster, & Christ, 2016; see also Chapter 3 of this book).

Making sense of language is a simple but useful definition of comprehension, and a similar definition can be applied to reading comprehension: *making sense of text*. From a cognitive perspective, making sense of text involves the reader's *construction of a coherent representation of text in memory* (Kendeou, van den Broek, Helder, & Karlsson, 2014; Kintsch, 1988; McNamara & Magliano, 2009; van den Broek, 1994). To construct a coherent mental representation of a text, the reader makes connections among the main events or ideas in the text, and between these events or ideas and prior knowledge (see Kendeou et al., 2014; Oakhill & Cain, 2012; Trabasso, Secco, & van den Broek, 1984). To make such connections, the reader often needs to make inferences, to help fill in gaps with information that might not be explicitly stated in the text. Sometimes such inferences seem to occur automatically—with little conscious thought—and at other times the reader must actively use a strategy to make a connection (Rapp & van den Broek, 2005; van den Broek, 1994; van den Broek, Rapp, & Kendeou, 2005). For example, think about the following text from the first two pages of the book *If You Give a Pig a Pancake* by Laura Numeroff:

> If you give a pig a pancake,
> she'll want some syrup to go with it.

Why would a pig want syrup to go with her pancake? Some readers (or listeners) will automatically draw the inference needed to connect these two ideas (that receiving a pancake might lead to wanting some syrup) and have a coherent representation of the text. These readers most likely have knowledge of, or experience with, eating pancakes with syrup to make them sweet and sticky. Other students might not be familiar with pancakes, or with this way of eating pancakes, and will need to strategically search for the connection between the two ideas. For example, students from some Asian cultures might eat pancakes as a savory dish with meat or vegetables, and might not automatically see a connection between receiving a pancake and wanting syrup to go with it. They might need to actively search the text, or their prior knowledge of other cultures, for more information to meaningfully connect the two ideas. Of course, this example is very simple—inferences are often much less obvious and require connecting more complex information. Yet students with intensive instructional needs related to comprehension might need support in making even this most basic type of inference, not to mention more complex inferences, in order to form coherent representations of texts that they encounter.

Students who require intensive instruction in language and reading comprehension may struggle for a variety of reasons—in fact, there is no one single predictor of comprehension difficulties, but rather a range of characteristics (alone or in combination) that might explain such difficulties (Cain & Oakhill, 2007). In addition to phonological awareness and word recognition skills, students might struggle with oral language skills, including syntactic skills, relating to their understanding of sentence structure and semantic skills, and also including vocabulary knowledge as well as efficiency in accessing and retrieving that knowledge (see Chapter 5). They might also struggle with metacognitive skills, like comprehension monitoring (e.g., recognizing when they do not comprehend, and recognizing that a strategy might help); with knowledge of different genres of text and text structures (such as differences between fiction and nonfiction); or with cognitive skills, such as working memory, which requires the simultaneous storage and processing of information.

Using the example above, a student with limited semantic skills might not understand or quickly access and retrieve the meaning of *syrup*. A student with limited knowledge of text genres may be unfamiliar with anthropomorphizing (attributing human characteristics to animals) in stories, and thus might be confused by the idea that a pig would want syrup for her pancake. A student with limited working memory might get further into the story and have difficulty comprehending how a rubber ducky (which the pig wants when she takes a bath) has anything to do with the pig's original desire for syrup, because this inference requires both holding in memory that the pig had some syrup *and* processing the causal sequence from eating syrup to getting sticky to needing a bath, and so on.

In addition to the skills described above, which comprise individual *reader characteristics*, other factors influence comprehension, including *text properties* and *instructional context* (McNamara & Kendeou, 2011; RAND Reading Study Group, 2002; van den Broek, Helder, & Van Leijenhorst, 2013). Text properties include the difficulty level, content (what the text is about), genre (e.g., fiction or nonfiction), sentence structure (e.g., sentence length and complexity), and text structure (the way the text is organized, such as using conventional story grammar often found in narrative text, or expository structures, such as compare–contrast or cause–effect). Instructional context includes the purpose for reading, the goals for instruction, the teacher's expectations, and the instructional environment, including whether there are distractions and whether the activities and materials are motivating for the student. In designing and intensifying comprehension instruction, it is important to consider how reader characteristics, text properties, and instructional context might interact with one another to promote successful comprehension (McMaster, Espin, & van den Broek, 2014).

Researchers have devoted significant efforts to designing and testing the effectiveness of a variety of interventions to support comprehension. A number of instructional approaches have been developed in the primary grades that do not rely on children's decoding skills, but rather focus on language comprehension (e.g., Al Otaiba, Connor, & Crowe, 2018; Connor, Alberto, Compton, & O'Connor, 2014; Santoro, Chard, Howard, & Baker, 2008), including a range of language interventions that focus on comprehension monitoring, story structure awareness, and morphological awareness, among other skills. Many of these interventions involve read-aloud approaches, which have been shown to have positive effects on the language comprehension skills of early readers (Swanson et al., 2011).

With respect to reading comprehension, research findings have been summarized in numerous literature syntheses (e.g., Berkeley, Scruggs, & Mastropieri, 2010; Gersten et al., 2001; Kim, Linan-Thompson, & Misquitta, 2012; National Reading Panel & National Institute of Child Health and Human Development, 2000; RAND Reading Study Group, 2002; Scammacca, Roberts, Vaughn, & Stuebing, 2015). Authors of these reviews agree on several points, including the importance of teaching vocabulary (discussed in Chapter 5); linking reading comprehension instruction to content learning; drawing upon an array of text genres; promoting students' use of comprehension strategies; and enhancing student engagement through choice, challenging texts, and peer-mediated learning (see RAND Reading Study Group, 2002).

With respect to both language and reading comprehension, researchers have noted the importance of inferencing and prior knowledge as central to comprehension in both reading and nonreading contexts, such as listening to stories or watching shows (Kendeou et al., 2016). Over the last 40 years, researchers have developed and examined an array of approaches that show promise to promote use of prior knowledge and inference making to support comprehension (see McMaster & Espin, 2017, for a review), including (1) preteaching activities designed to activate prior knowledge; (2) systematic questioning about key parts of text, with feedback; (3) teaching specific strategies, such as looking for clues and thinking aloud; (4) self-questioning; and (5) using graphic organizers.

WHAT ARE THE CRITICAL ELEMENTS OF LANGUAGE AND READING COMPREHENSION INSTRUCTION?

Given the research base described above, it is not surprising that the critical elements to include in language and reading comprehension instruction for elementary students include developing semantic and syntactic knowledge (not only in oral language, as covered in Chapter 5, but also during reading comprehension), knowledge of text structure, prior knowledge, inferencing skills, and cognitive and metacognitive strategies. Let's examine each critical element of comprehension, along with ways to provide intensive instruction in these elements.

Semantic Knowledge

Comprehension instruction should include intentional and explicit support for the development of semantic knowledge, which involves vocabulary knowledge as well as ways to efficiently retrieve and use relevant vocabulary knowledge to make sense of text. Vocabulary knowledge is supported by prior knowledge (it is easier to learn a new word if you already have some prior knowledge of the concept it represents), use of context, and knowledge of the English language. As covered in Chapter 5, vocabulary knowledge primarily develops by repeated exposure, and so students should be exposed to a wide variety of words through listening, speaking, reading, and writing (Graves & Silverman, 2011).

Explicit instruction can include teaching meanings of specific words and concepts needed to comprehend a text, as well as teaching strategies to learn new words independently. As we noted in Chapter 5, specific words and concepts can be taught using simple definitions, positive and negative examples, making connections between related words (including the use of graphic organizers), and extended instruction that promotes transfer by providing application or use of the word in varied contexts.

Syntactic Knowledge

As students advance through school, sentence structure and grammar (or syntactic knowledge, a critical language skill; see Chapter 5) become increasingly complex in grade-level text, and thus more difficult to comprehend. Students like Crystal who experience significant comprehension difficulties likely will need explicit instruction designed to support sentence-level comprehension (Carnine, Silbert, Kame'enui, & Tarver, 2004). Such instruction should show students that it is important to pay attention to the order in which different words and phrases appear within a sentence, because different word orders can change the meaning of that sentence. Consider the following two examples:

1. *The pig tricked the dog.* (active sentence structure)
   "Who was tricked?" ("The dog.")
   "Who did the tricking?" ("The pig.")

2. *The pig was tricked by the dog.* (passive sentence structure)
   "Who was tricked?" ("The pig.")
   "Who did the tricking?" ("The dog.")

Passive sentence structure is often more difficult to comprehend than active sentence structure. The questions for both sentences are the same, so the student must pay attention to the words *was* and *by,* which indicate who was tricked in the passive sentence. We recommend providing students with multiple opportunities for guided and independent practice with pairs of sentences like those in the example. Giving explicit instructions to listen to (or read) each word in the sentence very carefully can help students to distinguish the difference between an active and a passive voice. It may be necessary to emphasize key words: "The pig was tricked *by* the dog. Who was tricked?"

The example above illustrates active versus passive voice, but can also be applied to other elements of sentence structure, such as the use of participles (e.g., *The pig eating the pancake looked at the dog* vs. *The pig looked at the dog eating the pancake*), clauses (e.g., *The pig, who was eating the pancake, looked at the dog* vs. *The pig looked at the dog, who was eating the pancake*), or connectives (e.g., *Either the pig or the dog ate the pancake* vs. *Neither the pig nor the dog ate the pancake*). For each example, the answer to the question "Who was eating the pancake?" varies based on sentence structure. Again, providing pairs of sentences like these examples for practice can help students learn to attend to how words and phrases are used within the sentences to alter their meaning. It is also important to identify complex sentence structures within passages that students listen to or read, direct students to attend to the order of words and phrases, and ask questions in order to check for understanding. Doing so should support transfer from practicing syntactic skills in isolation to a more integrated context.

Knowledge of Text Structure

Students are expected to read a wide range of texts throughout school, and thus must attempt to comprehend texts following a variety of structures. Students with intensive needs related to comprehension likely will need explicit instruction focused on how to recognize and gain meaning from different types of text structures, such as compare–contrast and cause–effect structures. As with any explicit instruction, text structure instruction should move from simpler to more complex examples, with modeling, scaffolding, and guided practice with feedback that fades as the student becomes more independent. Instruction should include teaching of relevant vocabulary, including key words that signify a specific text structure, identifying where those words occur in a text, and using graphic organizers and questioning to help students identify key information that relates to the text structure (e.g., Williams & Pao, 2013).

For example, when teaching students to recognize and comprehend different types of expository texts, it is important to first define the specific type of text (e.g., compare–contrast texts discuss similarities and differences between two or more related concepts). Then teach students to look out for "clue words" that often appear in that type of text (e.g., in compare–contrast texts, the clue words *compare, contrast, same, different, but, and, however,* and *than* are often used). For students with intensive comprehension needs, it might be necessary to model finding clue words in text and provide extensive guided practice.

Students then might listen to or read short compare–contrast passages, labeling sentences based on whether they address similarities or differences, and identifying the clue words that helped them come up with these labels, again with modeling and guided practice with feedback. They then might use a graphic organizer (such as the semantic feature analysis described above, or a Venn diagram) to compare and contrast information from the text, and ask questions about the information, such as "What two things is this paragraph about? How are they the same? How are they different?" (Williams & Pao, 2013, p. 365). A similar process can be used for other text structures (see, e.g., Al Otaiba, Connor, et al., 2018, described in more detail in Chapter 7 of this book).

When one is teaching students to recognize and comprehend narrative texts, it is useful to teach *story grammar,* or the different elements that are typically included in stories. These elements include the characters, setting, problem and main events related to the problem, the solution, and the ending. There is also typically a temporal sequence— again, teaching relevant vocabulary (e.g., *first, next, last*) can help students recognize this sequence. A specific type of graphic organizer called a *story map* (see Figure 6.1)

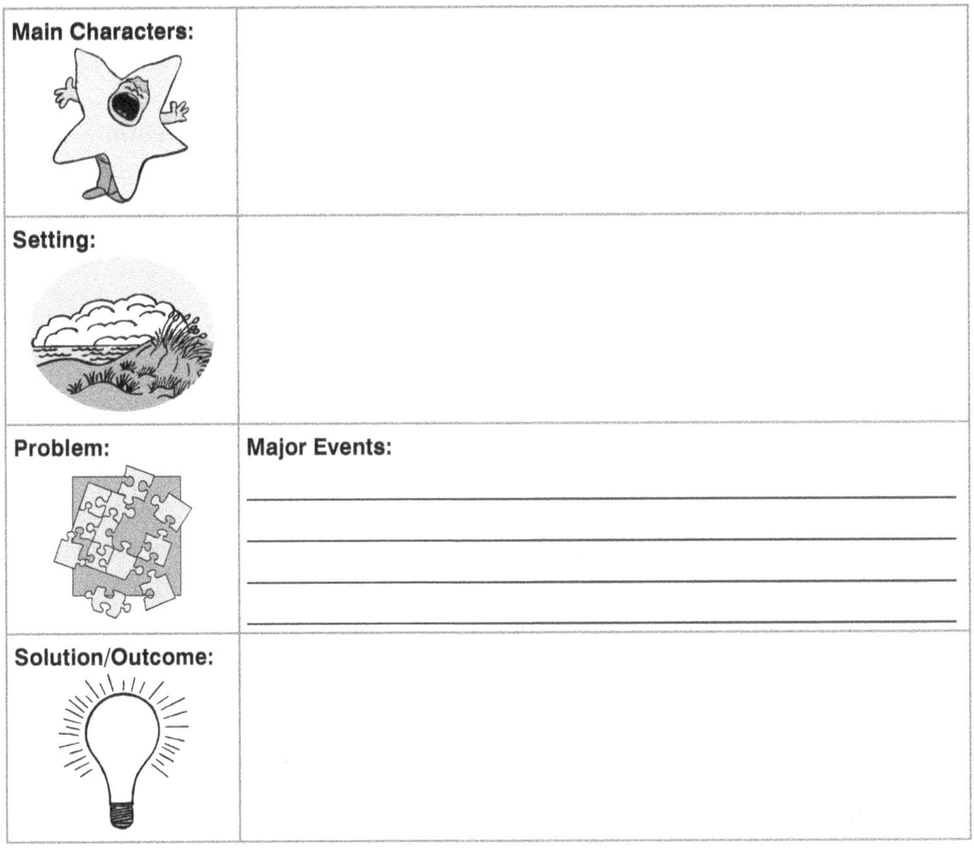

Main Characters:	
Setting:	
Problem:	Major Events:
Solution/Outcome:	

FIGURE 6.1. Example of a Story Map.

can help students identify, organize, and comprehend story elements. Again, instruction using these approaches can be intensified through extended modeling and guided practice with feedback.

Prior Knowledge

Many students with intensive comprehension needs do not have sufficient prior knowledge to form coherent mental representations of texts (Compton, Miller, Elleman, & Steacy, 2014), *or* they might have relevant knowledge, but may not know how to access it when it is needed. Although it is not always possible to provide students with the extensive background knowledge needed to form a completely coherent representation of every text that they listen to or read, it is worth spending time to activate relevant prior knowledge. In addition, when needed, it is helpful to teach explicitly at least the most relevant concepts that are necessary for students to comprehend specific texts. Activating or teaching relevant knowledge might include previewing the text by looking at the title, subheadings, pictures, or other graphics; asking questions about students' knowledge and experiences related to the text, and prompting students to ask questions or make predictions about the text using their prior knowledge; and explicitly teaching vocabulary and concepts relevant to the text. Background knowledge can also be built into the reading process itself, such as by reading multiple texts related to a specific topic and explicitly making connections across texts. Questioning techniques are useful for this process (e.g., "The pig got all sticky and needed a bath! What did we learn in the book we read about syrup that can help us understand why/how the pig got all sticky?").

Inferencing

As we discussed at the beginning of this chapter, inferencing is central to successful comprehension. Researchers have shown that students with intensive comprehension needs are often able to make inferences, and that these students often fail to do so while listening to or reading text (McMaster, Espin, & van den Broek, 2014). Instruction designed to prompt inference making can improve the likelihood that students will make connections among ideas in the text, or between the text and prior knowledge, that are needed to form a coherent representation of the text. Such instruction should include explicit teaching of what an inference is (connecting ideas in the text with one another, or with prior knowledge, to fill in gaps in the text), teaching relevant background knowledge and vocabulary (as described above), and modeling making connections through think-alouds (e.g., "Hmm, let me think. I know that syrup is sticky, and I know that pigs can be messy eaters. So, I think the pig got all sticky because she probably got syrup all over herself while eating the pancake!"). Inference making can also be prompted through questioning, scaffolding, and feedback. Figure 6.2 provides examples of ways to provide scaffolding and feedback depending on different ways that students might respond to comprehension questions.

Strategy Use

Students who experience significant difficulties with comprehension may benefit from learning strategies—or specific plans or steps that they can apply to a wide range of texts to help them understand what they read (Gersten et al., 2001). Research-based approaches to teaching strategies (e.g., Collaborative Strategic Reading [CSR]—Klingner & Vaughn, 1999; Peer-Assisted Learning Strategies [PALS]—Fuchs & Fuchs, 2005; Reciprocal Teaching—Palincsar & Brown, 1984) include common elements, such as questioning, retelling, summarizing, predicting, and monitoring comprehension of text. Strategy instruction, like other intensive instructional approaches, is likely to be most effective when done explicitly, including providing a purpose for using the strategy and when it might be used, modeling with examples and non-examples, and guided practice with scaffolding and feedback.

One example of strategy instruction is PALS (Fuchs & Fuchs, 2005). PALS has been validated for use as a classwide peer tutoring program, and is intended to supplement core instruction in the general education classroom. For some students, however, it may

NEEDS SCAFFOLDING
Provide up to two additional opportunities to make the right connection.
Allow the student who made the connection to attempt to respond, but involve
others in the group if needed.

PARTIALLY CORRECT:

Your connection makes sense/is on the right track *(restate correct part of answer if needed)*, but you're missing an important part of the connection.

What (ELSE) does it say in the text about why [insert question]?

OR ask follow-up Why questions. If needed, you may also ask Who, What, When, Where, How . . . questions.

After student responds: So, why [insert question]?

OVERLY LENGTHY:

You just said a lot.

Now, try to make your connection shorter, by saying the most important reason why [insert question].

IN TEXT BUT NOT CORRECT:

You connected to the text, but that doesn't make sense for why [insert question].

What ELSE does it say in the text about why [insert question]?

NOT IN TEXT, NOT CORRECT:

That makes sense/might be true, but didn't happen in the text.

Remember to connect to an important part of the TEXT.

Use the text to explain why [insert question]?

Award 1 point for the team.

CORRECT RESPONSE
If correct after first try
OR if correct after one to two scaffolding attempts

CORRECT:

Your connection makes sense!

OR

Your connection makes sense! Now, use the word BECAUSE to complete your connection.

Provide specific feedback (e.g., You remembered to use the word BECAUSE; You used your own words).

Can you show us the important part of the text that helped you make your connection? *(HELP as needed.)*

Award 1 point for the team.

SEEMS CORRECT, BUT NOT IN ANSWER KEY:

I think that makes sense. Can you show us the important part of the text that helped you make your connection?

If student can support the connection with text and the connection makes sense, say:

That connection DOES make sense. There (is/may be) another important reason why [insert sentence]. Did anyone think of another connection?

If student cannot support the connection with text, and/or no additional connections are made, move to scaffolding.

FIGURE 6.2. Sample of scaffolding and feedback. From McMaster, Espin, and van den Broek (2014).

also be a way to intensify instruction, as it allows for one-to-one interaction with a more proficient peer reader. PALS includes *partner reading* to build fluency (the stronger reader reads aloud for 5 minutes, then the weaker reader reads the same text aloud for 5 minutes); *retell* to support recall of details in sequence (the reader retells everything he or she has read so far to his or her partner); *paragraph shrinking* (each partner reads paragraphs and summarizes [1] the most important who or what, [2] the most important thing about the who or what, and [3] the main idea of the paragraph in 10 words or less); and *prediction relay* (partners take turns making predictions, reading segments of text, and then confirming whether their prediction came true). Critical to PALS success are (1) appropriate text selection (the struggling reader should be able to read about 90% of the text without errors), and (2) a strong partner who can support the struggling reader. It is also important that the teacher monitors the process to provide corrective feedback and support as needed.

Whereas strategy instruction has been beneficial for many students, including those who struggle with reading, they have typically been conducted in whole-class and peer-mediated contexts, and not all students with significant comprehension difficulties have responded well to strategy instruction under these conditions (cf. O'Connor & Jenkins, 2013). In such cases, strategy instruction may need to be intensified by increasing the amount of modeling and guided practice with scaffolding and corrective feedback. Further, even when students do respond well to strategy instruction, it can be extremely difficult to transfer strategy use to new contexts (Pressley, Graham, & Harris, 2006). Therefore, we emphasize the importance of explicitly teaching for transfer, by modeling and practicing the strategy across the multiple contexts in which it might be used (e.g., with different types of texts, in different settings, for different purposes, with different people) to maximize the benefits of strategy instruction.

Metacognitive Skills

A particular challenge associated with strategy use is that it requires cognitive resources (such as attention and memory) both to learn the strategy and to remember how and when to use it, reducing the cognitive resources available to actually read and comprehend text. Students who struggle with comprehension might benefit from learning to monitor their own comprehension in order to decide whether a strategy is actually needed. They can be taught, through explicit modeling with guided practice and feedback, to stop periodically (e.g., after each paragraph or other segment of text) and check their own comprehension using self-questioning (e.g., "Do I understand what I just read?"). If the answer is "No," they can choose a strategy that might help repair their comprehension.

One approach that has had considerable research as a way to support students' comprehension monitoring is self-regulated strategy development (SRSD; see Baker, Chard, Ketterlin-Geller, Apichatabutra, & Doabler, 2009, for a review; Mason, 2004). SRSD incorporates explicit instruction, modeling, mnemonics, and scaffolding for students until they reach mastery and can use a strategy with few or no supports (Baker et al., 2009). There are six basic stages of SRSD instruction: (1) *develop background knowledge,* which involves preteaching the skills needed for using the strategy (e.g., how to summarize the main idea); (2) *discuss it,* which involves discussing the benefits of the strategy and how and when to use it; (3) *model it,* which involves modeling the strategy using a think-aloud approach; (4) *memorize it,* in which students use mnemonics and self-instructions to recall the strategy; (5) *support it,* which involves scaffolding students' use of the strategy through collaborative writing and guided practice; and (6) *independent performance,* in which students apply the strategy independently to various reading tasks, and evaluate their own performance with teacher support. In addition, students learn self-regulation procedures, including goal setting, self-monitoring, and self-reinforcement to reward themselves when they are successful.

Cognitive Processes

Although evidence indicates that difficulties with comprehension are related to limits in areas of cognitive processing, such as working memory and executive functioning

(Cain & Oakhill, 2007; Swanson & Zheng, 2013), it is unclear whether specific interventions can *improve* these processes. Some researchers have shown that direct training (e.g., training focused on improving working memory) can improve cognitive processing, but there is limited evidence that such training also leads to improved comprehension outcomes (e.g., Peng & Fuchs, 2016; Swanson & Zheng, 2013). It is important, however, to keep in mind that individual differences in cognitive processing may influence some students' reading comprehension, and to consider addressing these individual differences when intensifying intervention by reducing the cognitive load needed to complete comprehension tasks.

If you notice that a student has difficulty following multistep instructions or procedures, or recalling a strategy and applying it to a new task, consider the following ways to reduce the cognitive load: (1) limit the amount of information presented at one time (e.g., present instructions in a step-by-step manner); (2) provide visual aids (e.g., list the steps of a comprehension strategy on a cue card, or templates for graphic organizers); (3) remove other cognitively taxing demands (e.g., read a text aloud if the primary goal is comprehension, rather than imposing decoding demands); and (4) teach memory strategies, such as mnemonics, rehearsal, clustering, and elaboration (see Table 6.1).

HOW DO I MONITOR PROGRESS IN LANGUAGE AND READING COMPREHENSION?

Monitoring student progress in comprehension can assist teachers in determining students' overall growth, as well as specific strengths and needs, something that in turn can help in planning for appropriate areas to focus on in instruction. In this section, we identify formal and informal progress monitoring techniques that intervention teachers can use to objectively monitor students' learning and make instructional decisions.

TABLE 6.1. Examples of Memory Strategies

Strategy	Description	Example
Mnemonics	An acronym or phrase to help recall information.	Dear King Philip Came Over For Good Soup (used to remember the taxonomic classification system: Domain, Kingdom, Phylum, Class, Order, Family, Genus, Species).
Rehearsal	Repetition (for low-level recall); creating graphic aids or explaining in own words (for high-level recall).	Student rehearses definitions of key vocabulary words, or practices explaining them in his or her own words.
Clustering	Organizing information into related groups.	Student organizes bat species according to similar features.
Elaboration	Assigning meaningful information to information to be recalled.	Student pictures a small bat sending out sound waves that bounce off bugs to be eaten.

Formal Measures

The most common and well-researched approach to monitoring overall reading prog-ress is CBM (Deno, 1985), using either an oral reading or maze selection approach. CBM oral reading is described in detail in Chapter 4. For maze, students silently read a pas-sage in which every seventh word is deleted and replaced with three response choices, only one of which is syntactically and semantically correct in the context of the passage. The student is to select the correct word. Students usually read for 1–3 minutes, and the number of correct selections is scored (Wayman, Wallace, Wiley, Tichá, & Espin, 2007). For either oral reading or maze, the passages should be at the level that represents the individualized goal for the student, and may or may not be grade-level text, depending on the individual student's needs.

Data from CBM oral reading can be used as an indicator of whether the student is on track to meet a long-term reading goal, or whether further diagnosis is needed (see "Other Approaches" below). Researchers have found that CBM in reading pro-vides a valid indicator of general reading proficiency as measured by standardized tests, including state achievement tests, with correlations reported to range from $r =$ .60 to .75 (Nese, Park, Alonzo, & Tindal, 2011) to over .80 (Wayman et al., 2007). CBM in reading has also been shown to relate specifically to reading comprehension, with correlations of $r = .63$ for oral reading and $r = .62$ for maze for primary-grade students (Shin & McMaster, 2019).

Other Approaches

Though CBM provides an overall indicator of students' reading proficiency, and is use-ful for monitoring RTI over relatively short periods of time, it does not necessarily pro-vide information about students' specific strengths and weaknesses, nor does it indicate what to teach or what instructional changes to make. Thus, when CBM data indicate that an instructional change is needed, additional informal assessments may be neces-sary to provide further insight regarding a student's specific needs for intensive inter-vention.

Miscue analysis involves systematically identifying error patterns in a student's reading. In miscue analysis, the examiner marks the student's oral reading errors and notes exactly what the student said, and then summarizes the errors to deter-mine whether they are code based (indicating needs specific to phonics) or meaning based (indicating needs specific to comprehension). We discussed ways to examine the code-based, graphophonetic errors in Chapter 3. Figure 6.3 shows an example of a student's meaning-based miscues during reading, and shows how these miscues can be categorized to determine the student's strengths and needs for intensive interven-tion. Although this information can be useful, miscue analysis is largely dependent on the specific passage that the student read. Thus, multiple samples from a variety of passages may give more reliable information about specific needs (but can be time-consuming to gather).

Muddy Buddy

            week

I took my dog Buddy out for a walk. He was so happy to be outside. When he got

    farm   sleep went   barn

to the park, Buddy was ready to play. I ^threw the ball over and over and Buddy

                        caught it

ran to get it. Then the ball went so far I couldn't see it but Buddy ran after it

                      a   bark   grass

anyway. All of a sudden, Buddy came out with the ball but was covered in mud!

                                           nap

"Buddy, you are so muddy!" I said. We ran home so Buddy could take a bath. It

                                   hug

took so long to get the mud off. Once Buddy was dry I gave him a treat for being a

good boy, even if he was a muddy buddy!

Word in text (+ for insertion)	Word student read (– for omission)	Graphophonetic Errors								Comprehension Errors		
		Irregular word	Beginning sound	Ending sound	Long/short vowel	Silent-e rule	Consonant blend	Letter combinations	Other:	Semantic	Syntactic	Other:
Walk	week							X		X		
Park	Farm										X	
Play	Sleep										X	
+	Went									X		
Ball	Barn										X	
Bath	Nap										X	
Mud	Grass										X	
treat	Hug										X	

FIGURE 6.3. Student passage and error analysis.

     Another approach to informally assessing language or reading comprehension is through retells, which can give insight into both a student's memory for text and the extent to which the student formed a coherent representation of that text. To conduct a retell, after the student listens to or reads a passage aloud or silently, ask the student to retell the text (orally or in writing) as if telling it to a friend who had never heard or read it before. Note each unique idea that the student recalls, and match it to the main events in the text. The retell can be scored as a percentage of details, main ideas, or story elements recalled. The sequence of the retell can also be noted to determine the extent to which the student recalled ideas from the text in the order in which they occurred. As with miscue analysis, however, recalls can be time-consuming and passage dependent. Additionally, if the student writes the retell (as opposed to delivering it orally), the student's writing skills might interact with his or her recall of the text, making a written retell at least partially a writing assessment.

Finally, another useful way to informally gauge student comprehension is through systematic and well-planned questioning. Questions can be asked *before* reading, to gain insight into relevant prior knowledge and provide information about how much preteaching of relevant words and concepts might be needed. Questions can also be asked *during* reading, to gain insight into whether the student is forming a coherent representation during the reading process (e.g., by identifying critical elements of the text, summarizing the main idea, or generating inferences). And, of course, questions can be asked *after* reading, to determine the student's overall comprehension of the text. Questions can be literal (often posed as *who, what, where, when* questions), inferential (often posed as *why* or *how* questions), or thematic (e.g., questions about the overall point or lesson learned from the text). Student responses to questions might be text dependent, and might not necessarily provide generalizable information about comprehension skills in general, but patterns in their responses (e.g., most literal questions answered correctly, but many inferential or thematic questions missed) can reveal specific needs that can be addressed as part of instruction.

INSTRUCTIONAL ACTIVITIES FOR LANGUAGE AND READING COMPREHENSION

Note: In this section, we provide examples of intensive comprehension instructional activities for children in the early to mid/late elementary grades. Books of two different genres (fiction and nonfiction) are used to illustrate these activities, but these are just examples—you can substitute in any text and mix and match activities. Note that both fiction and nonfiction can and should be used across all elementary-grade levels. Also note that it is not necessary to do all activities within the same lesson—rather, select activities that meet individual students' most significant needs. For each grade level, activities for before, during, and after reading are provided.

Early Elementary: Activating Prior Knowledge before Reading

Objective

The student will be able to identify prior knowledge that is relevant to today's story.

Materials

Book to be read aloud to or with the student.

Procedures

MODEL

1. Introduce the story. For example: "Today, we're going to read a book called *If You Give a Pig a Pancake* by Laura Numeroff."
2. Identify the genre. For example: "This book is *fiction*, which means it's a story made up by the author."
3. Model using a think-aloud while previewing the title and book cover. For example: "First, I'm going to think about what this book might be about. The title and the picture on the front of the book are both about a pig. So I think this story has something to do with this pig."

SUPPORTED PRACTICE

1. Ask the student to make predictions on what the story might be about. For example: "What else do you think this story might be about? What makes you think that?"
2. Provide feedback based on the student's responses. For example: "That was a great idea to look at the pictures to make your predictions."

Review

Remind the student that previewing a book by looking at the title and pictures, and making predictions on what the book will be about, will help with understanding the text.

Examples of Activity Intensifications

DOES THE STUDENT NEED MORE FREQUENT OPPORTUNITIES
FOR STUDENT RESPONSE, PRACTICE, AND REVIEW?

- When activating background knowledge, use questioning with additional probing as needed. For example: "What else is in the picture? What else is in the title? What do you know about pigs? What do you know about pancakes? Do pigs usually eat pancakes? What do you usually have with pancakes? What do you predict might happen to the pig?"
- Summarize the relevant information before moving on to the next activity.

Early Elementary: Provide Explicit Vocabulary Instruction before Reading

Note: Refer to Chapter 5 for additional details on providing explicit vocabulary instruction.

Objective

The student will pronounce, define, and use key vocabulary.

Materials

Three words that are key to understanding the story (e.g., *syrup, sticky, homesick*).

Pictures and/or objects that provide examples and non-examples of each word (e.g., for *syrup,* you might have pictures of different kinds of syrup, as well as non-examples, such as sugar and cooking oil).

Procedures

MODEL

1. Provide definitions of each word. For example: "Before we read, I'll teach you some words that will help you to understand the story. The first word is *syrup*. Say 'syrup' with me. Syrup is a thick liquid that you can put on pancakes or other foods to make them taste sweet and yummy."

2. Show the picture illustrating the word in the book, or in a separate picture or object.

SUPPORTED PRACTICE

1. Prompt the student to repeat the definition. For example: "What is syrup?"

2. Show another picture (or an actual item, such as a syrup bottle) and have the student confirm whether it represents the word. For example: "Is this syrup?" Provide corrective feedback as needed and elaborate on the picture. For example: "This picture shows a thick liquid that you can put on food to make it sweet and yummy."

3. Repeat with one or two more positive examples, then show a negative example (e.g., sugar) and have the student confirm whether it represents the word. For example: "Is this syrup?" Provide corrective feedback as needed. For example: "This is sugar! You can put sugar on food to make it sweet, but it is not a thick liquid," or "This is cooking oil! Cooking oil is a thick liquid, but people don't use it to make food taste sweet."

4. Repeat Steps 1–3 with the remaining words.

Review

Have the student record the key words in personal dictionaries, to be reviewed with guidance or independently on another day.

Examples of Activity Intensifications

DOES THE STUDENT NEED MORE EXPLICIT INSTRUCTION?

When teaching vocabulary meanings, provide additional positive and negative examples. Use "minimally different pairs," such that examples differ only on the key distinguishing feature. For example: "I'm sad because I lost my cat. Am I homesick?" [No.] "I'm sad because I'm at my grandma's house and I miss my cat, who's at my house. Am I homesick?" [Yes.]

Early Elementary: Deep Processing of Vocabulary during Reading

Objective

The student will be able to use knowledge of key vocabulary to comprehend the text.

Materials

Same book as for the activities above.

Procedures

MODEL

1. Before beginning to read, prompt the student to be on alert for the words taught above while listening to or reading the story, and to raise his or her hand whenever he or she hears or reads the words.

2. Provide a model of this behavior. For example: "I'll show you how. Let's say we were listening for the word *pancake*." Read, "If you give a pig a pancake . . . ," and raise your hand when you read *pancake*. "See, I raised my hand when I heard the word *pancake*."

SUPPORTED PRACTICE

1. Reinforce the student for raising his or her hand when he or she hears a vocabulary word. For example: "Oh, good. You raised your hand! What word did you hear? Yes, *syrup*."

2. Prompt the student to provide the definition. For example: "Do you remember what syrup is?"

3. Support the student in recalling the definition, and then reread the sentence with the definition: " 'If you give a pig a pancake, she'll want a thick liquid to make it sweet and yummy!' What will she want on her pancake?"

4. Support the student in pronouncing the word *syrup*. Repeat this process when you come to the other key words in the story.

Review

After reading, review the key vocabulary words and their meanings.

Examples of Activity Intensifications

DOES THE STUDENT NEED MORE EXPLICIT INSTRUCTION?

Instead of asking the student to produce the definition, remind him or her of the definition and examples/non-examples with modeling, as in the before-reading activity. Have the student generate examples and non-examples, as well.

DOES THE STUDENT NEED MORE FREQUENT OPPORTUNITIES
FOR STUDENT RESPONSE, PRACTICE, AND REVIEW?

Provide opportunities for the student to hear the word used in a variety of contexts (e.g., make up sentences using the word, have the student use the word in a sentence, have peers use the word in their own sentences).

DOES THE STUDENT NEED MORE SPECIFIC AND CORRECTIVE FEEDBACK?

If the student has trouble producing the correct word or definition, immediately say, "My turn," provide the word or definition, and have the student repeat it after you.

Early Elementary: Inferential Questioning with Scaffolding and Feedback during Reading

Objective

The student will be able to use information from the text and background knowledge to answer inferential questions about the text.

Materials

Same book as for the activities above.

Identify four to five points in the text where an inference is needed to understand the story.

Procedures

MODEL

1. Explain what an inference is. For example: "Today, while we read, I'm going to stop and ask questions about the story. The questions will help us make *inferences* that will help you understand what you read. To make an inference, we'll connect clues from the story with what we already know to help us understand what's happening in the story."

2. Model using a think-aloud. When you come to a part of the text where an inference is needed, ask a *why* question, and model using "clues" to answer the question. For

example: "Why would the pig want some syrup? To answer this question, I can find a clue in the text: We know that the pig has a pancake, right? And I can connect that clue to what I already know about syrup: It makes food taste sweet and yummy. So I think the pig would want some syrup because it would make her pancake taste sweet and yummy!"

SUPPORTED PRACTICE

1. When you come to the next part of the text where an inference is needed, ask another *why* question. For example, "Why would the pig need to find her rubber ducky?"

2. Prompt the student to identify clues from the text and/or background knowledge to answer the question.

3. If needed, provide scaffolding by giving one clue at a time. For example: "Clue 1 is, we know she's taking a bath, and Clue 2 is, we know that she wants a toy. Can you use those two clues to figure out why the pig needs to find her rubber ducky?"

Review

Remind the student that making inferences—or connecting clues from the text with background knowledge—can help with understanding the text. Encourage the student to use clues to make inferences during other reading activities throughout the day.

Examples of Activity Intensifications

DOES THE STUDENT NEED MORE SPECIFIC AND CORRECTIVE FEEDBACK?

If the student does not answer the question correctly even with scaffolding, use the examples in Figure 6.3 to provide feedback.

DOES THE STUDENT NEED DIRECT INSTRUCTION
FOR TRANSFER TO NEW CONTEXTS?

Use the same questioning approach across multiple contexts, including during discussions or while watching shows, listening to stories, and reading. Explain that asking *why* questions can help make inferences that can help the student understand what he or she is seeing, hearing, or reading.

Early Elementary: Deep Processing of Vocabulary after Reading

Objective

The student will be able to use knowledge of key vocabulary words to answer questions and formulate sentences.

Materials

Same book as for the activities above.

Procedures

MODEL

1. Reintroduce a target word. For example: "Remember how the pig was *homesick* and wanted to visit the farm where she was born?"

2. Provide examples. For example: "My sister felt sad and missed our family when we went away to summer camp. Would you say she was *homesick*? Why?"; "I was having so much fun at camp that I barely thought about anything else. Would you say that I was *homesick*? Why not?"

SUPPORTED PRACTICE

1. Ask questions to support the student's understanding and use of the word. For example: "Every night, the boy wished he could go home to his parents and dog. What word does this make you think of? Why?"

2. Support the student in formulating sentences. For example: "Everybody gets a turn making up a sentence with the word *homesick* in it. Start your sentence by saying, 'I might feel *homesick* if I _____.'"

Review

Review the target word one more time, and praise the student for using the word to answer questions and formulate sentences.

Examples of Activity Intensifications

DOES THE STUDENT NEED MORE EXPLICIT INSTRUCTION?

• Provide additional examples of sentences and questions before asking the student to generate his or her own.

• Provide a think-aloud in response to the student's answers to questions. For example: "If I was having so much fun at camp that I barely thought about anything else, I probably wouldn't feel *homesick* because I wouldn't be thinking very much about my home, or my parents and friends. I'd just be thinking about camp!"

DOES THE STUDENT NEED MORE SYSTEMATIC INSTRUCTION?

Break the activity steps into smaller parts:

- First, provide examples of sentences.
- Then, provide sentences with blanks and a word bank to complete them, and then sentence stems (as above).
- Last, have the student generate new sentences.

Mid- to Late Elementary: Introduce Text Structure before Reading

Objective

The student will be able to identify features of and key vocabulary common to compare–contrast texts.

Materials

A text describing similarities and differences related to a given subject or topic (e.g., bats).

Procedures

MODEL

1. Introduce the text. For example: "Today, we are going to read a book about bats. Did you know there are over 1,200 species of bats? There are two major kinds, or suborders, of bats: microbats and megabats. They mainly differ in size: Microbats can be smaller than the palm of my hand, and megabats can be huge! But there are lots of ways that microbats and megabats are *similar to* and *different from* each other."

2. Introduce the specific text structure. For example: "The text that we'll read today *compares* and *contrasts* different kinds of bats. To *compare* things means to identify ways that they are similar. What does it mean to compare things? To *contrast* things means to identify ways that they are different. What does it mean to contrast things? Today, we'll read about how different kinds of bats are the same, and also how they are different."

3. Introduce relevant vocabulary. For example: "When we read compare–contrast texts, it's helpful to look out for clue words that tell us about ways that things are the *same* or *different*. Here are some words that mean that things are the *same*, or nearly the same."

SUPPORTED PRACTICE

1. Discuss words that appear in the text, such as *similar, alike, identical,* and *equal.* Give examples of how they might be used in a sentence, and support the student in using the word. For example: "So, if I say that my friend and I dressed *alike,* what does that mean? Right—it means we dressed the *same.* Now, here are some words and phrases that indicate that things are *not the same.*"

2. Repeat with additional words that appear in the text, such as *differ, different, from/ than, dissimilar, unalike, in contrast.* Again, give examples of sentences, and support the student in using the word. For example: "So, if I say that today's lunch menu is *different from* yesterday's menu, what does that mean? Right—it means lunch is *not the same* today as it was yesterday."

Review

Remind the student that, during reading, it is helpful to look for clue words in the text that signal what type of text it is, such as a *compare and contrast* text.

Examples of Activity Intensifications

DOES THE STUDENT NEED MORE FREQUENT OPPORTUNITIES FOR STUDENT RESPONSE, PRACTICE, AND REVIEW?

• Provide support to ensure that the student understands *compare* and *contrast.* Discuss examples, comparing and contrasting characteristics of students or objects in the classroom.

• Provide additional opportunities to discuss terms related to *compare* and *contrast,* using examples of pictures or objects to identify similarities and differences.

DOES THE STUDENT NEED DIRECT INSTRUCTION FOR TRANSFER TO NEW CONTEXTS?

• Explain the different contexts in which the student might need to compare and contrast things, and the words to look out or listen for.

• Have the student generate examples of other contexts in which comparing and contrasting is useful.

• Model, and have the student practice, comparing and contrasting across multiple texts and other contexts.

Mid- to Late Elementary: Apply Text Structure Knowledge during Reading

Objective

The student will be able to label sentences as *comparing* or *contrasting.*

Materials

A text comparing and contrasting features related to a given subject (e.g., bats).

Procedures

MODEL

Model use of text structure knowledge—show the student how to identify text that is comparing and contrasting. For example: Read the sentences in the text with the student, and label them as *comparing* or *contrasting*: "Each species of bats belongs to one of two suborders: megabats or microbats. Megabats are *much bigger than* microbats. I know this sentence is *contrasting* megabats and microbats, because it has the clue words *much bigger than*."

SUPPORTED PRACTICE

1. Provide practice opportunities to the student by having him or her read additional sentences and labeling them as comparing or contrasting. For example: "One of the main *differences* among bat species is their diet. Many microbats mainly eat insects, while many megabats mainly eat fruit." [contrasting] "However, some megabats eat insects, just *like* microbats do!" [comparing] "Another way that megabats and microbats are *similar* is that they all have good eyesight." [comparing]

2. Continue to practice labeling sentences until the student can reliably identify them as comparing or contrasting.

Review

In later lessons with compare–contrast text structures, remind the student about the purpose of compare–contrast texts and test his or her knowledge of relevant clue words. If needed, practice labeling additional sentences.

Examples of Activity Intensifications

DOES THE STUDENT NEED MORE FREQUENT OPPORTUNITIES FOR STUDENT RESPONSE, PRACTICE, AND REVIEW?

- If the student has difficulty identifying comparing and contrasting words, help him or her identify clue words in the sentence, and ask whether the clue words likely mean *the same* or *different*. Reinforce that words that mean *the same* are likely comparing, whereas words that mean *different* are likely contrasting.

- Provide worksheets with multiple examples of compare–contrast statements, using a variety of clue words, for the student to practice labeling.

Mid- to Late Elementary: Use Strategies to Support Comprehension during Reading

Objective

The student will be able to use the paragraph-shrinking strategy to identify the main idea in text (Fuchs et al., 1997).

Materials

Any text at the student's instructional level (i.e., the student can read about 90% of the words without errors).

A cue card with the three paragraph-shrinking steps:

1. Name the most important *who* or *what*.
2. Tell the most important thing about the *who* or *what*.
3. Say the main idea in 10 words or less.

Procedures

MODEL

1. Model paragraph-shrinking use with a think-aloud. For example: "I'm going to read this paragraph and then show you a strategy that can help you identify the *main idea* of the paragraph." If needed, also teach what a strategy is, and/or what a main idea is.

2. Read the paragraph:

   > "Bats are *not* blind; in fact, they can see almost as well as humans. But to fly around and hunt for insects in the dark, they use a remarkable high frequency system called echo-location. Echolocation works in a similar way to sonar. Bats make calls as they fly and listen to the returning echoes to build up a sonic map of their surroundings. The bat can tell how far away something is by how long it takes the sounds to return to them." (*www. bats.org.uk/pages/echolocation.html*)

3. Continue to model using a think-aloud. For example: "Now, to identify the main idea, I'm going to do three steps." Point to each step on the cue card as you model them. "First, I'll name who or what the paragraph is mostly about. I think this paragraph is mostly about bats. Next, I'll name the most important thing about the *who* or *what*. I think this paragraph is telling us that bats use a special system called echolocation to help them find their food in the dark. Now that I've said the main *who* or *what*, and the most important thing about the *who* or *what*, I'll put those parts together to say the main idea in 10 words or less: Bats use echolocation to find their food in the dark." Put up one finger for each word. "Did I get it? Yes! Now it's your turn to try."

SUPPORTED PRACTICE

1. Have the student read or listen to another paragraph. At the end of the paragraph, have the student complete each paragraph-shrinking step (if you are working with a small group, have each student share with a partner, and then call on one student to share with the group).

2. If the student's answer is not quite right, provide scaffolding. For example: Ask *who, what, where, when,* and *why* questions that guide the student to the main idea.

3. If the student is still not able to identify the main idea, provide part of the response. For example: "I think the main *what* in the paragraph are bats. So what do you think is important about bats in this paragraph?" If needed, provide the correct response, and a brief explanation of why the response is correct. For example: "Since most of this paragraph is describing how bats use echolocation, I think that's the most important thing about the bats."

4. If the student has trouble saying the main idea in 10 words or less, say "Shrink it," and, if needed, model saying only the most important words needed to express the idea.

5. Practice with additional paragraphs as needed.

6. For additional practice, add a peer-mediated component. The paragraph-shrinking strategy is one of several peer-mediated strategies that are included in PALS, discussed earlier in the chapter. The paragraph-shrinking strategy can be implemented by a peer as follows:

   a. The first reader (the stronger reader in the pair) reads aloud for 5 minutes, stopping after each paragraph. The second reader (weaker reader) acts as the "coach."

   b. After each paragraph, the coach uses the cue card to prompt the reader to summarize the paragraph using the three paragraph-shrinking steps. If the reader needs help, the coach can prompt the reader to skim the paragraph and try again, give a hint, and finally share his or her own ideas if needed.

   c. After 5 minutes, the students switch jobs. The second reader picks up where the first reader left off, and stops after each paragraph to summarize. The first reader (now the coach) gives the prompts and helps as needed.

More information about PALS is provided in the "Resources" section of this chapter.

Review

On multiple days each week, review the strategy using the cue card, and have the student practice the strategy on multiple texts. Explain and model how the strategy can be used across a wide variety of texts that are read for different purposes.

Examples of Activity Intensifications

DOES THE STUDENT NEED MORE SYSTEMATIC INSTRUCTION?

Teach each step of the strategy as a separate lesson until the student has mastered that step.

DOES THE STUDENT NEED COGNITIVE PROCESSING STRATEGIES?

If the student has difficulty keeping track of the three steps on the cue card, turn it into a checklist. You can laminate the card and provide a dry-erase marker, so that the student can check off each step, and then wipe it clean for the next paragraph, or teach the student a mnemonic to recall the steps, such as "WIM-10:" W = *who* or *what*, I = important thing about the *who* or *what*, M-10 = main idea in 10 words or less. Just make sure that recalling the mnemonic does not distract the student from the primary task (recalling the main idea).

Mid- to Late Elementary:
Use Semantic and Text Structure Knowledge after Reading

Objective

The student will be able to complete a semantic feature analysis to compare and contrast different species of bats.

Materials

Template for completing a semantic feature analysis (see Figure 5.1 in Chapter 5 for an example).

Procedures

MODEL

1. Introduce the semantic feature analysis. For example: "Now, we're going to use what we learned in our text to compare and contrast different bat species. We're going to make a chart that shows how some bat species are the same and different, based on their diets, how they navigate and find food, and whether they hibernate."

2. Model using a think-aloud. Demonstrate completing the chart by modeling one row, using the text to find out needed information. For example: Point to the first row in the chart shown in Figure 5.1 in Chapter 5 and say, "I'll show you how. Our first microbat is the long-eared myotis. First, we need to find out about the diet of the long-eared myotis—or what it eats. Hmm; I remember the text saying that the long-eared myotis eats insects, or bugs. I'm going to check the text to make sure I'm right. Here it is in the text: 'The long-eared myotis is an insectivore!' That means it eats insects, so I'm going to put a (+) under the 'Insects' column and a (−) under the

'Fruit' and 'Blood' columns. That shows that it *does* eat insects and does *not* eat fruit or blood." Repeat this modeling with the "navigation/finding" and "hibernation" components of the chart.

SUPPORTED PRACTICE

1. Have the student help you complete the second row of the chart, encouraging him or her to use the text as needed.

2. Then have the student complete a row on his or her own, providing guidance and feedback as needed. For example: "Do you remember what the text said about what tricolored bats eat? Is their diet the same or different from the long-eared myotis and little brown bat? Where did we learn about bats' diets in our text?"

3. Have the student complete the remainder of the chart independently, or with a partner.

Review

Review the purpose of the semantic feature analysis: to help compare and contrast features of a text. Have the student summarize what was learned about different types of bats, encouraging him or her to use words that signal comparing and contrasting.

Examples of Activity Intensifications

DOES THE STUDENT NEED MORE EXPLICIT INSTRUCTION?

- Increase the amount of modeling and guided practice before the student completes the remainder of the chart on his or her own. For example, after modeling an entire row, prompt the student to try the first cell of the next row.

- If the student has difficulty finding the information, model going back to the text to look for the information, or ask questions such as "Do you remember when the text explained the diets of different types of bats? Let's go back to that part to see what it says about the tricolored bat." Show the student how you might look back to that part of the text to find the answer.

- Then move to the next cell in the row, encouraging the student to find the information in the text, and modeling this part as needed.

DOES THE STUDENT NEED MORE SYSTEMATIC INSTRUCTION?

- Break the task into smaller steps. For example, show the student a highlighting approach in which he or she (1) finds a bat species in the text (e.g., long-eared myotis); (2) finds and highlights specific information about diet, navigation, and hibernation; and (3) uses the highlighted text to record the relevant information on the chart.

- Have the student complete one section of the chart at a time (either by rows or columns), and provide specific feedback before the student completes the next section.

RESOURCES

Foorman, B., Beyler, N., Borradaile, K., Coyne, M., Denton, C. A., Dimino, J., et al. (2016). *Foundational skills to support reading for understanding in kindergarten through 3rd grade: Educator's practice guide* (NCEE 2016-4008). Washington, DC: National Center for Education Evaluation and Regional Assistance. Available at *https://ies.ed.gov/ncee/wwc/Docs/PracticeGuide/wwc_foundationalreading_070516.pdf*.

This guide, provided by What Works Clearinghouse, includes recommendations with supporting research to build understanding in reading for students in kindergarten through third grade. These recommendations can be applied both in the classroom and at home for parents.

IRIS Center Module on Graphic Organizers *https://iris.peabody.vanderbilt.edu/module/di/cresource/q2/p06/di_06_link_organizers*.

The IRIS Center provides examples of graphic organizers that can be used before, during, and after reading to assist in comprehension. The examples provided can be easily differentiated and adapted to meet specific text features, genres, and student needs.

Klingner, J. K., Vaughn, S., & Boardman, A. (2015). *Teaching reading comprehension to students with learning disabilities*. New York: Guilford Press.

K–12 teacher evidence-based tools are provided in this book, including supporting research, discussion questions, assessment tools, reproducibles, and sample lessons. Downloadable graphic organizers are also provided for teachers to access easily.

Semantic Mapping—Teach with Tech | Power Up What Works. Available at *https://powerupwhatworks.org/strategy-guide/semantic-mapping-teach-tech*.

PowerUp provides tips on incorporating the use of semantic maps in reading instruction while providing supporting research, along with lessons in action and incorporating the use of technology. Additional links for word analysis, self-questioning, and connection to words are included.

Vadasy, P. F., & Nelson, J. R. (2012). *Vocabulary instruction for struggling students*. New York: Guilford Press.

This book provides a variety of evidence-based approaches for students with difficulty in vocabulary. Assessment tools, as well as an intervention framework and small-group to individual student interventions, are provided for students beginning in preschool and older.

CHAPTER 7

Intensive Interventions to Support Writing to Read

Many teachers feel unprepared to teach writing, often because teacher preparation programs and inservice professional development workshops do not emphasize this critical skill. And writing often seems to be a lower priority, with less time devoted during literacy blocks to writing than to reading, and little explicit or systematic instruction implemented in this area. Some teachers wonder what they should focus on for writing instruction—Is it necessary to worry about handwriting? Spelling? Grammar? Or is it more important to focus on generating ideas and the writing process itself? How do we know which aspect of writing to focus on? It can quickly become overwhelming to determine what to do, and to know whether spending time on writing instruction is worth the precious resource of time. It *is* worth the time and effort, particularly for students who experience significant writing difficulties.

Intensive instruction in writing supports students in gaining transcription, text generation, and self-regulation skills at the letter, word, sentence, and passage levels, all of which support not only writing skill development but also overall literacy and learning (Biancarosa & Snow, 2004). Writing provides students with the means to integrate knowledge and think critically (Shanahan, 2004), as well as to communicate what they know (Graham & Perin, 2007). There is a strong connection between reading and writing (Graham & Hebert, 2011), and evidence indicates that fostering students' writing skills can strengthen their reading skills and vice versa.

WHAT DOES THE RESEARCH SAY ABOUT WRITING TO READ?

Researchers have shown that teaching writing can have an important impact on reading achievement in the following ways: (1) teaching spelling skills improves word-reading skills (in fact, Ehri [2000] referred to learning to read and learning to spell as "two sides of a coin" [p. 19]); (2) teaching spelling and sentence construction skills improves reading fluency; and (3) teaching the writing process, as well as teaching about sentence construction and text structures, improves reading comprehension (Graham & Hebert, 2010, 2011). Furthermore, increasing how much students write overall can improve their reading comprehension, and having students write about texts they read can improve comprehension of content-area texts (Graham & Hebert, 2010).

Teaching reading and writing to support development in both areas makes sense, because learning in both domains relies on similar knowledge and processes (Graham & Hebert, 2011). For example, teaching spelling can support both reading and writing because it fosters students' ability to see and remember connections between letters and sounds that form words. Teaching students to combine simple sentences into more complex sentences can help them understand complex sentence structures in reading, and teaching the process of composing text should help students gain insights into how text can be used to convey meaning (Graham & Hebert, 2011).

Researchers have proposed a *simple view of writing* (Berninger & Amtmann, 2003) that is helpful for thinking about how to assess and provide instruction that supports writing development in children. In this simple view, writing comprises three components: *text generation*, which involves the process of selecting words and producing sentences, paragraphs, and longer units of text in order to express ideas; *transcription*, which involves translating those words, sentences, and passages into print, and includes handwriting or typing and spelling; and *self-regulation*, which includes processes related to planning, reviewing, revising, and other self-regulatory skills.

Development in each of these areas requires cognitive resources, such as attention and memory (Berninger, 2009; McCutchen, 2006). When students struggle with one component of writing (such as handwriting and spelling skills involved in transcription), they have limited cognitive resources to devote to other components (such as word selection and sentence construction involved in text generation). Because each of these components is important to the overall quantity and quality of students' writing (e.g., Berninger, 2009; Graham, McKeown, Kiuhara, & Harris, 2012; McCutchen, 2006), writing instruction that targets skills within each component is needed to improve students' overall writing development. Furthermore, instruction should target students' skills at each level of language, including subword (e.g., letter and letter sound), word, sentence, and passage levels (Whitaker, Berninger, Johnston, & Swanson, 1994).

Types of Interventions to Support Writing Development

Students with intensive needs related to writing are more likely to benefit from instruction if it is explicit and systematic, and if connections to reading are made very clear

(Berninger, Nielsen, Abbott, Wijsman, & Raskind, 2008). Syntheses of writing instruction indicate that interventions with the strongest effects include explicit teaching of transcription skills (e.g., handwriting and spelling; Datchuk & Kubina, 2012; Graham, McKeown, Kiuhara, & Harris, 2012; McMaster, Kunkel, Shin, Jung, & Lembke, 2017); explicit teaching of writing processes and knowledge, writing strategies, text structure, and creativity/imagery (Graham, Bollinger, et al., 2012); and self-regulated strategy development (Baker et al., 2009; Graham, McKeown, et al., 2012; McMaster et al., 2017). Graham, McKeown, et al. also found that interventions that include prewriting activities, peer-assisted learning, goal setting, and assessing writing can improve student outcomes, as can instruction that incorporates word processing and extra writing time.

Bringing all of these findings together, researchers (Graham, Bollinger, et al., 2012) recommend that comprehensive writing instruction should include the following elements: (1) provide students with time to write every day, (2) teach students to use the writing process for a variety of purposes, (3) teach students to develop fluency in transcription and sentence construction skills, and (4) create an engaged community of writers. For students with intensive writing needs, explicit instruction and supports in each of these elements are likely needed.

WHAT ARE THE CRITICAL ELEMENTS OF WRITING-TO-READ INSTRUCTION?

Following the simple view of writing and the research base described above, it is not surprising that the critical elements to include in writing instruction for elementary students include developing transcription, text generation, and self-regulation skills. Let's examine each critical element of writing, along with ways to provide intensive instruction in these elements.

Transcription

Many students who struggle with writing may have a lot of great ideas in mind to write about, but experience significant difficulties in transcribing those ideas into print—for example, by spelling words, and by forming the letters using handwriting skills. Therefore, when students become so focused on forming letters or spelling words, they have relatively less attention or memory left to generate words and sentences that clearly convey their ideas. Thus, their writing might end up seeming simplistic, disorganized, or even incoherent. Such difficulties can be addressed by explicit instruction that promotes fluent handwriting and spelling, something that can then free up the cognitive resources needed to engage in higher-level writing processes.

Fortunately, researchers have developed and validated interventions that address handwriting (e.g., Graham, Harris, & Fink, 2000) and spelling (e.g., Graham, Harris, & Chorzempa, 2002). These interventions include carefully sequenced lessons that can be implemented alone or in combination with writing instruction in other areas (such as sentence construction). The "Resources" section of this chapter indicates where you can obtain full sets of lessons that are briefly described below (see also "Instructional Activities" for sample lessons).

Handwriting

Effective handwriting interventions typically include some combination of visual cues and verbal modeling, with opportunities to trace and copy example letters and then write them independently. It is important to limit the number of letters to be practiced in a given session (e.g., three letters at a time). Frequently used, easier letters should be taught first (e.g., *t, a, s*), before letters that are less frequent (e.g., *q, z*), and letters that have easily confused or reversible letters (e.g., *b, d, p, q*) should be taught separately.

The "Instructional Activities" section provides a sample lesson adapted from handwriting instruction developed by Graham et al. (2000). Each lesson consists of four activities. First, in *Alphabet Warm-Up,* the student identifies letters by singing the alphabet song and playing alphabet games. Next, in *Alphabet Practice,* the teacher models how to form each letter, and then the student copies the teacher's model. The teacher then prompts the student to compare and contrast the forms of the letters. The student practices writing the letters using visual cues, first by tracing the letter, then by writing the letter within guiding or dotted lines, and then by writing the letter independently. Last, the student identifies his or her best-written letter. During *Alphabet Rockets,* the student copies a sentence containing multiples of the three letters for 3 minutes (e.g., *Little kids like letters*), and counts and graphs the number of letters copied. Last, in *Alphabet Fun,* the student writes the letters in unusual ways (e.g., long and tall, short and fat).

Spelling

Effective spelling interventions typically include a focus on phonemic awareness, with word building, word sorting, word hunting, and word study that focus on spelling patterns that are frequently encountered in text or used by students in their own writing. Chapter 3 also addresses spelling, underscoring the strong connection between reading and writing.

The "Instructional Activities" section provides a sample lesson adapted from spelling instruction developed by Graham et al. (2002). This program includes five activities that can be implemented in different combinations on different days. In *Phonics Warm-Up,* students identify letters corresponding to sounds using picture cards. For *Word Building,* they build words that correspond to the spelling patterns in that unit by placing a card including consonant, blend, or diagraph at the front of a rime card (e.g., placing *b, p,* or *d* in front of *ig*). During *Word Sort,* students categorize words by spelling patterns, and identify spelling patterns or rules. For *Word Hunt,* they hunt for words with the target spelling patterns. During *Word Study,* they study words using a four-step process: (1) say the word and study the letters, (2) spell the word by saying the letters with eyes closed, (3) cover the word and write it three times without looking at the correct spelling, and (4) uncover the word and correct any misspellings.

Text Generation

Students with intensive needs related to writing might also struggle to generate text. Generating texts includes coming up with ideas to write about (something that requires either creativity or content knowledge, depending on the genre), finding the words to express those ideas, and using knowledge of sentence and text structure to organize ideas into a coherent form. Generating texts also requires an understanding of the various purposes for writing, and of the audience for whom the writing is intended.

Sentence Construction

At a very basic level, students with intensive needs in writing often need explicit instruction in how to construct simple (and later, more complex) sentences. To do so, students can be taught five rules for writing sentences (Schumaker & Sheldon, 2005): Every complete sentence (1) starts with a capital letter, (2) ends with a punctuation mark, (3) has a subject, (4) has a verb, and (5) should make sense. Each rule is then taught explicitly with modeling, demonstration, guided practice with scaffolding and feedback, and independent practice. See "Instructional Activities" for procedures for teaching each rule.

Sentence Combining

Once students can identify the components of sentences and generate their own simple sentences, they can begin to generate more complex sentences. Students who struggle with writing will likely need explicit instruction focused on grammatical strategies that they can use, such as combining simple sentences into more complex sentences. Learning to use such strategies can help to improve the quantity and quality of students' writing (Saddler, Behforooz, & Asaro, 2008; Saddler & Graham, 2005). Sentence-combining instruction should start with a simple focus, by combining sentences using words like *and, but,* and *because.* Once students master simple combining, they can learn to embed adjectives and adverbs, and later, adjectival and adverbial phrases, to create more complex sentences. Table 7.1 lists example kernel sentences that can be used for sentence-combining activities.

Text Structure Instruction

Just as students should learn to identify important elements of different text structures in reading (e.g., story grammar for narrative texts; clue words such as *first, next,* and *last* for sequence; *same* and *different* for compare–contrast; *because* for cause–effect), they can also learn to use these elements in their own writing (cf. Al Otaiba, Connor, et al., 2018). Further, because writing about texts that students have read can lead to better writing *and* reading comprehension outcomes, teaching text structure in the context of texts that students are reading provides a great opportunity to emphasize writing to read. Having students create story maps or semantic (concept) maps as described in Chapters

TABLE 7.1. Sample Kernel Sentences for Sentence-Combining Activity

Kernel sentences	Possible combined sentence
Combining using and	
The book was long. The book was boring.	The book was long and boring.
The water was cool. The water was refreshing.	The water was cool and refreshing.
When they hibernate, bats need a place with an ideal temperature. When they hibernate, bats need a place with ideal humidity.	When they hibernate, bats need a place with an ideal temperature and humidity.
Combining using but	
The house was falling apart. No one seemed to care.	The house was falling apart, but no one seemed to care.
I wanted to visit my friends. No one was home.	I wanted to visit my friends, but no one was home.
Combining using because	
The girl fell off the log. She lost her balance.	The girl fell off the log because she lost her balance
The car stalled. The car ran out of gas.	The car stalled because it ran out of gas.
The glaciers began to melt. The earth's average temperature increased.	The glaciers began to melt because the earth's average temperature increased.

5 and 6, and using information from texts they are reading, is one way to integrate reading and writing skills. Similarly, having students write summaries or responses to questions about what they have read and using key words that align with specific text structures (e.g., a summary of what comes first, next, and last in a particular sequence of steps) can support understanding of text structures through both reading and writing.

Building Fluency

Both writing and reading outcomes improve when students write a lot, and so it is critical to provide many opportunities to practice writing in ways that integrate text generation and transcription of that text into print. The aim, of course, is to improve both the quantity *and* quality of writing, and so building fluency should occur in the context of increasing production of *quality* writing. Fluency-building activities can also help build stamina, something that is important when sustained writing is required (as in the general education classroom, or during state test taking). Fluency-building activities can be particularly effective with a goal-setting component (Parker, Dickey, Burns, & McMaster, 2012)—for example, start by providing the students with a writing prompt. Provide a short time (no more than 1 minute) to plan, and then ask the students to begin writing. After 3 minutes, tell the students to stop writing, and count the number of words written. Have the students graph this number. Then, repeat this activity with another prompt, encouraging the students to write more words the second time. Count and graph the number of words written the second time, and celebrate improvement.

Self-Regulated Strategy Development

A critical element of writing instruction involves teaching the writing process, something that typically involves generating ideas around a particular topic, planning and organizing writing, drafting, and revising. Many students benefit from strategy instruction—or instruction that teaches systematic ways to remember and execute specific writing processes. For students who struggle with writing, remembering and executing strategies can be a cognitively demanding task in and of itself, and so finding ways to support this process that enables students to focus on writing is important.

As mentioned in Chapter 6, one well-researched way to support students' effective strategy use is SRSD, which involves teaching students to use strategies that help them to remember important text-generation processes, and to regulate their use of these writing processes. SRSD incorporates explicit instruction, modeling, mnemonics, and scaffolding for students until they reach mastery and can use the strategies with few or no supports (Baker et al., 2009). SRSD was developed by Graham and Harris (1996), and has been shown to improve students' writing quality and quantity across a wide range of grade levels. The six basic stages of SRSD instruction are described in Chapter 6.

A number of different strategies are taught using the SRSD approach (see Harris, Graham, Mason, & Friedlander, 2008). Among the most common and well researched are strategies for planning and organizing writing—for example, the POW strategy is designed to support students' planning in writing in different genres. POW is a mnemonic that stands for Pick my idea, Organize my notes, and Write and say more. This mnemonic is designed to help students remember planning steps in drafting a paper. Additional strategies can be added to POW for specific genres—for example, for writing stories, during the organize my notes step of POW, students can use the strategy WWW, what = 2, how = 2 to describe Who, When, Where, what the characters do, What happens to the main character and What happens then (What = 2), How the characters feel, and How the story ends (How = 2). For opinion essays, students use the mnemonic TREE (Topic sentence, Reasons—three or more, Ending, and Examine) to organize their ideas. See "Instructional Activities" at the end of this chapter for a detailed example.

Connecting Writing and Reading

As we mentioned at the beginning of this chapter, learning to read and learning to write involve many similar processes, and supporting development in one area should support development in the other. Nonetheless, especially for students with intensive needs, explicit and systematic instruction in both areas is critical. Reading and writing do not need to be taught separately, and indeed it often makes sense to combine instruction in both areas—for example, phonics and spelling instruction can be integrated, as the spelling of words reinforces the letter–sound correspondences needed to sound out and read them, and vice versa. When students generate text, whether at the sentence, paragraph, or passage level (e.g., as part of sentence or text structure instruction), having them read their own writing aloud can promote reading fluency and comprehension. Similarly, encouraging students to write in response to the texts that they read can also promote fluency and comprehension while also improving writing skills. In Chapter 8, we provide examples of comprehensive lesson plans that incorporate both reading and writing for students with intensive needs.

HOW DO I MONITOR PROGRESS IN WRITING TO READ?

Monitoring student progress in writing can assist teachers in determining students' overall growth as well as specific strengths and needs, which in turn can help in planning for appropriate areas to focus on in instruction—for example, a teacher might select a progress monitoring task that reflects a student's writing goal for an instructional period (such as a school year). If the goal is for the student to write words quickly and accurately, the teacher might select a word-level task for progress monitoring. If the goal is to write coherent sentences, the teacher might select a sentence-level task, and if the goal is to write paragraphs or longer passages, the teacher might select a passage-level task. Below, we identify formal and informal progress monitoring techniques that intervention teachers can use to objectively monitor students' writing at the word, sentence, and passage levels to determine the effectiveness of instruction and to further individualize and intensify instruction when needed.

Formal Measures

Just as CBM is a well-researched and validated approach to monitoring student progress and making data-based decisions in reading, there is also support for using CBM to monitor student writing progress (McMaster, Ritchey, & Lembke, 2011; Ritchey et al., 2016). Below, we review three CBM approaches that can be used to monitor student writing progress at the word, sentence, and passage levels. Each type of task has multiple forms that are designed to be equivalent in difficulty, so that progress can be seen over time. We recommend selecting one type of task and scoring procedure that best represents the student's goal over a specific instructional period (e.g., school year or IEP cycle), to administer and score the task weekly, and to graph the data regularly to obtain a picture of progress over time (such as the graph shown in Chapter 1, Figure 1.2). Graphing the data can be a powerful way to show the effectiveness of instruction, and can also signal the need for an instructional change in a timely fashion.

Word Dictation

Measures at the word level are typically designed to capture transcription skills, and are appropriate for students who are just beginning to write words (Hampton & Lembke, 2016; Lembke, Carlisle, & Poch, 2015; Lembke, Deno, & Hall, 2003). Word dictation is one measure that is individually administered for 3 minutes. The examiner dictates words (using spelling patterns found in many core reading and writing curricula) with one repeat, and students write each word (see Figure 7.1). Scores include words written (WW), words spelled correctly (WSC), correct letter sequences (CLS; any two adjacent letters that are correctly placed according to the correct spelling of the word), and correct minus incorrect letter sequences (CILS). Complete scoring directions can be found at *http://arc.missouri.edu/dbi_early.aspx*.

Picture–Word

Measures at the sentence level are designed to capture transcription and text generation at the sentence level, and are appropriate for students who are learning to connect words into sentences (Lembke et al., 2015; McMaster, Du, & Petursdottir, 2009). A picture–word measure is a group-administered prompt consisting of words with a picture above (see Figure 7.2). After providing students with practice, the examiner instructs them to write sentences using the prompts. After 3 minutes, the examiner instructs students to stop, and scores the writing sample for WW, WSC, and correct word sequences (CWS; two adjacent words that are spelled correctly, and that were used correctly in the context of the sentence). Complete scoring directions can be found at *http://arc.missouri.edu/dbi_early.aspx* or *www.progressmonitoring.org/pdf/ewscoring.pdf*.

Story Prompts

Story prompts capture transcription and text generation at the passage level, and can be individually or group administered with students across the elementary grades (e.g., Lembke et al., 2003, 2015; McMaster & Campbell, 2008; McMaster et al., 2009, 2011). Story prompts are designed to reflect experiences that students attending U.S. schools will be able to relate to, and to have simple vocabulary and sentence structure. Each prompt is printed at the top of a page, followed by lines to write on. The examiner provides 30 seconds for students to think about what they will write, and then 3 minutes to respond to the prompt. Students' samples are scored for WW, WSC, and CWS. Scoring directions can be found at *http://arc.missouri.edu/dbi_early.aspx* or *www.progressmonitoring.org*.

Word Dictation Examiner Form

Word List

1. hat
2. drop
3. list
4. bed
5. plus
6. sock
7. game
8. dig
9. clap
10. just
11. mine
12. score
13. gear
14. swim
15. ramp
16. zone
17. frame
18. goal
19. flop
20. next
21. tube
22. sleep
23. flash
24. prize
25. loop
26. wake
27. cloud
28. blend
29. globe
30. raid

Word Dictation Student Response Form

Name: _____   Date: _____   Form: _____

Example: _____

1. _____
2. _____
3. _____
4. _____
5. _____
6. _____
7. _____
8. _____
9. _____
10. _____
11. _____
12. _____
13. _____
14. _____
15. _____
16. _____
17. _____
18. _____
19. _____
20. _____
21. _____
22. _____
23. _____
24. _____
25. _____
26. _____
27. _____
28. _____
29. _____
30. _____

WW: _____   WSC: _____   CLS: _____   ILS: _____

FIGURE 7.1. Sample word dictation examiner (left) and student (right) forms. From McMaster and Lembke (2016).

Form 1

GRAND TOTAL: WW = ____   Page 1 Total: WW = ____

Name: _____   WSC = ____   WSC = ____

Date: _____   CWS = ____   CWS = ____

IWS = ____   IWS = ____

TR = ____   TR = ____

wash

school

mouse

FIGURE 7.2. Sample picture–word form.

Informal Measures

While CBM provides an overall indicator of students' reading proficiency, and is useful for monitoring responsiveness to intervention, additional informal assessments might be helpful to provide further insight regarding a student's needs in intensive intervention. Thus, when CBM data indicate the need to make an instructional change, it is important to collect additional information to inform what type of change is likely to meet the student's needs. For writing, it is useful both to observe the student during the writing process, and to collect samples of the student's writing products, in order to gain insights into a student's writing strengths and needs. Such information can help determine whether writing instruction should focus on transcription, text generation, self-regulation, or some combination of the three.

Various checklists and inventories exist to identify areas of strength and needs related to handwriting and spelling, and rubrics exist to identify areas of strength and needs related to text generation and composition (see the "Resources" section of this chapter). For example, handwriting checklists prompt observations to determine whether the student holds the pen or pencil comfortably, writes without excessive erasing or scribbling, forms letters independently without a model, produces letters and words without considerable effort, and sustains writing for an extended time period (all related to process). In terms of product, such checklists include whether the student writes letters legibly in upper and lower case, in the correct direction, with smooth strokes in a regular size and with proper slant, and evenly on lines with correct spacing between letters and words. Spelling inventories provide a way to examine students' knowledge of different spelling patterns in order to determine where they are in their spelling development—something that can be useful for identifying the focus of spelling instruction. Writing rubrics are designed to distinguish among beginning and more proficient writers based on composition elements, such as idea generation, organization, voice, word choice, sentence fluency, conventions, and presentation.

Curriculum-Based Assessment

CBM and informal assessments of students' writing processes and products can be used as part of an integrated curriculum-based assessment (CBA) approach to assessing students' writing (Parker, Burns, McMaster, & Shapiro, 2012). This CBA approach includes the following four steps. Step 1 is to assess the instructional environment, by completing rating scales, direct observations, and permanent product reviews. Step 2 is to assess a student's instructional level, by administering rate- and accuracy-based writing probes (such as CBM). Step 3 is to determine the instructional modifications that are needed, based on the assessment data collected within Steps 1 and 2, and Step 4 is to monitor student progress using CBM.

INSTRUCTIONAL ACTIVITIES FOR WRITING TO READ

Note: In this section, we provide sample activities in the areas of transcription (handwriting and spelling), text generation, and self-regulation. Activities in each area can be implemented in isolation or combined with each other to form a more comprehensive writing lesson, depending on the student's strengths and needs. We strongly recommend pairing writing activities with reading instruction to reinforce the reading–writing connection.

Transcription Activities (Pair with Phonemic Awareness and Phonics Activities): Handwriting Alphabet Practice and Alphabet Rockets (Graham et al., 2000)

Objective

The student will be able to write letters of the alphabet quickly and correctly by tracing, copying, writing the letters from memory, and writing the letters in sentences.

Materials

Paper with letters to trace and practice for Alphabet Practice.

Alphabet Rockets worksheet; Create a worksheet with sentences that have multiple target letters to practice—for example, *Little kids like letters* for practicing *l, i, t.*

Chart for graphing number of letters written correctly.

Pencil.

Procedures

MODEL

1. Show each letter, and model how to form each letter by tracing the letter with your index finger while describing the process aloud.

2. Point to the letter and tell the student the letter's name. For example: "This letter's name is *l*. What is the letter's name? I'll show you how to write this letter."

3. Demonstrate how to write the letter while providing directions. For example: "Start at the top and pull down to the bottom."

SUPPORTED PRACTICE

1. Have the student trace each letter.

2. Discuss how the target letters are similar and different, comparing two letters at a time.

3. Have the student practice one letter at a time by (a) tracing each letter with a pencil, while saying the letter aloud; (b) writing the letter within guided or dashed lines, while saying it aloud; (c) writing the letter three times, while saying it aloud; and (d) covering the letter examples and writing the letter three times from memory.

4. If the student makes an error, provide immediate corrective feedback. For example: If the student says the incorrect letter, say, "That letter is *A*. Say it with me: *A*. What letter?" If the student writes the letter incorrectly, model writing the letter correctly, and have the student write the letter again.

5. Have the student circle his or her best letter written.

6. Build fluency: Using the Alphabet Rockets worksheet, read the sentence, and then have the student read the sentence. Then ask the student to copy the sentence as many times as possible, writing quickly and accurately, for 3 minutes. After 3 minutes, have the student count up the number of letters written correctly, and graph this number. The goal is to increase the number of letters written correctly each time the student completes this activity.

Review

Each day that the student practices handwriting, review previously practiced letters to ensure maintenance. Review could include using a new copy of the same worksheet as was used in the above activities, or a blank sheet of paper, to write the letters in isolation or in sentences.

Examples of Activity Intensifications

DOES THE STUDENT NEED MORE FREQUENT OPPORTUNITIES
FOR STUDENT RESPONSE, PRACTICE, AND REVIEW?

• If the student has difficulty tracing and copying letters, provide hand-over-hand guidance, then gradually release support to tracing (with additional opportunities to trace), copying (with additional opportunities to copy), and then finally writing the letters from memory, with immediate corrective feedback, until the student can produce the letters independently.

• If the student needs additional practice to build fluency, provide additional sentences for the student to practice copying with frequent repetitions of the target letters.

DOES THE STUDENT NEED DIRECT INSTRUCTION FOR TRANSFER
TO NEW CONTEXTS?

Modify the Alphabet Practice and/or Alphabet Rockets worksheets so that they resemble material that is used in other contexts during the child's school day. For example: If the child's general education classroom uses paper with a different type of lines than those on the worksheet, provide opportunities to practice tracing, copying, and writing letters and sentences on the paper used in class.

Transcription Activities: Spelling—Word Building (Graham et al., 2002)

Objective

The student will be able to make words by adding consonants/digraphs to rimes using letter and rime cards.

Materials

Word-building cards with rimes and consonants/digraphs.
Timer.
Paper or whiteboard for writing words.
Pencil.

Procedures

MODEL

1. Introduce a new rime (e.g., /an/) and model building words.

2. Place a card with the rime on it in front of the student, and model blending the sounds together. For example: "These letters say /an/." Have the student repeat the rime and spell it.

3. Model how to make a word by adding a consonant or digraph (e.g., /c/) to the rime. For example: "Let's add the letter *c*. The letter *c* makes the /c/ sound." Then ask the student to say the sound.

4. Say the sounds for the letter card and rime card, pointing to the letters. Model reading the word. For example: Say "/c/ /an/."

SUPPORTED PRACTICE

1. Select several onset–rime cards. Have the student say the onset and the rime, then blend the sounds into the word. For example, "What word do these sounds make? That's right, *can*!" Have the student write the word while saying it out loud.

2. Have the student compose more real words using the rime and additional consonants/ digraphs. Encourage the student to build each word using the cards, then write each word while saying it out loud. Provide immediate corrective feedback as needed.

3. Tell the student to write as many words as possible in 1 minute. Use the timer. If time permits, repeat and challenge the student to beat his or her first time by writing even more words in 1 minute.

Review

Review the two rimes. Have the student say and spell each rime independently, or with supported practice as needed. Then make words using both rimes, following the same procedure as above.

Examples of Activity Intensifications

DOES THE STUDENT NEED MORE EXPLICIT INSTRUCTION?

- Model each step, having the student repeat each step after (or with) you. For example:
  - ○ "These letters say /an/. Say it with me: /an/."
  - ○ "The letter *c* says /c/. Say it with me: /c/."
  - ○ "When I add the letter *c* to /an/, I make a new word: /c/ /an/. [Point to the letters as you say them.] Say it with me: /c/ /an/."
  - ○ "Now I'll write the word [model writing the word]."
  - ○ "Now you write the word [have the student either trace over your model or copy the word on the next line]."

- Provide additional supported practice.
  - "Now it's your turn to write the word."
  - Provide corrective feedback and additional practice as needed.
- Repeat this intensified modeling and practice with several words before having the student practice with more typical support (Step 2) and work on building automaticity (Step 3).

DOES THE STUDENT NEED MORE SPECIFIC AND CORRECTIVE FEEDBACK?

When correcting an error, be sure to state the specific error and how to correct it, and then praise the correct answer. For example:

- If the student says the wrong sound or rime, say, "Oops, you said the wrong sound. That sound is /c/. Say it with me: /c/. What sound? That's right, /c/!"
- If the student builds a word that is not real, say, "Oops, you made the word /s/ /an/, *san*. *San* is not a real word. Let's find another letter and make a real word. Great job, you made the word *tan*! *Tan* is a real word."
- If the student writes a word incorrectly, say, "Oops, you wrote *car* but we're making the word *can*. Let's spell the word *can* together: *c-a-n*. Now write *can* and say the letters out loud: *c-a-n*. Way to go! You wrote the word *can*!"

DOES THE STUDENT NEED DIRECT INSTRUCTION FOR TRANSFER TO NEW CONTEXTS?

- Show the student how to build words without using word cards. For example: List two rimes at the top of a sheet of paper or on a whiteboard, and several consonants and digraphs below them. Have the student write new words by pairing the consonants/digraphs with the rimes, and read them aloud.
- Write out sentences, leaving blanks where words with the rime would fit. For example: I _____ to the house. Have the student build a word that makes sense in the sentence (e.g., *ran*).
- Have the student write his or her own sentences using words with the target rime in his or her journal.

Text Generation Activities (Pair with Reading Fluency and Comprehension Activities): Sentence Construction

Objectives

The student will be able to identify the five components of a complete sentence, correct prewritten sentences to include these components, and generate new sentences including these components.

Materials

Sample sentences for each rule.

Paper and pencil.

Procedures

MODEL

1. Teach Rule 1: "All complete sentences begin with a capital letter," and define what a capital letter is, providing examples to compare and contrast capital and lower-case letters. Then explain that a capital letter serves as a "signal" that a new sentence is beginning (the way a traffic light signals when to start or stop driving).

2. Model writing a sentence using a capital letter. For example: "Let's say I wanted to write the sentence *My dog is big*. The first word is *my*. So what letter should I start with? [M] Should I write a capital *M* or a lower-case *m*? [capital *M*]." Model writing a capital *M*, and then the rest of the sentence.

3. Teach Rule 2: "Every sentence ends with a punctuation mark," in the same way as you taught Rule 1. Explain that punctuation serves as a "signal" that the sentence has come to an end, and model writing a period at the end of the sample sentence used above: *My dog is big.*

4. Provide the student with a variety of sentences that are missing capital letters and/or punctuation. Model working through an example or two, by identifying which part(s) of the sentence need to be corrected, and then rewriting the sentence with correct capitalization and punctuation.

SUPPORTED PRACTICE

1. Provide guided practice with feedback until the student can correctly capitalize and punctuate, and then provide independent practice.

2. Practice with Rules 1 and 2 should continue until the student can consistently produce correct capitalization and punctuation, and then move on to teaching Rule 3.

MODEL

1. Teach Rule 3: "Every complete sentence has a subject," in a similar way to Rules 1 and 2. First, explain that a complete sentence has two types of words. The first type is called a "subject"—the person, place, thing, or idea that the sentence is about. Brainstorm words that fit into each of those categories, and explain that each of those words is a "noun." When a noun is a word that the whole sentence is about, it is the subject. Explain that the subject in a sentence can be labeled with an *S*.

2. Teach Rule 4: "Every complete sentence has a verb"—a word that shows the action of the subject in the sentence. Brainstorm action verbs (something a person can do with

his or her body or mind), and explain that the verb in a sentence can be labeled with a *V*.

SUPPORTED PRACTICE

1. After teaching Rules 3 and 4, work with the student to generate sentences with subjects and verbs, and label those words with *S* and *V*, respectively.

2. Provide additional sentences for practice. This time, the student should still fix capitalization and punctuation errors, but should also label the subjects and verbs in sentences. The student can then generate his or her own sentences and identify the subjects and verbs.

3. Continue to practice Rules 3 and 4 until the student can consistently and correctly identify subjects and verbs in sentences, and then move to Rule 5.

MODEL

1. Teach Rule 5: "A complete sentence has a subject and a verb that work together to make sense." To teach this rule, provide positive and negative examples (e.g., *The boy jumped, The book smiled*), and discuss whether or not they make sense, and why or why not.

2. Show how the student can draw an arrow between the subject and verb to show that they make sense:

$$S \leftrightarrow V$$
$$\text{The \quad boy \quad jumped.}$$

SUPPORTED PRACTICE

Practice with additional sentences, in which the student determines correct capitalization and punctuation, identifies subjects and verbs, and confirms whether the sentence makes sense.

Review

Review and practice all five rules until the student can consistently and correctly identify and produce capitals, end punctuation, subjects, and verbs, and can determine whether sentences make sense.

Examples of Activity Intensifications

DOES THE STUDENT NEED MORE SYSTEMATIC INSTRUCTION?

Break instruction into even smaller steps and isolate skills. Practice one rule at a time until it is mastered, then practice the next rule until it is mastered, and then put the two rules together. For example, use the following sequence:

- Teach Rules 1 and 2 (capitalization and punctuation) until mastery is achieved.
- Teach Rule 3 (subjects) to mastery, using examples for practice that are correctly capitalized and punctuated, and focus only on subjects.
- Teach Rule 4 (verbs) to mastery, using examples for practice that are correctly capitalized and punctuated, and focus only on verbs.
- Practice Rules 3 and 4 together until mastery is achieved.
- Practice Rules 1–4 together until mastery is achieved.
- Teach Rule 5 (makes sense) until mastery is achieved, using practice examples that are correctly capitalized and punctuated, and focus only on whether the subjects and verbs make sense.
- Practice Rules 1–5 together until mastery is achieved.

Text Generation Activities: Sentence Combining

Objective

The student will be able to combine sentences using the words *and, but, because,* and other coordinating conjunctions, adjectives and adverbs, and adjectival and adverbial clauses.

Materials

Sample sentences for each rule.

Paper and pencil.

Procedures

MODEL

1. Start by explaining that good writers often play with their sentences to make them sound better, by changing words, moving words around, or adding or removing words.
2. Model applying a sentence-combining strategy by thinking aloud. For example: "I'm going to combine these two sentences. [Read them aloud.] I'll put these sentences together by using the word *and*."
3. Write the new combined sentence, and then read it aloud.

SUPPORTED PRACTICE

1. Have the student generate more examples, writing them and reading them aloud. Discuss whether the sentences make sense.
2. Provide the student with kernel sentences (see examples in Table 7.1) to practice

combining. Do several together, fading support and providing immediate corrective feedback, until the student can carry out the activity independently.

3. Have the student combine sentences independently, and then provide specific corrective feedback.

4. Once the student masters sentence combining using *and, but*, and *because*, you can introduce other coordinating conjunctions, adjectives and adverbs, and adjectival and adverbial clauses.

Review

Each day that the student writes, review the different ways that sentences can be combined using *and, but*, and *because*, and other types of words and clauses. Encourage the student to revise writing by using the sentence-combining strategy.

Examples of Activity Intensifications

DOES THE STUDENT NEED DIRECT INSTRUCTION FOR TRANSFER
TO NEW CONTEXTS?

Apply the sentence-combining approach to editing passage-level writing.

- You could start with a sample of your own writing or a sample of a peer's writing, and then use a sample of the student's own writing.

- Help the student identify simple sentences that could be combined into more complex sentences.

- Model how you can use the sentence-combining approach to revise sentences within the passage.

- Read the sentences aloud before and after the revision, and discuss how the combined sentences improve the way the passage sounds to the reader.

Self-Regulated Strategy Development (Pair with Reading Comprehension Activities): POW + TREE Strategy for Writing Opinion Essays (Adapted from Harris et al., 2008)

Objectives

The student will be able to identify parts of an opinion essay, learn the POW + TREE mnemonic, and write an opinion essay (first collaboratively, then independently).

Materials

POW mnemonic: Create a chart that lists what each letter stands for—<u>P</u> = pick my idea, <u>O</u> = organize my notes, <u>W</u> = write and say more.

TREE graphic organizer: Create a chart or worksheet on which the student can write notes for each letter—T = topic sentence, R = reasons—three or more, E = ending, E = examine—Do I have all the parts?

Essay samples.

Paper and pencil.

Procedures

Note: The following procedures should be divided across multiple sessions/days.

Model

1. Develop background knowledge: Describe what an opinion essay is (i.e., an essay that explains the writer's beliefs about an issue and his or her reasons). Explain that powerful opinion essays include several parts.

2. Introduce the POW + TREE mnemonic: Show the mnemonic chart. Explain that POW stands for Pick my idea, Organize my notes, Write and say more (this strategy can apply to a wide range of writing). Then introduce TREE:

   T = Topic sentence, represented by the trunk. The topic sentence should be strong, and everything else in the essay should be connected to it.

   R = Reasons, represented by the roots. The reasons provide support for the topic sentence, just as the roots support the tree.

   E = Ending (to wrap it up), represented by the earth, which wraps around the tree.

   E = Examine, which is what we do to make sure all the parts are there.

3. Model finding the parts in a sample essay: Provide a sample essay and read it aloud with the student. Encourage the student to listen/look for each part as you read. When you come to each part (topic sentence, reasons, and ending), identify the part and underline and label it. As you read the essay, also identify *transition words* that the writer used to show that a reason is being given (e.g., *first, second, third; another, also, furthermore*). After reading the entire essay, support the student in "examining" it to make sure all the parts are there.

4. Introduce the graphic organizer: Model writing the parts found in the essay on the graphic organizer.

SUPPORTED PRACTICE

1. Practice using TREE: Review the TREE mnemonic, including what each letter represents. Then have the student memorize the mnemonic by hiding the chart and having the student write as many components as possible, and then check his or her work by looking back at the chart. Keep doing this until the student can explain the entire mnemonic from memory.

2. Practice finding the parts: Provide another sample essay and have the student practice underlining and labeling the parts, providing corrective feedback as needed. Repeat this step with multiple essay samples until the student can identify all of the parts correctly and independently (this step might occur across multiple sessions).

MODEL

1. Model writing an essay using the POW + TREE strategy: Use the POW + TREE graphic organizer to model writing an opinion essay. Think aloud as you go through each step. For example: "The first letter in POW is *P*, and it stands for 'pick my idea.' Today I'm going to write an opinion essay about recess. I came up with this idea because I believe we should have recess two times each day, not just one time."

2. Continue to think aloud and model *O* and *W* and explain that you'll use the TREE strategy to help you organize your notes and write your paper. Model using the graphic organizer to organize your notes, and then write your paper, thinking aloud as you go.

3. Emphasize the use of transition words (e.g., *first, next, last*) as you write each reason supporting the topic sentence. Allow the student to help as much as possible.

4. Model developing self-statements: Help the student think of self-statements to say to him- or herself while working on writing essays. Have the student write the self-statements for future reference. Examples of self-statements include:

   • *Before writing:* "What is my assignment? I need to write an opinion essay about _____" and "I can use POW + TREE to write my essay."
   • *During writing:* "I can use transition words to signal that I am introducing a new reason to support my opinion."
   • *After writing:* "Did I include all the parts of an opinion essay?"

SUPPORTED PRACTICE

1. Use the POW + TREE graphic organizer to collaboratively write an opinion essay. Have the student help pick an idea and generate the parts that go onto the organizer, and then work together to write the essay.

2. Provide feedback and guidance as you write.

3. Have the student use the POW + TREE strategy, including self-statements, to write an opinion essay independently.

Review

Review the POW + TREE strategy, including self-statements, each time the student writes an opinion essay. Keep copies of the graphic organizer in a place where the student knows how to find them, so that they are always available for use when needed.

Examples of Activity Intensifications

DOES THE STUDENT NEED COGNITIVE PROCESSING STRATEGIES?

- Provide two or three choices for the student to write about.
- With the student, identify a goal in terms of an area of writing to improve, such as number of reasons generated to support the opinion, number of words written, and so on.
- After writing each essay, have the student graph his or her progress toward this goal.
- Celebrate when the student reaches the goal (this could include some type of meaningful reward, such as computer time or other activity that is reinforcing to the student).

DOES THE STUDENT NEED MORE SPECIFIC AND CORRECTIVE FEEDBACK?

- During supported practice activities, provide specific and corrective feedback for each step. For example, for picking an idea: "That's a great idea to write your opinion essay about recycling at school, because I know that's something you feel strongly about." For writing a topic sentence: "I think you could make this topic sentence stronger by using a more powerful word." For writing three reasons: "I'm not sure that reason completely supports your topic sentence. Do you mean to say . . . ?"
- As needed, provide additional modeling and practice to demonstrate and reinforce how to use the specific feedback.

RESOURCES

DBI-TLC for Early Writing manual and tools

http://arc.missouri.edu/dbi_early.aspx

The Assessment Resource Center, provided by the University of Missouri, provides assessments and surveys for purchase. The DBI-TLC materials include early writing instructional materials, manuals, and decision-making tools.

Research Institute on Progress Monitoring

www.progressmonitoring.org

The Research Institute on Progress Monitoring provides tools to evaluate individualized instruction while also providing research behind early writing measures. Additionally, products to score writing samples and informational guides on CBM are provided.

Harris, K. R., Graham, S., Mason, L. H., & Friedlander, B. (2008). *Powerful writing strategies for all students*. Baltimore: Brookes.

This book provides for students in elementary and middle school evidence-based lesson plans that can act as a supplement to an existing writing curriculum. Reproducible pages are included to guide the writing process from the planning stage through revising.

Graham, S., Bollinger, A., Booth Olson, C., D'Aoust, C., MacArthur, C., McCutchen, D., et al. (2012). *Teaching elementary school students to be effective writers: A practice guide* (NCEE 2012-4058). Washington, DC: National Center for Education Evaluation and Regional Assistance, Institute of Education Sciences, U.S. Department of Education. Available at *http://ies.ed.gov/ncee/wwc/publications_reviews.aspx#pubsearch*.

This practice guide provides evidence-based recommendations for teaching elementary school students to be more effective writers, as well as information on how to create an engaged community of writers within your classroom. Research and supplemental evidence to support each recommendation is provided.

Harris, K. R., & Graham, S. (1992). *Helping young writers master the craft: Strategy instruction and self-regulation in the writing process.* Northampton, MA: Brookline Books.

This book focuses on strategies to assist students with planning their writing, and on the research behind self-regulation strategies. The research-backed tips and tricks in the book can be adapted to both classwide and individual instruction.

CHAPTER 8

Multicomponent Reading Interventions

WHAT DOES THE RESEARCH SAY
ABOUT MULTICOMPONENT READING INTERVENTIONS?

Many children with intensive needs in reading struggle with multiple aspects of read-ing, and thus will require multicomponent interventions—or interventions that address and integrate several reading skills. For example, young children who are struggling to learn to read may need intensive phonemic awareness and letter-sound instruction, but might also struggle with oral language skills that are foundational to later reading comprehension success. Other students, including some students diagnosed with dys-lexia, might have relative strengths in oral language and listening comprehension, but might have significant struggles with phonics and spelling. Some students in the upper-elementary grades might present gaps in phonics and morphological awareness skills that impact their spelling and writing, but might also have needs related to develop-ing reading fluency and comprehension. To provide the most comprehensive intensive intervention possible, it is critical to evaluate students' strengths and needs in all areas of reading—and, when data indicate that a multicomponent intervention is needed, to build this intervention around those specific areas of relative strength and need.

Findings from a growing body of research demonstrate the efficacy and efficiency of multicomponent interventions for both early grades (Wanzek & Vaughn, 2007) and upper grades (e.g., O'Connor et al., 2002; Ritchey, Silverman, Montanaro, Speece, & Schatschneider, 2012; Vadasy & Sanders, 2008; Wanzek & Roberts, 2012; Wanzek et al., 2010). Multicomponent interventions are generally implemented by teachers, although some involve computer-assisted instruction, or peer-mediated practice. In addition to the focus on reading skills, some students with intensive reading needs may also need sup-port for how they approach learning, including their attention, engagement, motivation or eagerness to learn, organization, and task persistence (e.g., Matthews, Kizzie, Rowley, & Cortina, 2010; Morgan, Farkas, Tufis, & Sperling, 2008). In fact, researchers have shown that by first grade, students rated as having weak learning skills were found to be four times more likely to be poor readers by fourth grade (Morgan et al., 2008). Notably, this research controlled for students' initial reading scores, socioeconomic status, and demographics.

WHAT ARE THE CRITICAL ELEMENTS OF MULTICOMPONENT READING INTERVENTIONS?

When one is compiling a multicomponent instructional program for a student (or group of students) with intensive needs in reading, it is helpful to use a basic instructional plan that includes the following common elements: (1) specific objectives, (2) grouping strategies, (3) a plan for reinforcing positive behavior and motivating the student to try his or her best, (4) the specific activities and materials needed to conduct those activities, (5) plans for further intensifying activities as needed, and (6) plans for monitoring student progress on a frequent and regular basis, along with space to record these data. We also strongly recommend including space to reflect on what went well in the lesson, areas for improvement, and elements that might need to be retaught or delivered in a new way. Examples for two students with intensive needs (Laura and Calvin) are provided in Figures 8.1 and 8.2, respectively. Below, we elaborate on the common elements for Laura's and Calvin's basic instructional plans for their intensive interventions. We then provide information on how their interventions were further intensified as needed to accelerate progress.

Laura

Laura is a first-grade girl who struggles with phonemic awareness, decoding, and spelling skills, and also has needs in the areas of oral language and comprehension. Since preschool, she has received speech and language services for articulation problems and language delays. Her current speech and language IEP goals include pronouncing blends, speaking in longer and more complex sentences, and listening comprehension, particularly with regard to her ability to draw inferences. Although Laura is a bright girl, she recently asked her teacher if she is stupid, because the early reading skills that seem to come so easy for her peers are such a struggle for her. She loves listening to books, browses and pretend-reads books during center time, and has many favorite authors. Her sight-word reading is relatively stronger than her decoding skills. She likes to draw pictures during journaling time, mostly about animals. She seems embarrassed when asked to read aloud, and is shy to respond to questions. Her teacher, however, reported that Laura can answer many literal questions that involve recall or summarization, but also that she does not correctly draw inferences and struggles to use her own background knowledge to answer *why* or *how* questions. Furthermore, even when her answers are correct, they are generally brief.

To date, Laura's first-grade classroom teacher has provided her with biweekly small-group phonics intervention during the fall of first grade. This intervention involved CVC word study and work with flash cards to build her automaticity in reading the words. However, Laura has not demonstrated adequate progress. The RTI team met, discussed the concerns with Laura's speech and language therapist, and conducted some additional assessments. They determined that Laura had not caught up to grade level in phonics and also that her other literacy skills were about a year behind her classmates'. The team hypothesized that she needs more intensive instruction that incorporates multiple components, to be delivered with greater frequency in a smaller group size by a reading specialist. The team recommended additional objectives to include more explicit instruction for phonemic awareness, decoding, spelling, oral language, and listening comprehension. Laura's new multicomponent intensive reading intervention will be provided by a reading specialist for 45 minutes daily in a small group of two students. The intervention teacher, Mrs. R, will provide more explicit instruction in each component and more frequent opportunities for responding, practicing, and reviewing. Mrs. R will also collaborate with Laura's speech and language therapist, Ms. SLP. An example of Laura's basic instructional plan is shown in Figure 8.1.

Specific Objectives

The team suggested specific objectives for the intensive multicomponent intervention. In the area of phonemic awareness, Laura is working toward blending and segmenting words with three to five phonemes; these words include blends and digraphs (e.g., the /bl/ in *blend* is a blend, and the /ph/ in *digraphs* is a digraph). Similarly, in phonics and spelling, she is working to master decoding and spelling CCVC and CVCC words. These objectives are more aligned with the skills taught in the core curriculum in the fall of first grade, so the intensive intervention is designed to help her catch up by providing explicit instruction in how to decode these word types. The RTI team also suggested that Laura have more opportunities to read and practice to fluency in connected text, rather than only the limited word study her teacher had provided. Another objective related to oral language is for her to speak in more complex and grammatically correct sentences, and her final objective is to increase her ability to answer inferential questions within the area of listening comprehension. In order to provide explicit instruction with frequent opportunities for response and practice for these two later objectives, Mrs. R plans to implement dialogic reading. Her plan also involves frequent oral reading fluency progress monitoring to inform whether Laura's progress is adequate, or whether the plan needs to be changed.

Behavioral Supports and Motivation Plan

The RTI team also hypothesized that Laura would benefit from behavioral supports to increase her learning skills for reading. They noted that Laura is motivated to draw animals, and that her favorite books are by authors who write fiction and nonfiction texts about animals. She also loves to listen to e-books. Mrs. R plans to reinforce Laura for

Student's Name: Laura

Teacher: Ms. R

Grade: 1

Date: March 18

Objective(s)/learning target(s): Laura will (1) blend and segment words with consonant blends (e.g., bl, cl, br, and cr) correctly on three consecutive trials, (2) decode and spell CVCC and CCVCC words with blends correctly on three consecutive trials, (3) orally connect two simple sentences to form a longer sentence that is grammatically correct, and (4) after listening to a story read aloud, will correctly answer inferential questions on three correct trials.

Grouping strategy: 1:2 instruction, with peer-mediated practice as needed.

Behavioral supports and motivation plan: Laura will earn one ticket for staying on task and for correct responding during each activity. 15 tickets = 10 minutes of e-reading time.

Activity	Time	Materials	Possible intensifications if needed
Each session: review objectives and rules ☑ Introduce/review purpose and objectives. ☑ Introduce/review rules and behavior/motivation plan.	<1 minute	☑ Rules ☑ Motivational materials	☐ Change dosage or group size. ☐ Increase explicit, systematic instruction. ☐ Include more opportunities for responding, practice, and review. ☐ Provide more specific, corrective feedback. ☐ Embed cognitive processes. ☐ Teach for transfer.
Warm-up: speed game to practice fluent reading CVC, CCVC, CCVCC patterns	5 minutes	✓ Laura's "mastered words" cards	NA
ACTIVITY 1: phonemic awareness, phonics/spelling ✓ Word-building activity - Laura orally blends and segments words with initial or final blends. - Laura builds words with initial or final blends (letter tiles, writing on whiteboard, or spelling with iPad). - Laura sorts words with blends versus digraphs. - Laura spells words. - Laura reads words quickly and correctly. - Add mastered words to "mastered words" pile.	15 minutes	✓ Word cards (e.g., black, clap, stop, flag and non-example: with digraphs shop, that) ✓ Letter tiles, whiteboard, or iPad for spelling words	If needed, provide additional modeling and guided practice with immediate feedback. Use Elkonin boxes with four to five boxes and letter tiles. Scaffold to independence.

ACTIVITY 2: transfer of word reading to connected text reading and fluency building ✓ Laura will practice phonetic patterns. ✓ She will identify words in text with blends. ✓ The teacher models fluent reading of the passage. ✓ Laura reads three times, earns two tickets when she beats her first or second time.	10 minutes	✓ Passage from Bob Books by Maslen ✓ Timer ✓ Rocket chart and markers	Provide additional practice via partner reading on Bob Books with blends.
ACTIVITY 3: dialogic reading ✓ Read to Laura. ✓ Pause and ask dialogic reading questions (CROWD–HS). ✓ Why did Sally Ride want girls to achieve their dreams? ✓ Why did she persist to become the first American woman in space? ✓ How could you be a role model at home for your little sister? ✓ How have you persisted today during reading? ✓ Use the PEER strategy to elongate Laura's answers and to help her combine sentences.	10 minutes	✓ Passage from She Persisted: 13 American Women Who Changed the World by Clinton ✓ Vocabulary: persisted, role model, opportunity, achieve	✓ Model by thinking aloud how to answer. ✓ Review text that supports inferential questions (show text that supports correct answer to the "why" question). ✓ Remind Laura that an inference is when we connect something we see or hear in the story to something we already know (like from home or school) to make a brand new idea.
Each session: closing Lesson wrap-up—Laura reflects: What is she proud of? What will she keep working on? Laura draws a picture of herself persisting.	5 minutes		NA
Once per week: progress monitoring ☑ Administer a progress monitoring prompt to student. ☑ Score and graph as soon as possible after lesson.	3 minutes	✓ Prompt grade 1 oral reading fluency ✓ Timer	
Reflection What went well? What could I do to improve? Other reflections:		What do I need to reteach?	Do I need to regroup?

FIGURE 8.1. Laura's basic instructional plan.

153

volunteering to answer more inferential questions, for answering correctly, and also for using more complete and complex sentences when responding. Mrs. R has downloaded a new series of decodable e-books with engaging pictures about animals, with phonics patterns ranging from CVC to CCVCC and some CVC*e* patterns; she intends that these will double as a reinforcer, and will provide extra scaffolding for independent practice. Mrs. R uses tickets to reinforce Laura, and Laura can earn up to 15 tickets within a reading lesson—each ticket earns her time on her e-book. At the close of each lesson, Mrs. R will ask Laura to reflect on her goals and her persistence.

Calvin

Calvin is a fourth-grade boy who struggles with both phonics and comprehension skills. He would like to do well and generally tries hard, but can easily get frustrated and tends to revert to off-task behaviors (looking out the window, doodling in his notebook) when he is experiencing difficulty during reading instruction. He received supplemental intervention of varying intensities in third grade, and that intervention did help him improve in his decoding skills, though not to consistent grade-level performance. He also struggles with comprehension, but did not receive targeted intervention in this area in third grade (his teachers felt that addressing his decoding difficulties would ameliorate any comprehension problems). At the end of third grade, Calvin was identified with a specific learning disability in reading, and was deemed eligible for special education services. The IEP team hypothesized that he needs intensive instruction that incorporates multiple components, to be delivered daily in a one-on-one setting. His IEP specifies goals related to phonics, reading fluency and comprehension, and written expression, with intervention to be provided one-on-one or in small groups by the special education teacher, Ms. K, daily for 60 minutes. Ms. K will provide explicit instruction in each component, along with more frequent opportunities for responding, practicing, and reviewing. An example of Calvin's basic instructional plan is shown in Figure 8.2.

Specific Objectives

Calvin's objectives target the areas identified on his IEP. In the area of phonics, Calvin is working to master conventions for adding endings to words (in this lesson, focusing on /ing/). This objective aligns with his core curriculum, and the intensive intervention is designed to support his mastery of this skill. Note that the objective incorporates both reading and spelling, emphasizing the strong connection between decoding, encoding, and transcription of letter sounds into printed words. In the area of reading fluency and comprehension, several components are addressed: vocabulary learning, which will help Calvin focus on the meaning of text, as well as on quick and accurate word recognition; fluency building within grade-level text; and reading comprehension focusing on identifying specific text structure elements—in this case, story elements. Calvin also has objectives related to writing, in that he will be required to write about text that he reads (by filling out a story map), and then generate his own text using both vocabulary and text structure knowledge learned during the lesson.

Grouping Strategies

In this example, the teacher plans to work with Calvin individually (thus increasing intensity by working one-on-one rather than in whole-class or small-group settings). Note, however, that these activities could also be conducted in a small group of students with similar needs, or in a peer-mediated format (e.g., partner reading during repeated reading in Activity 2).

Behavioral Supports and Motivation Plan

Calvin is highly motivated to earn time to play games on his iPad, and so Ms. K plans to reinforce on-task behavior and correct responding during his reading lesson with a simple point system. When he earns 100 points, he can bank those to equal 5 minutes on his iPad. He usually likes to bank a few 5-minute blocks, and uses 15–20 of those minutes on Fridays.

Specific Activities and Materials

Calvin's five objectives are addressed in three main activities (phonics/spelling, vocabulary and fluency building, and comprehension/writing). Each activity includes explicit instruction (e.g., providing the rule for *-ing* in spelling and modeling its application using positive and negative examples, followed by guided and independent practice for Calvin to build words with *-ing*; preteaching vocabulary words with positive and negative examples, followed by guided practice for Calvin to apply use of the words; repeated reading with modeling to build fluency; and modeling and guided practice for Calvin to complete a story map of *James and the Giant Peach*). These activities are followed by an integrated practice activity that incorporates additional practice across the reading fluency, comprehension, and writing skills that are addressed throughout the lesson. Note that each activity is broken into a specific time block, with some flexibility for the longer, more complex activities (including the idea that the integrated practice could extend into a separate day).

Intensifications for Laura and Calvin

This element of the basic instructional plan provides Ms. K and Mrs. R with the opportunity to think of ways to intensify the activities if Calvin or Laura experience difficulty with specific skills, or if their progress monitoring data indicate that they are not making sufficient growth. Both teachers draw from the options for intensifications presented in Chapter 1, including organizational changes (e.g., dosage, group size) and instructional delivery changes, such as (1) making instruction more explicit and

Student's Name: *Calvin*

Grade: *4*

Teacher: *Ms. K*

Date: *September 21*

Objective(s)/learning target(s): *Calvin will (1) read and spell –ing words using conventional ending rules correctly on three consecutive trials, (2) identify and define key vocabulary words in a third-grade passage, (3) read at least 110 words correctly in 1 minute in a third-grade passage, (4) complete a story map using complete sentences, and (5) plan, write, revise, and read aloud his own story using key vocabulary words and story elements.*

Grouping strategy: *1:1 instruction, with peer-mediated practice as needed.*

Behavioral supports and motivation plan: Calvin will earn points on his point sheet for staying on task and for correct responding during each activity. 100 points = 5 minutes of iPad time.

Activity	Time	Materials	Possible intensifications if needed
Each session: review objectives and rules ☑ Introduce/review purpose and objectives. ☑ Introduce/review rules and behavior/motivation plan.	<1 minute	☑ Rules ☑ Motivational materials	☐ Change dosage or group size. ☐ Increase explicit, systematic instruction. ☐ Include more opportunities for responding, practice, and review. ☐ Provide more specific, corrective feedback. ☐ Embed cognitive processes. ☐ Teach for transfer.
Warm-up: *flash-card drill*	2 minutes	✓ Calvin's "mastered words" cards	*NA*

ACTIVITY 1: phonics/spelling
✓ *Teach ending rule for –ing.*
✓ *Word-building activity*
  – Calvin builds words with –ing.
  – Calvin writes words, doubling the consonant or dropping the silent e.
  – Calvin reads words quickly and correctly.
  – Add mastered words to "mastered words" pile.
	7 minutes	✓ Word cards (+ -ing card)
		✓ Worksheet for writing words
			If needed, increase explicit instruction and more specific, corrective feedback by providing additional modeling and guided practice with immediate feedback for each step of word building. Scaffold to independence.

ACTIVITY 2: vocabulary and fluency building ✓ Preteach vocabulary: enormous, nasty, jiffy. Have Calvin use each word in a sentence. ✓ Model reading the passage. ✓ Calvin reads three times, colors rocket chart when he beats his first or second time.	10 minutes	✓ Passage from James and the Giant Peach by Dahl ✓ Timer ✓ Rocket chart and markers	Provide additional opportunities for responding, practice, and review via partner reading.

INTEGRATED PRACTICE: writing a story (complete over 2 days if needed)
✓ Have Calvin plan out a story that includes key vocabulary practiced earlier. Use a story map to plan story elements.
✓ Have Calvin write his story using a story map.
✓ Have Calvin check and revise work:
  – Every sentence capitalized/punctuated
  – Every sentence has subject and verb
  – Every sentence makes sense
✓ Have Calvin read story aloud to a partner.
	15–20 minutes	✓ Blank story map
		✓ Paper and pencil
			Provide a cognitive strategy by working with Calvin to make up a mnemonic to remember the five sentence components (capitalized, punctuated, subject, verb, makes sense).

Each session: closing Lesson wrap-up—Calvin reflects: What is he proud of? What will he keep working on?	<1 minute	NA	NA
Once per week: progress monitoring ☑ Administer a progress monitoring prompt to student. ☑ Score and graph as soon as possible after lesson.	5 minutes	✓ Prompt grade 4 oral reading fluency ✓ Timer	
Reflection What went well? What could I do to improve? What do I need to reteach? Do I need to regroup? Other reflections:			

FIGURE 8.2. Calvin's basic instructional plan.

157

systematic; (2) increasing the frequency of opportunities for student responding, practice, and review; (3) providing specific and corrective feedback; (4) embedding cognitive processes; and (5) teaching for transfer to other contexts. We recommend that teachers select from these options based on hypotheses that they generate based on student progress monitoring data (described in more detail in the next section).

Progress Monitoring

It's important to explicitly plan for progress monitoring, as progress monitoring is an essential element of intensifying intervention and evaluating whether the hypotheses and possible intervention solutions are effective for the individual student. Progress monitoring should be done on a frequent (e.g., weekly) and routine (e.g., every Wednesday at 10:00 A.M.) basis, so that it is a seamless part of instruction. For some students, it might work best to administer progress monitoring tasks at the beginning of the lesson, whereas others might do better with progress monitoring saved for the end. Additionally, for some students, the teacher might administer progress monitoring in multiple areas. In Laura's case, Mrs. R will monitor progress in terms of phonological awareness, phonics, and spelling, and she will use a rubric to keep track of the number of inferential and other question types that Laura can answer correctly. She will also ask for input from Ms. SLP. In Calvin's case, the example lesson specifies oral reading, but on another day, he also completes progress monitoring in writing using story prompts.

Other Considerations

Whereas Laura's and Calvin's instructional plans are quite comprehensive, there might be times when a focus on a smaller set of skills is warranted for a limited period of time. A student like Laura or Calvin may be so far behind that, for a period of time, the teacher might focus on certain components, such as building basic skills in phonics and sight-word reading, so that the student can read well enough to participate in a multicomponent intervention. For example, in a recent case study (Al Otaiba, Jones, Levy, Rivas, & Wanzek, 2019), we described two fourth-grade students whose decoding skills were so weak (they had not yet mastered all short vowel patterns) that they could not read connected text in a commercially available multicomponent intervention. Initially, this intervention provided word study with application to text reading, but over time the emphasis shifted to relatively more comprehension and vocabulary instruction. To address their individual needs, with consultation from their teacher, Al Otaiba, Jones, and colleagues developed a different instructional plan that focused on intensive decoding and sight-word instruction, and also included fluency instruction at their word-reading level. This plan was still multicomponent in that it addressed multiple skills, but was narrower in its focus, to allow the student to build sufficient word-level skills necessary to engage in comprehension and vocabulary instruction more successfully. The ultimate goal was to help the students accelerate their growth on basic skills, so that they could access grade-level multicomponent instruction.

HOW DO I USE DATA TO INTENSIFY INSTRUCTION?

Critical to intensifying instruction in ways that effectively and efficiently accelerate student learning is using progress monitoring data in a data-based individualization framework, an idea introduced in Chapter 1. To illustrate this process, let's consider Calvin's basic instructional plan in the context of his progress monitoring. First, Calvin was identified as in need of intensive reading instruction, and Ms. K and Calvin's IEP team used existing reading assessment data to determine his areas of specific need, write his objectives, and develop his basic instructional plan. Next, before starting to implement this plan, Ms. K administered three CBM oral reading prompts to determine his current level of performance. She scored the prompts and determined the median (middle) score, a way of ensuring a stable and reliable estimate of current performance. Calvin's median score was 40 words read correctly in 1 minute. She plotted this baseline score on a graph (see the first data point on the graph in Figure 8.3 [the same as Figure 1.2, introduced in Chapter 1]), and then determined a long-term goal for Calvin, using district benchmark data. Because Calvin was currently performing at the 10th percentile in terms of oral reading fluency, Ms. K thought it would be both reasonable and ambitious to move him up to the 25th percentile by the end of the school year. Benchmarking data indicated that, to score at the 25th percentile by the end of the school year, Calvin would need to read 98 words correctly in 1 minute. In other words, he would need to increase his oral reading fluency score by approximately 1.61 words read correctly each week to meet the long-term goal. Ms. K plotted the goal on the graph (indicated by a star in Figure 8.3), and drew a line between Calvin's baseline score and his goal. This line would serve as Calvin's "goal line."

Next, Ms. K began to implement Calvin's basic instructional plan (the panel labeled "Basic Instructional Plan" in Figure 8.3), monitoring his progress each week and charting his weekly data on his graph. Doing so would allow her to see whether he was on track to meet his goal, or whether he needed an instructional change. She monitored his progress for 8 weeks—enough time to observe a stable and reliable trend line (to show Calvin's actual rate of progress; e.g., Ardoin, Christ, Morena, Cormier, & Klingbeil, 2013). As shown on the graph, Calvin made good progress at first, but started to level off after a few weeks. Ms. K considered the following decision rules to determine whether and when to make an instructional change:

- If the student's trend line is even with the goal line, keep instruction as is.
- If the student's trend line is above the goal line, raise the goal.
- If the student's trend line is below the goal line, make an instructional change.

Because it was clear after 8 weeks that Calvin's trend line was below the goal line, Ms. K decided to make a change in order to intensify his instruction. To do so, she generated hypotheses about what would be beneficial for Calvin. Using the intensification elements on the instructional plan, she thought about whether he might need a change in dosage or group size, or an instructional delivery change, such as increasing the explicitness of instruction or opportunities to respond. She noticed that, while Calvin

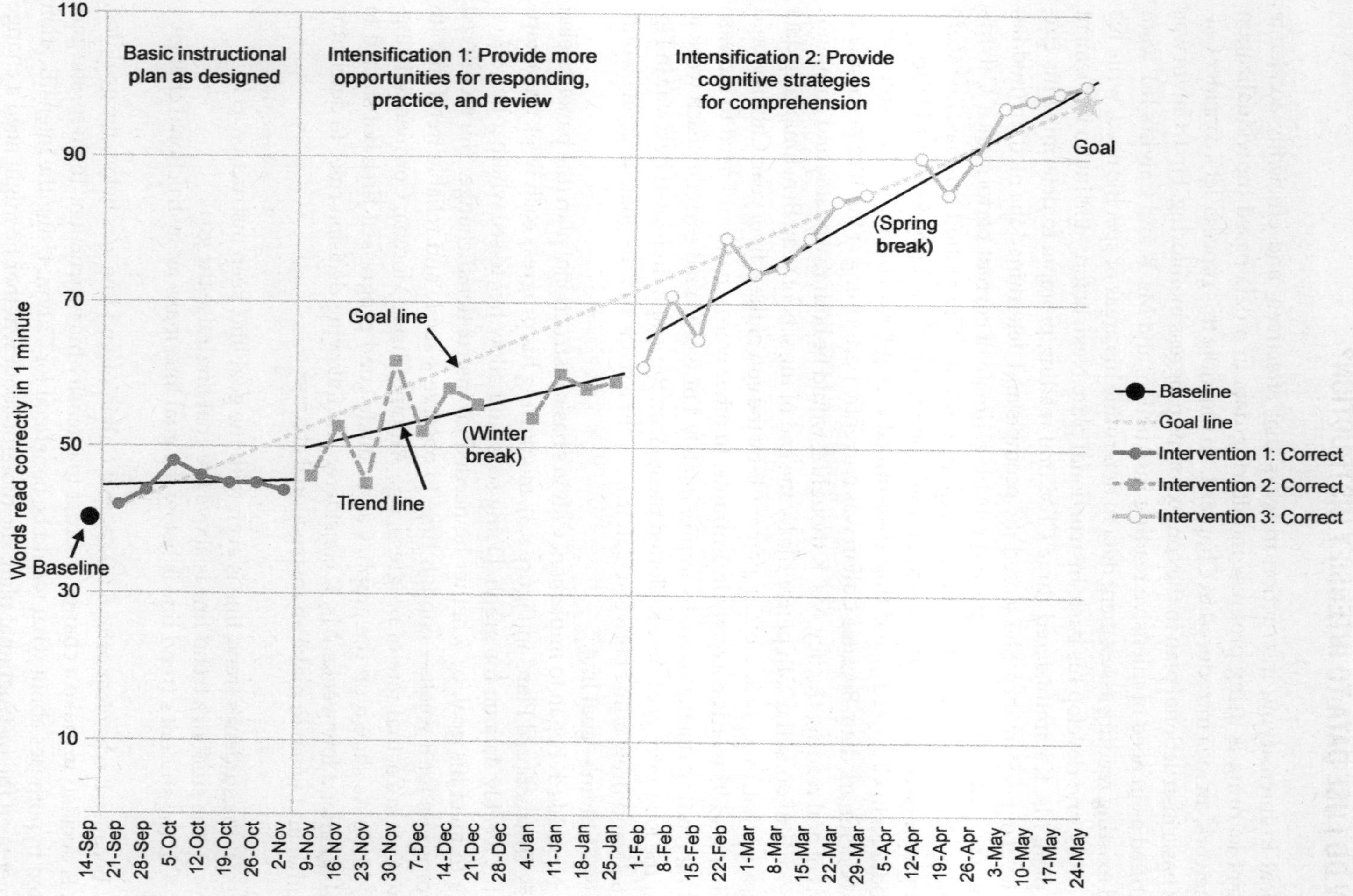

FIGURE 8.3. Calvin's progress monitoring graph.

160

seemed to be mastering the phonics and spelling skills covered in Activity 1 of his plan, this mastery was not translating into fluent reading during Activity 2. She hypothesized that he might benefit from more frequent opportunities for response and practice in fluency, but he seemed reluctant to practice reading with her one-on-one. Because she also knew that Calvin enjoyed interacting with peers and tended to be more engaged when his peers were around, she decided to have him practice reading with a peer during the fluency-building component of his lesson.

Having selected this instructional change, Ms. K inserted a vertical line on Calvin's graph to show that she was implementing a new intervention, and labeled it "Intensification 1." She then introduced the change to Calvin, and continued to monitor his progress. She repeated the whole process of examining Calvin's data, using decision rules to determine whether the intervention was effective. In late January, it again became clear that Calvin's progress was not sufficient to meet his goal, so again Ms. K generated hypotheses about what to change. She noticed that he was having trouble remembering the elements of a story map when applying this approach to different texts, so she decided to teach a cognitive strategy, using a mnemonic to help him with this task. Again, she noted "Intensification 2" on his graph, and continued monitoring his progress. By late spring, it was clear that Calvin was finally on track to meet his goal!

FIDELITY VERSUS FLEXIBILITY

Throughout this book, we have emphasized implementing *intensive* instruction in reading for children with the most significant learning needs—that is, those students with the most severe reading difficulties who have not made adequate progress in standard reading interventions. We have also given suggestions for ways to further intensify instructional activities provided in each chapter. Here, we emphasize the need to balance fidelity of implementation of research-based practices with flexibility in modifying those practices to meet individual student needs.

Intervention researchers and educational administrators often emphasize the importance of implementing interventions with *fidelity*—that is, interventions should be implemented as they were designed, by following the manual, protocol, or training provided by the developers. Fidelity is critical, because if an intervention is not implemented the way it was designed, it is difficult to determine whether a student is not making progress because the intervention is not effective for that student, or because it was not implemented properly. Thus, a first step in delivering intensive intervention is to ensure that it is implemented as designed. The educator can ask the following self-questions to determine whether the intervention was implemented with fidelity:

- "Did I implement the intervention as it was intended—for example, did I follow the manual or script provided by the developers?"
- "Did I implement all of the components?"
- "Did I incorporate all of the materials prescribed by the developer?"
- "Did I implement the intervention for the amount of time prescribed by the

developer (including the duration of each session, the number of sessions per week, and the total number of sessions)? Was the student present for the majority of the sessions?"

If the answer to any of the above questions is "No," we encourage correcting that aspect of implementation before determining that a modification is needed.

On the other hand, children with intensive learning needs are often those for whom even the strongest research-based approaches are not sufficient—thus, they need something more individualized. If an intervention has been implemented with fidelity and a child hasn't responded, the educator might hypothesize that a specific modification is needed to make that intervention more effective. We have discussed many such modifications throughout this book. Yet an important question arises: How can (or should) a teacher balance the importance of fidelity with the need to make modifications for students with intensive needs?

Researchers have studied this question (e.g., Johnson & McMaster, 2013; McMaster, Jung, et al., 2014) and have identified some important considerations. First, as much as possible, the teacher should attempt to retain the *core elements* of the intervention. Core elements are those features that are key to the intervention's effectiveness; other noncore elements might be helpful but not necessary for a child to benefit from that intervention. It is up to researchers to articulate what the core elements are—these might be found in the introductory material in intervention manuals, highlighted in research articles about the intervention, or presented during professional development sessions. If not, the teacher might be able to ascertain the core elements by examining which features appear to be most prevalent throughout the intervention. These features might include a specific scope and sequence, presentation format, or instructional routine—features that often have general support in the research (e.g., explicit instruction with modeling, guided practice with scaffolding, and immediate corrective feedback). Therefore, in modifying a research-based intervention, the teacher might consider the following: "What are the core elements, should they be retained, and if so, how can I retain them while modifying other, noncore elements?"

After identifying core elements and considering whether and how to retain them as part of the intervention, the teacher should articulate clearly the aspects that are going to be modified. In doing so, the teacher should justify the modification, using progress monitoring data that indicate the need for an intervention change, along with any other diagnostic data that informed the teacher's hypothesis for how the intervention should be intensified. The teacher should describe the following: "What is the modification, and why am I making it?"

Finally, after clearly articulating the modification and its rationale, the teacher should define what the modification looks like, such that an observer would be able to judge whether the modification is being implemented as intended. This way, if the student continues to struggle, it will not be because the modification was not actually carried out as designed. The teacher should be able to answer this question: "Did I implement the modification with fidelity?"

When an instructional intervention is intensified with a well-justified modification that preserves core intervention elements (to the extent possible) and is delivered with fidelity, then it is possible to examine ongoing progress monitoring data and answer the following question: "Is the modified, intensified intervention effective for this student?" If the student is now making progress in line with his or her goal, then it is safe to assume that the answer is "Yes." If the student continues to make insufficient progress, then the answer is likely "No," and further hypothesis testing and modification is needed. By following this process, the teacher can determine systematically how to optimize the effectiveness of an intervention for an individual student—maintaining fidelity to core elements and to well-justified modifications, while at the same time introducing flexibility to adapt the intervention to a specific student's needs.

PROFESSIONAL LEARNING COMMUNITIES AND RESOURCES

As you finish reading our book, we hope that you will continue on a path toward learning more about intensive interventions. We also hope that you might feel empowered to reach out to other educator colleagues and share the information you have learned. Thus, it seems appropriate to highlight the resources across the chapters, particularly those that are web based and are updated in an ongoing fashion. For example, the practice guides from the Institute of Education Sciences might provide teachers with more reliable guidance for instructional planning than Pinterest. In addition, the professional learning community guides, developed by some of the Regional Educational Laboratories, provide very helpful materials for self-study, and also provide professional development to other educators. The PowerPoint slides, videos, and other materials provide a wealth of information for preservice and inservice teachers. We hope you find these resources useful as you intensify instruction to accelerate learning for students with the most significant reading needs.

References

Adams, A., & Gathercole, S. (1995). Phonological working memory and speech production in preschool children. *Journal of Speech and Hearing Research, 38,* 403–414.

Al Otaiba, S., Connor, C. M., & Crowe, E. (2018). Promise and feasibility of teaching expository text structure: A primary grade pilot study. *Reading and Writing, 31*(9), 1997–2015.

Al Otaiba, S., & Fuchs, D. (2002). Characteristics of children who are unresponsive to early literacy intervention: A review of the literature. *Remedial and Special Education, 23,* 300–316.

Al Otaiba, S., Jones, F., Levy, D., Rivas, B., & Wanzek, J. (2019). Building a growth mindset within data-based individualization: A case study of two students with reading disabilities learning to learn. In P. C. Pullen & M. J. Kennedy (Eds.), *Handbook of response to intervention and multi-tiered systems of support* (pp. 249–268). New York: Routledge.

Al Otaiba, S., Lake, V. E., Greulich, L., & Folsom, J. S. (2012). Preparing beginning reading teachers: An experimental comparison of initial early literacy field experiences. *Reading and Writing, 25,* 109–129.

Al Otaiba, S., Puranik, C., Ziolkowski, R., & Curran, T. (2009). Effectiveness of early phonological awareness interventions for students with speech or language impairments. *Journal of Special Education, 43,* 107–128.

Apel, K., Brimo, D., Diehm, E., & Apel, L. (2013). Morphological awareness intervention with kindergartners and first- and second-grade students from low socioeconomic status homes: A feasibility study. *Language, Speech, and Hearing Services in Schools, 44,* 161–173.

Apel, K., & Diehm, E. (2014). Morphological awareness intervention with kindergarteners and first and second grade students from low SES homes: A small efficacy study. *Journal of Learning Disabilities, 47,* 65–75.

Archer, A. L., Gleason, M. M., & Vachon, V. L. (2003). Decoding and fluency: Foundation skills for struggling older readers. *Learning Disability Quarterly, 26,* 89–101.

Ardoin, S. P., Christ, T. J., Morena, L. S., Cormier, D. C., & Klingbeil, D. A. (2013). A systematic review and summarization of the recommendations and research surrounding curriculum-based measurement of oral reading fluency (CBM-R) decision rules. *Journal of School Psychology, 51,* 1–18.

Arnold, D. H., Lonigan, C. J., Whitehurst, G. J., & Epstein, J. N. (1994). Accelerating language development through picture book reading: Replication and extension to a videotape training format. *Journal of Educational Psychology, 86*, 235–243.

Baker, S. K., Chard, D. J., Ketterlin-Geller, L. R., Apichatabutra, C., & Doabler, C. (2009). Teaching writing to at-risk students: The quality of evidence for self-regulated strategy development. *Exceptional Children, 75*, 303–318.

Baker, S. K., Santoro, L. E., Chard, D. J., Fien, H., Park, Y., & Otterstedt, J. (2013). An evaluation of an explicit read aloud intervention taught in whole-classroom formats in first grade. *Elementary School Journal, 113*(3), 331–358.

Beck, I. L., McKeown, M., & Kucan, L. (2002). Choosing words to teach. In *Bringing words to life: Robust vocabulary instruction* (pp. 15–30). New York: Guilford Press.

Berkeley, S., Scruggs, T., & Mastropieri, M. (2010). Reading comprehension instruction for students with learning disabilities, 1995–2006: A meta-analysis. *Remedial and Special Education, 31*, 423–436.

Berninger, V. (2009). Highlights of programmatic, interdisciplinary research on writing. *Learning Disabilities Research and Practice, 24*, 69–80.

Berninger, V. W., & Amtmann, D. (2003). Preventing written expression disabilities through early and continuing assessment and intervention for handwriting and/or spelling problems: Research into practice. In H. L. Swanson, K. R. Harris, & S. Graham (Eds.), *Handbook of learning disabilities* (pp. 345–363). New York: Guilford Press.

Berninger, V. W., Nielsen, K. H., Abbott, R. D., Wijsman, E., & Raskind, W. (2008). Writing problems in developmental dyslexia: Under-recognized and under-treated. *Journal of School Psychology, 46*(1), 1–21.

Bhattacharya, A., & Ehri, L. C. (2004). Graphosyllabic analysis helps adolescent struggling readers read and spell words. *Journal of Learning Disabilities, 37*, 313–348.

Biancarosa, C., & Snow, C. E. (2004). *Reading next: A vision for action and research in middle and high school literacy: A report to Carnegie Corporation of New York.* Washington, DC: Alliance for Excellent Education.

Biemiller, A. (1999). *Language and reading success.* Cambridge, MA: Brookline Books.

Blachman, B. A. (2013). *Foundations of reading acquisition and dyslexia: Implications for early intervention.* New York: Routledge.

Bloom, L., & Lahey, M. (1978). *Language development and language disorders.* New York: Wiley.

Bowers, P. N., Kirby, J. R., & Deacon, S. H. (2010). The effects of morphological instruction on literacy skills: A systematic review of the literature. *Review of Educational Research, 80*, 144–179.

Branum-Martin, L., Tao, S., Garnaat, S., Bunta, F., & Francis, D. (2012). Meta-analysis of bilingual phonological awareness: Language, age, and psycholinguistic grain size. *Journal of Educational Psychology, 104*, 932–944.

Brown, A. L. (1978). Knowing when, where, and how to remember: A problem of metacognition. In R. Glaser (Ed.), *Advances in instructional psychology* (Vol. 1, pp. 77–165). Hillsdale, NJ: Erlbaum.

Cain, K., & Oakhill, J. (Eds.). (2007). *Children's comprehension problems in oral and written language: A cognitive perspective.* New York: Guilford Press.

Carlisle, J. F. (1988). Knowledge of derivational morphology and spelling ability in fourth, sixth, and eighth graders. *Applied Psycholinguistics, 9*, 247–266.

Carlisle, J. F. (1995). Morphological awareness and early reading achievement. In L. B. Feldman (Ed.), *Morphological aspects of language processing* (pp. 189–209). Hillsdale, NJ: Erlbaum.

Carnine, D. W., Silbert, J., Kame'enui, E. J., & Tarver, S. G. (2004). *Direct instruction in reading* (4th ed.). Upper Saddle River, NJ: Pearson-Prentice Hall.

Catts, H. (1989). Defining dyslexia as a developmental language disorder. *Annals of Dyslexia, 39,* 50–64.

Catts, H. (1991). Early identification of reading disabilities. *Topics in Language Disorders, 12,* 1–16.

Catts, H. W., & Hogan, T. P. (2003). Language basis of reading disabilities and implications for early identification and remediation. *Reading Psychology, 24*(3–4), 223–246.

Catts, H. W., Hogan, T. P., & Adlof, S. M. (2005). Developmental changes in reading and reading disabilities. In H. W. Catts & A. G. Kamhi (Eds.), *The connections between language and reading disabilities* (pp. 24–38). Mahwah, NJ: Erlbaum.

Chard, D. J., & Dickson, S. V. (1999). Phonological awareness: Instructional and assessment guidelines. *Intervention in School and Clinic, 34*(5), 261–270.

Chard, D. J., Vaughn, S., & Tyler, B. J. (2002). A synthesis on effective interventions for building reading fluency with elementary students with learning disabilities. *Journal of Learning Disabilities, 35,* 386–406.

Compton, D. L., Miller, A. C., Elleman, A. M., & Steacy, L. M. (2014). Have we forsaken reading theory in the name of "quick fix" interventions for children with reading disability? *Scientific Studies of Reading, 18,* 55–73.

Connor, C. M., Alberto, P. A., Compton, D. L., & O'Connor, R. E. (2014). *Improving reading outcomes for students with or at risk for reading disabilities: A synthesis of the contributions from the Institute of Education Sciences Research Centers* (NCSER 2014-3000). Washington, DC: National Center for Special Education Research, Institute of Education Sciences, U.S. Department of Education.

Conte, K., & Hintze, J. (2000). The effects of performance feedback and goal setting on oral reading fluency within curriculum-based measurement. *Assessment for Effective Intervention, 25,* 85–98.

Coyne, M., McCoach, D., & Kapp, S. (2007). Vocabulary intervention for kindergarten students: Comparing extended instruction to embedded instruction and incidental exposure. *Learning Disability Quarterly, 30,* 74–88.

Craig, H. K., Connor, C. M., & Washington, J. A. (2003). Early positive predictors of later reading comprehension for African American students: A preliminary investigation. *Language, Speech, and Hearing Services in Schools, 34*(1), 31–43.

Cunningham, A. E., & Stanovich, K. E. (1998). The impact of print exposure on word recognition. In J. L. Metsala & L. C. Ehri (Eds.), *Word recognition in beginning literacy* (pp. 235–262). Mahwah, NJ: Erlbaum.

Dale, P. S., Crain-Thoreson, C., Notari-Syverson, A., & Cole, K. (1996). Parent–child book reading as an intervention technique for young children with language delays. *Topics in Early Childhood Special Education, 16,* 213–235.

Datchuk, S., & Kubina, R. (2012). A review of teaching sentence-level writing skills to students with writing difficulties and learning disabilities. *Remedial and Special Education, 34,* 180–192.

Deno, S. L. (1985). Curriculum-based measurement: The emerging alternative. *Exceptional Children, 52,* 219–232.

Denton, C. A., Fletcher, J. M., Anthony, J. L., & Francis, D. J. (2006). An evaluation of intensive intervention for students with persistent reading difficulties. *Journal of Learning Disabilities, 39,* 447–466.

Diliberto, J. A., Beattie, J. R., Flowers, C. P., & Algozzine, R. F. (2008). Effects of teaching syllable skills instruction on reading achievement in struggling middle school readers. *Literacy Research and Instruction, 48*(1), 14–27.

Dolch Word List. (n.d.). Retrieved April 27, 2018, from *www.k12reader.com/dolch/dolch_combined_by_frequency.pdf.*

Eden, G., Jones, K., Cappell, K., Gareau, L., Wood, F., Zeffiro, T., et al. (2004). Neural changes following remediation in adult developmental dyslexia. *Neuron, 44*, 411–422.

Ehri, L. C. (1995). Phases of development in learning to read words by sight. *Journal of Research in Reading, 18*, 116–125.

Ehri, L. (2000). Learning to read and learning to spell: Two sides of a coin. *Topics in Language Disorders, 20*, 19–36.

Ehri, L. (2002). Phases of acquisition in learning to read words and implication for teaching. *British Journal of Educational Psychology: Monograph Series, 1*, 7–28.

Ehri, L. C., Nunes, S. R., Willows, D. M., Schuster, B. V., Yaghoub Zadeh, Z., & Shanahan, T. (2001). Phonemic awareness instruction helps children learn to read: Evidence from the National Reading Panel's meta-analysis. *Reading Research Quarterly, 36*(3), 250–287.

Elkonin, D. (1971). Development of speech. In A. V. Zaporozhets & D. B. Elkonin (Eds.), *The psychology of preschool children* (pp. 111–185). Cambridge, MA: MIT Press.

Fang, Z. (2012). Approaches to developing content area literacies: A synthesis and a critique. *Journal of Adolescent and Adult Literacy, 56*, 103–108.

Fletcher, J. M., Lyon, G. R., Fuchs, L. S., & Barnes, M. A. (2007). *Learning disabilities: From identification to intervention.* New York: Guilford Press.

Flynn, K. S. (2011). Developing children's oral language skills through dialogic reading: Guidelines for implementation. *Teaching Exceptional Children, 44*(2), 8–16

Foorman, B., Beyler, N., Borradaile, K., Coyne, M., Denton, C. A., Dimino, J., et al. (2016). *Foundational skills to support reading for understanding in kindergarten through 3rd grade* (NCEE 2016-4008). Washington, DC: National Center for Education Evaluation and Regional Assistance, Institute of Education Sciences, U.S. Department of Education.

Foorman, B. R., Francis, D. J., Fletcher, J. M., Schatschneider, C., & Mehta, P. (1998). The role of instruction in learning to read: Preventing reading failure in at-risk children. *Journal of Educational Psychology, 90*, 37–55.

Fowler, A. E., & Liberman, I. Y. (1995). The role of phonology and orthography in morphological awareness. In L. B. Feldman (Ed.), *Morphological aspects of language processing* (pp. 157–188). Hillsdale, NJ: Erlbaum.

Francis, D. J., Shaywitz, S. E., Stuebing, K. K., Shaywitz, B. A., & Fletcher, J. M. (1996). Developmental lag versus deficit models of reading disability: A longitudinal, individual growth curves analysis. *Journal of Educational Psychology, 88*, 3–17.

Fry, E., & Kress, J. E. (2006). *The reading teacher's book of lists* (5th ed.). San Francisco: Jossey-Bass.

Fuchs, D., & Fuchs, L. S. (2005). Peer-assisted learning strategies: Promoting word recognition, fluency, and reading comprehension in young children. *Journal of Special Education, 39*, 34–44.

Fuchs, L. S., Fuchs, D., Hamlett, C. L., & Allinder, R. M. (1991). The contribution of skills analysis to curriculum-based measurement in spelling. *Exceptional Children, 57*, 443–452.

Fuchs, L. S., Fuchs, D., & Malone, A. S. (2017). The taxonomy of intervention intensity. *Teaching Exceptional Children, 50*, 35–43.

Fuchs, L. S., Fuchs, D., Mathes, P., & Simmons, D. (1997). Peer-assisted learning strategies: Making classrooms more responsive to diversity. *American Educational Research Journal, 34*, 174–206.

Gersten, R., Compton, D., Connor, C. M., Dimino, J., Santoro, L., Linan-Thompson, S., et al. (2008). *Assisting students struggling with reading: Response to intervention and multi-tier intervention for reading in the primary grades: A practice guide* (NCEE 2009-4045). Washington, DC: National Center for Education Evaluation and Regional Assistance, Institute of Education Sciences, U.S. Department of Education.

Gersten, R., Fuchs, L., Williams, J., & Baker, S. (2001). Teaching reading comprehension strategies to students with learning disabilities: A review of research. *Review of Educational Research, 71,* 279–320.

Good, R. H., Simmons, D., & Kame'enui, E. J. (2001). The importance and decision-making utility of a continuum of fluency-based indicators of foundational reading skills for third-grade high-stakes outcomes. *Scientific Studies of Reading, 5,* 257–288.

Goodwin, A., & Ahn, S. (2013). A meta-analysis of morphological interventions in English: Effects on literacy outcomes for school-age children. *Scientific Studies of Reading, 17,* 257–285.

Gough, P. B., & Tunmer, W. (1986). Decoding, reading, and reading disability. *Remedial and Special Education, 7,* 6–10.

Graham, S., Bollinger, A., Booth Olson, C., D'Aoust, C., MacArthur, C., McCutchen, D., et al. (2012). *Teaching elementary school students to be effective writers: A practice guide* (NCEE 2012-4058). Washington, DC: National Center for Education Evaluation and Regional Assistance, Institute of Education Sciences, U.S. Department of Education. Retrieved from *http://ies.ed.gov/ncee/wwc/publications_reviews.aspx#pubsearch.*

Graham, S., & Harris, K. R. (1996). Self-regulation and strategy instruction for students who find writing and learning challenging. In C. M. Levy & S. Ransdell (Eds.), *The science of writing: Theories, methods, individual differences, and applications* (pp. 347–360). New York: Routledge.

Graham, S., Harris, K. R., & Chorzempa, B. F. (2002). Contribution of spelling instruction to the spelling, writing, and reading of poor spellers. *Journal of Educational Psychology, 94,* 669–686.

Graham, S., Harris, K. R., & Fink, B. (2000). Extra handwriting instruction: Prevent writing difficulties right from the start. *Teaching Exceptional Children, 33*(2), 88–91.

Graham, S., & Hebert, M. A. (2010). *Writing to read: Evidence for how writing can improve reading* (Carnegie Corporation Time to Act Report). Washington, DC: Alliance for Excellent Education.

Graham, S., & Hebert, M. (2011). Writing to read: A meta-analysis of the impact of writing and writing instruction on reading. *Harvard Educational Review, 81,* 710–744.

Graham, S., McKeown, D., Kiuhara, S., & Harris, K. R. (2012). A meta-analysis of writing instruction for students in the elementary grades. *Journal of Educational Psychology, 104,* 879–896.

Graham, S., & Perin, D. (2007). *Writing next: Effective strategies to improve writing of adolescents in middle and high schools: A report to Carnegie Corporation of New York.* Washington, DC: Alliance for Excellent Education.

Graves, M. F., & Silverman, R. (2011). Interventions to enhance vocabulary development. In A. McGill Franzen & R. Allington (Eds.), *Handbook of reading disability research* (pp. 315–328). New York: Routledge.

Hampton, D. D., & Lembke, E. S. (2016). Examining the technical adequacy of progress monitoring using early writing curriculum-based measures. *Reading and Writing Quarterly, 32,* 336–352.

Harris, K. R., Graham, S., Mason, L. H., & Friedlander, B. (2008). *Powerful writing strategies for all students.* Baltimore: Brookes.

Hart, B., & Risley, T. (1995). *Meaningful differences in the everyday experience of young American children.* Baltimore: Brookes.

Hart, B., & Risley, T. (2003). The early catastrophe: The 30 million word gap by age 3. *American Educator, 27,* 4–9.

Hasbrouck, J. E., Ihnot, C., & Rogers, G. H. (1999). "Read naturally": A strategy to increase oral reading fluency. *Reading Research and Instruction, 39,* 27–38.

Hasbrouck, J., & Tindal, G. (2017). *An update to compiled ORF norms* (Technical Report No. 1702). Eugene: Behavioral Research and Teaching, University of Oregon.

Hattie, J., & Timperley, H. (2007). The power of feedback. *Review of Educational Research, 77,* 81–112.

Hong, G., & Hong, Y. (2009). Reading instruction time and homogeneous grouping in kindergarten: An application of marginal mean weighting through stratification. *Educational Evaluation and Policy Analysis, 31,* 54–81.

Hoover, W. A., & Gough, P. B. (1990). The simple view of reading. *Reading and Writing, 2,* 127–160.

Hosp, M. K., Hosp, J. L., & Howell, K. W. (2016). *The ABCs of CBM: A practical guide to curriculum-based measurement* (2nd ed.). New York: Guilford Press.

Jacob, R., & Parkinson, J. (2015). The potential for school-based interventions that target executive function to improve academic achievement: A review. *Review of Educational Research, 85,* 512–552.

Johnson, L. D., & McMaster, K. L. (2013). Adapting research-based practices with fidelity: Flexibility by design. In B. G. Cook, M. Tankersley, & T. J. Landrum (Eds.), *Advances in learning and behavioral disabilities: Evidence-based practices* (Vol. 26, pp. 65–91). Bingley, UK: Emerald.

Johnston, T. C., & Kirby, J. R. (2006). The contribution of naming speed to the simple view of reading. *Reading and Writing, 19,* 339–361.

Joseph, L. M. (2000). Using word boxes as a large group phonics approach in a first grade classroom. *Reading Horizons, 41,* 117–127.

Joshi, R. M., & Aaron, P. G. (2000). The component model of reading: Simple view of reading made a little more complex. *Reading Psychology, 21,* 85–97.

Justice, L., & Ezell, H. (2008). *The syntax handbook.* Austin, TX: PRO-ED.

Kamhi, A. G., & Catts, H. W. (Eds.). (2012). *Language and reading disabilities.* Boston: Pearson.

Kendeou, P., McMaster, K. L., & Christ, T. J. (2016). Reading comprehension: Core components and processes. *Policy Insights from the Behavioral and Brain Sciences, 3,* 62–69.

Kendeou, P., van den Broek, P., Helder, A., & Karlsson, J. (2014). A cognitive view of reading comprehension: Implications for reading difficulties. *Learning Disabilities Research and Practice, 29*(1), 10–16.

Kim, W., Linan-Thompson, S., & Misquitta, R. (2012). Critical factors in reading comprehension instruction for students with learning disabilities: A research synthesis. *Learning Disabilities Research and Practice, 27,* 66–78.

Kim, Y.-S., Petscher, Y., Schatschneider, C., & Foorman, B. (2010). Does growth rate in oral reading fluency matter in predicting reading comprehension achievement? *Journal of Educational Psychology, 102*(3), 652–667.

Kim, Y.-S., & Wagner, R. K. (2015). Text (oral) reading fluency as a construct in reading development: An investigation of its mediating role for children from grades 1 to 4. *Scientific Studies of Reading, 19*(3), 224–242.

Kintsch, W. (1988). The role of knowledge in discourse comprehension: A construction-integration model. *Psychological Review, 95,* 163–182.

Klauda, S., & Guthrie, J. (2008). Relationships of three components of reading fluency to reading comprehension. *Journal of Educational Psychology, 100,* 310–321.

Klingner, J., & Vaughn, S. (1999). Promoting reading comprehension, content learning, and English acquisition though collaborative strategic reading (CSR). *The Reading Teacher, 52,* 738–747.

Lam, E. A., & McMaster, K. L. (2014). Predictors of responsiveness to early literacy intervention: A ten-year update. *Learning Disabilities Quarterly, 37,* 134–147.

Leach, J. M., Scarborough, H. S., & Rescorla, L. (2003). Late-emerging reading disabilities. *Journal of Educational Psychology, 95*(2), 211–224.

Lembke, E., Carlisle, A., & Poch, A. (2015, June 1). *Technical report 1 for the DBI-TLC project: Curriculum-based measurement screening study 1.* Minneapolis: University of Minnesota.

Lembke, E., Deno, S. L., & Hall, K. (2003). Identifying an indicator of growth in early writing proficiency for elementary school students. *Assessment for Effective Intervention, 28,* 23–35.

Light, J., & Binger, C. (1998). *Building communicative competence with individuals who use augmentative and alternative communication.* Baltimore: Brookes.

Lou, Y., Abrami, P. C., Spence, J. C., Poulsen, C., Chambers, B., & d'Apollonia, S. (1996). Within-class grouping: A meta-analysis. *Review of Educational Research, 66,* 423–458.

Lovett, M., Steinbach, K., & Frijters, J. (2000). Remediating the core deficits of developmental reading disability: A double-deficit perspective. *Journal of Learning Disabilities, 33,* 334–358.

Mason, L. H. (2004). Explicit self-regulated strategy development versus reciprocal questioning: Effects on expository reading comprehension among struggling readers. *Journal of Educational Psychology, 96,* 283–296.

Matthews, J. S., Kizzie, K. T., Rowley, S. J., & Cortina, K. (2010). African Americans and boys: Understanding the literacy gap, tracing academic trajectories, and evaluating the role of learning-related skills. *Journal of Educational Psychology, 102*(3), 757–771.

McCutchen, D. (2006). Cognitive factors in the development of children's writing. In C. MacArthur, S. Graham, & J. Fitzgerald (Eds.), *Handbook of writing research* (pp. 115–130). New York: Guilford Press.

McMaster, K. L., & Campbell, H. (2008). New and existing curriculum-based writing measures: Technical features within and across grades. *School Psychology Review, 37,* 550–556.

McMaster, K. L., Du, X., & Petursdottir, A. (2009). Technical features of curriculum-based measures for beginning writers. *Journal of Learning Disabilities, 42,* 41–60.

McMaster, K. L., & Espin, C. A. (2017). Reading comprehension instruction and intervention: Promoting inference making. In D. Compton, R. Partial, & K. Cain (Eds.), *Theories of reading development* (pp. 463–488). Amsterdam: John Benjamins.

McMaster, K. L., Espin, C. A., & van den Broek, P. (2014). Making connections: Linking cognitive psychology and intervention research to improve comprehension of struggling readers. *Learning Disabilities Research and Practice, 29*(1), 17–24.

McMaster, K. L., Jung, P.-G., Brandes, D., Pinto, V., Fuchs, D., Kearns, D., et al. (2014). Customizing an evidence-based reading practice: Balancing fidelity and flexibility. *The Reading Teacher, 68*(3), 173–183.

McMaster, K. L., Kunkel, A., Shin, J., Jung, P.-G., & Lembke, E. (2017). Early writing intervention: A best evidence synthesis. *Journal of Learning Disabilities, 51*(4), 363–380.

McMaster, K. L., & Lembke, E. (2016). *Data-based instruction in beginning writing: A manual.* Minneapolis: University of Minnesota.

McMaster, K. L., Ritchey, K. D., & Lembke, E. (2011). Curriculum-based measurement of elementary students' writing: Recent developments and future directions. In T. Scruggs & M. A. Mastropieri (Eds.), *Assessment and intervention: Advances in learning and behavioral disabilities* (pp. 111–148). Bingley, UK: Emerald.

McNamara, D., & Kendeou, P. (2011). Translating advances in reading comprehension research to educational practice. *International Electronic Journal of Elementary Education, 4*(1), 33–46.

McNamara, D. S., & Magliano, J. (2009). Toward a comprehensive model of comprehension. *Psychology of Learning and Motivation, 51,* 297–384.

McNamara, J. K., Scissons, M., & Gutknecht, N. (2011). A longitudinal study of kindergarten children at risk for reading disabilities: The poor really are getting poorer. *Journal of Learning Disabilities, 44,* 421–430.

Moats, L. (2010). *Speech to print: Language essentials for teachers* (2nd ed.). Baltimore: Brookes.

Morgan, P. L., Farkas, G., Tufis, P. A., & Sperling, R. A. (2008). Are reading and behavior problems risk factors for each other? *Journal of Learning Disabilities, 41*(5), 417–436.

Morgan, P. L., & Sideridis, G. D. (2006). Contrasting the effectiveness of fluency interventions for students with or at risk for learning disabilities: A multilevel random coefficient modeling meta-analysis. *Learning Disabilities Research and Practice, 21*(4), 191–210.

Mountain, L. (2005). Rooting out meaning: More morphemic analysis for primary pupils. *The Reading Teacher, 58,* 742–749.

National Center for Family Literacy. (2009). *Developing early literacy: Report of the National Early Literacy Panel.* Washington, DC: National Institute for Literacy.

National Reading Panel & National Institute of Child Health and Human Development. (2000). *Report of the National Reading Panel: Teaching children to read: An evidence-based assessment of the scientific research literature on reading and its implications for reading instruction.* Washington, DC: National Institute of Child Health and Human Development, National Institutes of Health.

Nese, J. F., Park, B. J., Alonzo, J., & Tindal, G. (2011). Applied curriculum-based measurement as a predictor of high-stakes assessment. *Elementary School Journal, 111,* 608–624.

Oakhill, J. V., & Cain, K. (2012). The precursors of reading ability in young readers: Evidence from a four-year longitudinal study. *Scientific Studies of Reading, 16,* 91–121.

O'Connor, R. E., Bell, K. M., Harty, K. R., Larkin, L. K., Sackor, S. M., & Zigmond, N. (2002). Teaching reading to poor readers in the intermediate grades: A comparison of text difficulty. *Journal of Educational Psychology, 94,* 474–485.

O'Connor, R. E., & Jenkins, J. R. (2013). Cooperative learning for students with learning disabilities: Advice and caution derived from the evidence. In L. Swanson, K. Harris, & S. Graham (Eds.), *Handbook of learning disabilities* (2nd ed., pp. 507–525). New York: Guilford Press.

O'Connor, R. E., White, A., & Swanson, H. L. (2007). Repeated reading versus continuous reading: Influences on reading fluency and comprehension. *Exceptional Children, 74,* 31–46.

O'Shaughnessy, T. E., & Swanson, H. L. (2000). A comparison of two reading interventions for children with reading disabilities. *Journal of Learning Disabilities, 33,* 257–277.

Palincsar, A. S., & Brown, A. L. (1984). Reciprocal teaching of comprehension-fostering and comprehension-monitoring activities. *Cognition and Instruction, 2,* 117–175.

Parker, D. C., Burns, M. K., McMaster, K. L., & Shapiro, E. S. (2012). Extending curriculum-based assessment to early writing. *Learning Disabilities Research and Practice, 27*(1), 33–43.

Parker, D. C., Dickey, B. N., Burns, M. K., & McMaster, K. L. (2012). An application of brief experimental analysis with early writing. *Journal of Behavioral Education, 21,* 329–349.

Peng, P., & Fuchs, D. (2016). A meta-analysis of working memory deficits in children with learning difficulties: Is there a difference between verbal domain and numerical domain? *Journal of Learning Disabilities, 49,* 3–20.

Perfetti, C. A. (2011). Phonology is critical in reading: But a phonological deficit is not the only source of low reading skill. In S. A. Brady, D. Braze, & C. A. Fowler (Eds.), *Explaining individual differences in reading* (pp. 153–171). New York: Routledge.

Pressley, M., Graham, S., & Harris, K. (2006). The state of educational intervention research as viewed through the lens of literacy intervention. *British Journal of Educational Psychology, 76*(1), 1–19.

RAND Reading Study Group. (2002). *Reading for understanding: Toward an R&D program in reading comprehension.* Santa Monica, CA: RAND Corporation.

Rapp, D. N., & van den Broek, P. (2005). Dynamic text comprehension: An integrative view of reading. *Current Directions in Psychological Science, 14,* 276–279.

Ritchey, K. D., McMaster, L. K., Al Otaiba, S., Puranik, S. C., Grace Kim, Y.-S., Parker, C. D., et al. (2016). Indicators of fluent writing in beginning writers. In D. K. Cummings & Y. Petscher (Eds.), *The fluency construct: Curriculum-based measurement concepts and applications* (pp. 21–66). New York: Springer.

Ritchey, K. D., Silverman, R. D., Montanaro, E. A., Speece, D. L., & Schatschneider, C. (2012). Effects of a tier 2 supplemental reading intervention for at-risk fourth-grade students. *Exceptional Children, 78,* 318–334.

Robertson, J. S. (2000). Is attribution theory a worthwhile classroom intervention for K–12 students with learning difficulties? *Educational Psychology Review, 12,* 111–134.

Saddler, B., Behforooz, B., & Asaro, K. (2008). The effects of sentence-combining instruction on the writing of fourth-grade students with writing difficulties. *Journal of Special Education, 42,* 79–90.

Saddler, B., & Graham, S. (2005). The effects of peer-assisted sentence-combining instruction on the writing performance of more and less skilled young writers. *Journal of Educational Psychology, 97,* 43–54.

Samuels, S. J. (1979). The method of repeated readings. *The Reading Teacher, 32,* 403–408.

Samuels, S. J. (2006). Toward a model of reading fluency. In S. J. Samuels & A. E. Farstrup (Eds.), *What research has to say about fluency instruction* (pp. 24–46). Newark, DE: International Reading Association.

Santoro, L., Chard, D., Howard, L., & Baker, S. (2008). Making the very most of classroom read-alouds to promote comprehension and vocabulary. *The Reading Teacher, 61,* 396–408.

Savage, R. (2006). Reading comprehension is not always the product of nonsense word decoding and linguistic comprehension: Evidence from teenagers who are extremely poor readers. *Scientific Studies of Reading, 10,* 143–164.

Scammacca, N., Roberts, G., Vaughn, S., & Stuebing, K. (2015). A meta-analysis of interventions for struggling readers in grades 4–12: 1980–2011. *Journal of Learning Disabilities, 48,* 369–390.

Schumaker, J. B., & Sheldon, J. B. (2005). *Fundamentals in the sentence writing strategy.* Lawrence, KS: Edge Enterprises.

Schwanenflugel, P. J., Hamilton, A. M., Wisenbaker, J. M., Kuhn, M. R., & Stahl, S. A. (2004). Becoming a fluent reader: Reading skill and prosodic features in the oral reading of young readers. *Journal of Educational Psychology, 96,* 119–129.

Schwanenflugel, P. J., Meisinger, E. B., Wisenbaker, J. M., Kuhn, M. R., Strauss, G. P., & Morris, R. D. (2006). Becoming a fluent and automatic reader in the early elementary school years. *Reading Research Quarterly, 41*(4), 496–522.

Scott, C., & Balthazar, C. (2013). The role of complex sentence knowledge in children with reading and writing difficulties. *Perspectives on Language and Literacy, 39*(3), 18–30.

Shanahan, T. (2004). Overcoming the dominance of communication: Writing to think and to learn. In T. L. Jetton & J. A. Dole (Eds.), *Adolescent literacy research and practice* (pp. 59–73). New York: Guilford Press.

Shin, J., & McMaster, K. L. (2019). *Relations between CBM (oral reading and maze) and reading comprehension on state achievement tests: A meta-analysis.* Journal of School Psychology, 73, 131–149.

Silverman, R. D., Speece, D. L., Harring, J. R., & Ritchey, K. D. (2013). Fluency has a role in the simple view of reading. *Scientific Studies of Reading, 17,* 108–133.

Snider, V. (1995). Primer on phonemic awareness: What it is, why it's important, and how to teach it. *School Psychology Review, 24,* 443–455.

Snowling, M., Duff, F., Nash, H., & Hulme, C. (2016). Language profiles and literacy outcomes of children with resolving, emerging, or persisting language impairments. *Journal of Child Psychology and Psychiatry, 57,* 1360–1369.

Soifer, L. H. (1999). Development of oral language and its relationship to literacy. In J. R. Birsh (Ed.), *Multisensory teaching of basic language skills* (pp. 19–62). Baltimore: Brookes.

Stanovich, K. (1986). Matthew effects in reading: Some consequences of individual differences in the acquisition of literacy. *Reading Research Quarterly, 21,* 360–407.

Stanovich, K. (2009). Matthew effects in reading: Some consequences of individual differences in the acquisition of literacy. *Journal of Education, 189*(1–2), 23–55.

Stecker, P. M., Fuchs, L. S., & Fuchs, D. (2005). Using curriculum-based measurement to improve student achievement: Review of research. *Psychology in the Schools, 42,* 795–819.

Stecker, P. M., Lembke, E., & Foegen, A. (2008). Using progress-monitoring data to improve instructional decision making. *Preventing School Failure, 52*(2), 48–58.

Storch, S., & Whitehurst, G. (2002). Oral language and code-related precursors to reading: Evidence from a longitudinal structural model. *Developmental Psychology, 38,* 934–947.

Swanson, E., Vaughn, S., Wanzek, J., Petscher, Y., Heckert, J., Cavanaugh, C., et al. (2011). A synthesis of read-aloud interventions on early reading outcomes among preschool through third graders at risk for reading difficulties. *Journal of Learning Disabilities, 44,* 258–275.

Swanson, H. L. (2000). What instruction works for students with learning disabilities?: Summarizing the results from a meta-analysis of intervention studies. In R. M. Gersten, E. P. Schiller, & S. Vaughn (Eds.), *Contemporary special education research: Syntheses of the knowledge base on critical instructional issues* (pp. 1–30). Mahwah, NJ: Erlbaum.

Swanson, H. L., Hoskyn, M., & Lee, C. (1999). *Intervention for students with learning disabilities: A meta-analysis of treatment outcomes.* New York: Guilford Press.

Swanson, H. L., & Zheng, X. (2013). Memory difficulties in children and adults with learning disabilities. In H. L. Swanson, K. R. Harris, & S. Graham (Eds.), *Handbook of learning disabilities* (2nd ed., pp. 214–238). New York: Guilford Press.

Swanson, H. L., Zheng, X., & Jerman, O. (2009). Working memory, short-term memory, and reading disabilities: A selective meta-analysis of the literature. *Journal of Learning Disabilities, 42*(3), 260–287.

Terry, N. P., Connor, C. M., Petscher, Y., & Conlin, C. (2012). Dialect variation and reading: Is change in nonmainstream American English use related to reading achievement in first and second grade? *Journal of Speech, Language, and Hearing Research, 55,* 55–69.

Therrien, W. (2004). Fluency and comprehension gains as a result of repeated reading. *Remedial and Special Education, 25,* 252–261.

Torgesen, J. K. (2002). The prevention of reading difficulties. *Journal of School Psychology, 40,* 7–26.

Torgesen, J. K., Alexander, A. W., Wagner, R. K., Rashotte, C. A., Voeller, K. K., & Conway, T. (2001). Intensive remedial instruction for children with severe reading disabilities: Immediate and long-term outcomes from two instructional approaches. *Journal of Learning Disabilities, 34*(1), 33–58, 78.

Torgesen, J. K., Wagner, R. K., Rashotte, C. A., Burgess, S., & Hecht, S. (1997). Contributions of phonological awareness and rapid automatic naming ability to the growth of word-reading skills in second- to fifth-grade children. *Scientific Studies of Reading, 1,* 161–185.

Toste, J. R., Capin, P., Vaughn, S., Roberts, G. J., & Kearns, D. M. (2017). Multisyllabic word-reading instruction with and without motivational beliefs training for struggling readers in the upper elementary grades: A pilot investigation. *Elementary School Journal, 117,* 593–615.

Trabasso, T., Secco, T., & van den Broek, P. W. (1984). Causal cohesion and story coherence. In H. Mandl, N. L. Stein, & T. Trabasso (Eds.), *Learning and comprehension of text* (pp. 83–111). Hillsdale, NJ: Erlbaum.

Uhry, J. (1999). Invented spelling in kindergarten: The relationship with finger-point reading. *Reading and Writing, 11,* 441–464.

Vadasy, P. F., & Sanders, E. A. (2008). Repeated reading intervention: Outcomes and interactions with readers' skills and classroom instruction. *Journal of Educational Psychology, 100,* 272–290.

Vadasy, P. F., & Sanders, E. A. (2009). Supplemental fluency intervention and determinants of reading outcomes. *Scientific Studies of Reading, 13,* 383–425.

Vadasy, P. F., Sanders, E. A., & Peyton, J. A. (2005). Relative effectiveness of reading practice or word-level instruction in supplemental tutoring: How text matters. *Journal of Learning Disabilities, 38,* 364–380.

van den Broek, P. (1994). Comprehension and memory of narrative texts: Inferences and coherence. In M. A. Gernsbacher (Ed.), *Handbook of psycholinguistics* (pp. 539–588). San Diego, CA: Academic Press.

van den Broek, P. W., Helder, A., & Van Leijenhorst, L. (2013). Sensitivity to structural centrality: Developmental and individual differences in reading comprehension skills. In M. A. Britt, S. R. Goldman, & J.-F. Rouet (Eds.), *Reading: From words to multiple texts* (pp. 132–146). New York: Routledge, Taylor & Francis.

van den Broek, P., Rapp, D. N., & Kendeou, P. (2005). Integrating memory-based and constructionist processes in accounts of reading comprehension. *Discourse Processes, 39*(2–3), 299–316.

Vaughn, S., Linan-Thompson, S., & Hickman, P. (2003). Response to instruction as a means of identifying students with reading/learning disabilities. *Exceptional Children, 69,* 391–409.

Vaughn, S., Linan-Thompson, S., Kouzekanani, K., Bryant, D. P., Dickson, S., & Blozis, S. A. (2003). Grouping for reading instruction for students with reading difficulties. *Remedial and Special Education, 24,* 301–315.

Vaughn, S., Wanzek, J., Murray, C. S., & Roberts, G. (2012). *Intensive interventions for students struggling in reading and mathematics: A practice guide.* Portsmouth, NH: RMC Research Corporation, Center on Instruction.

Vellutino, F. R., Fletcher, J. M., Snowling, M. J., & Scanlon, D. M. (2004). Specific reading disability (dyslexia): What have we learned in the past four decades? *Journal of Child Psychology and Psychiatry, 45,* 2–40.

Vellutino, F. R., Scanlon, D. M., Sipay, E. R., Small, S. G., Chen, R., Pratt, A., et al. (1996). Cognitive profiles of difficult-to-remediate and readily remediated poor readers: Early intervention as a vehicle for distinguishing between cognitive and experiential deficits as basic causes of specific reading disability. *Journal of Educational Psychology, 88*(4), 601–638.

Wanzek, J., & Roberts, G. (2012). Reading interventions with varying instructional emphases for fourth graders with reading difficulties. *Learning Disability Quarterly, 35,* 90–101.

Wanzek, J., Stevens, E. A., Williams, K. J., Scammacca, N., Vaughn, S., & Sargent, K. (2018). Current evidence on the effects of intensive early reading interventions. *Journal of Learning Disabilities, 51*(6), 612–624.

Wanzek, J., & Vaughn, S. (2007). Research-based implications from extensive early reading interventions. *School Psychology Review, 36,* 541–561.

Wanzek, J., Wexler, J., Vaughn, S., & Ciullo, S. (2010). Reading interventions for struggling readers in the upper elementary grades: A synthesis of 20 years of research. *Reading and Writing, 23,* 889–912.

Wayman, M., Wallace, T., Wiley, H., Tichá, R., & Espin, C. (2007). Literature synthesis on curriculum-based measurement in reading. *Journal of Special Education, 41,* 85–120.

Whitaker, D., Berninger, V. W., Johnston, J., & Swanson, H. L. (1994). Intraindividual differences in levels of language in intermediate grade writers: Implications for the translating process. *Learning and Individual Differences, 6,* 107–130.

Whitehurst, G. J., Arnold, D. S., Epstein, J. N., Angell, A. L., Smith, M., & Fischel, J. E. (1994). A picture book reading intervention in day care and home for children from low-income families. *Developmental Psychology, 30,* 679–689.

Whitehurst, G. J., Falco, F., Lonigan, C. J., Fischel, J. E., DeBaryshe, B. D., Valdez-Menchaca, M. C., et al. (1988). Accelerating language development through picture-book reading. *Developmental Psychology, 24,* 552–558.

Williams, J. P., & Pao, L. S. (2013). Developing a new intervention to teach text structure at the elementary level. In H. L. Swanson, K. R. Harris, & S. Graham (Eds.), *Handbook of learning disabilities* (2nd ed., pp. 361–374). New York: Guilford Press.

Wolf, M., & Bowers, P. G. (1999). The double-deficit hypothesis for the developmental dyslexias. *Journal of Educational Psychology, 91,* 415–438.

Zirkel, P., & Thomas, L. (2010). State laws and guidelines for implementing RTI. *Teaching Exceptional Children, 43,* 60–73.

Index